MW01482905

**Studies in Comparative Political Economy and Public Policy**

Editors: MICHAEL HOWLETT, DAVID LAYCOCK (Simon Fraser University), and STEPHEN MCBRIDE (McMaster University)

*Studies in Comparative Political Economy and Public Policy* is designed to showcase innovative approaches to political economy and public policy from a comparative perspective. While originating in Canada, the series will provide attractive offerings to a wide international audience, featuring studies with local, subnational, cross-national, and international empirical bases and theoretical frameworks.

*Editorial Advisory Board*

For a list of books published in the series, see page 219.

# Ideas and the Pace of Change

*National Pharmaceutical Insurance
in Canada, Australia, and the United
Kingdom*

KATHERINE BOOTHE

UNIVERSITY OF TORONTO PRESS
Toronto Buffalo London

© University of Toronto Press 2015
Toronto Buffalo London
www.utppublishing.com
Printed in the U.S.A.

ISBN 978-1-4426-4863-0

Printed on acid-free, 100% post-consumer recycled paper with vegetable-based inks.

**Library and Archives Canada Cataloguing in Publication**

Boothe, Katherine, 1982–, author
Ideas and the pace of change : national pharmaceutical insurance in Canada, Australia, and the United Kingdom / Katherine Boothe.

(Studies in comparative political economy and public policy)
Includes bibliographical references and index.
ISBN 978-1-4426-4863-0 (bound)

1. Pharmaceutical services insurance – Government policy – Canada.   2. Pharmaceutical services insurance – Government policy – Australia.   3. Pharmaceutical services insurance – Government policy – Great Britain.   4. Pharmaceutical policy – Canada.
5. Pharmaceutical policy – Australia.   6. Pharmaceutical policy – Great Britain.
I. Title.   II. Series: Studies in comparative political economy and public policy

RA401.A1B65 2015     362.17'82     C2014-907759-9

University of Toronto Press acknowledges the financial assistance to its publishing program of the Canada Council for the Arts and the Ontario Arts Council, an agency of the Government of Ontario.

 **Canada Council** **Conseil des Arts**
**for the Arts** **du Canada**

University of Toronto Press acknowledges the financial support of the Government of Canada through the Canada Book Fund for its publishing activities.

This book has been published with the help of a grant from the Federation for the Humanities and Social Sciences, through the Awards to Scholarly Publications Program, using funds provided by the Social Sciences and Humanities Research Council of Canada.

# Contents

# Preface and Acknowledgments

When I embarked on this research project, mentioning Canada's lack of a broad public pharmaceutical program generally elicited two responses. The first was, "Really, no public insurance? But my drugs are mostly covered." The second, which often came from those with an interest in Canadian health policy, was, "Well, the Hall Commission [the Royal Commission on Health Services] proposed it in 1964, but it was too late, of course."

The people who were *least* likely to be surprised by the exclusion of pharmaceuticals from Canada's supposedly universal and comprehensive system of public health insurance were those who had chronic illnesses or had a family member who experienced a catastrophic medical diagnosis or who worked in a job that did not provide extended health benefits. This anecdotal evidence aligns with the well-documented and unfortunate reality that the lack of a nationwide, universal program of public drug insurance in Canada causes real hardship to those Canadians who are not well served by the patchwork of limited provincial plans and private insurance. The lack of a broad public program also represents significant forgone benefits in governments' ability to negotiate drug prices, make expensive new drugs available to patients equitably, and provide integrated health services that seamlessly support patients, regardless of the type of therapy they require or the location in which it is delivered.

As I write this preface, there are a number of new sources of public information and advocacy about Canada's lack of pharmacare and its consequences. "Pharmacare 2020," a conference organized by the University of British Columbia's Centre for Health Services and Policy Research and the Pharmaceutical Policy Research Collaboration in February 2013, has now developed a website and a series of public information videos designed to inform the public of the benefits of universal pharmacare in access, equity, quality, and sustainability (Pharmacare 2020 2014). In May 2013, the Canadian Health Coalition sponsored a conference entitled "Rethinking Drug Coverage: Time for Universal Pharmacare?" that brought together experts, patient advocates, and industry representatives to discuss policy needs and options, and the group now maintains a public campaign for a national drug plan (Canadian Health Coalition 2013, 2014). Broadly organized public interest groups are also taking an interest in the issue. For example, Public Interest Alberta's Seniors Task Force became engaged in pharmacare questions in 2013, when the provincial government mused about moving from its current universal public drug coverage for seniors to an income-based scheme, as many other provinces have done (Public Interest Alberta 2014). In September 2013, the task force published a position paper that made an eloquent argument for truly universal pharmacare starting at the provincial level, summarizing benefits in efficiency and equity, and finally contending that "income is a proper basis for determining taxation, not medication" (ibid.).

I hope this book will contribute to dispelling the second problematic piece of accepted wisdom about pharmacare, that it was simply proposed "too late" in Canada. This claim has an unfortunate air of fatality to it, and although drugs did become more expensive and thus more challenging to provide publicly after the therapeutic revolution of the 1960s, it is also inaccurate. I argue that when considered in comparative perspective, the failure of nationwide pharmacare in Canada has a longer and more complicated history, one that can be traced before and after the therapeutic revolution, through good and bad economic times, and collegial and confrontational federal-provincial relations.

A primary theoretical message of the book is that a slow, incremental pace of policy development, such as Canada took toward its health system, makes a radical change like the adoption of universal pharmacare very difficult. Despite this finding, I am not a pessimist. I take the fact that health reformers and advocates have returned to the idea of broad public pharmaceutical insurance time and again as a good sign, that those with a passion for better and more equitable health services will not give up on a good idea. I also hope that, beyond any theoretical contribution it makes, the present work will provide some guidance to reformers, by giving them a road map of the barriers to policy change

– some of which they know well, and some they may not have considered systematically.

I began this research hoping to learn something about the way the framing of political issues interacts with institutions to affect policy outcomes. I finish it now convinced that change will be as difficult as it is important, and that by understanding barriers to meaningful change in Canadian pharmaceutical policy, we might be better positioned to overcome them.

No academic endeavour is a solo act, and this book was no exception. It started as a doctoral thesis at the University of British Columbia, where I received invaluable advice and support from Steve Morgan, Alan Jacobs, and especially Kathryn Harrison, who provided encouragement, guidance, and the best kind of constructive criticism throughout my graduate program. I could not have asked for a better committee. The many busy experts and professionals who agreed to be interviewed for this project also deserve special thanks – their generosity with their time and insights was a crucial element of the research.

My fieldwork was made much easier and more enjoyable by my visits to LSE Health, at the London School of Economics, and the Political Science program in the Research School of Social Sciences at the Australian National University. These institutions generously supplied workspace, library access, and a chance to connect with other graduate students and faculty who made me feel welcome and at home. At UBC, I was fortunate to participate in the Pharmaceutical Policy Group at the Centre for Health Services and Policy Research, whose members taught me more about current issues in pharmaceuticals and pharmaceutical policy than I could have ever learned on my own, and who kindly provided timely and thoughtful feedback on my work. I am also grateful for the feedback I received from the UBC Department of Political Science's graduate writing group and Canadian-Comparative Workshop, and particularly for the help of Campbell Sharman in reading the Australian case material, suggesting resources, and pushing me to clarify my conclusions.

At McMaster University, I was lucky to find another supportive and engaged academic home, and I thank especially Stephen McBride, Michelle Dion, Greg Flynn, and Peter Graefe for their criticism and advice. I benefited from the chance to present this work at McMaster's Centre for Health Economics and Policy Research, and to discuss the work in progress with more than one cohort of graduate students in the

Comparative Politics of Health Policy seminar. I am also grateful for the suggestions of two anonymous reviewers, and for the guidance of Daniel Quinlan at the University of Toronto Press, who made the publication process smoother and more worry-free than I would have thought possible. All remaining errors and omissions are, of course, my own.

Finally, I thank my family. I could not do this work without their love, support, and above all, their patience. Kevin and Naomi, this book is for you.

# IDEAS AND THE PACE OF CHANGE

National Pharmaceutical Insurance in Canada, Australia, and the United Kingdom

# Chapter 1

# Re-examining Health System Variation

Canada prides itself on its universal, comprehensive, public health care system, which guarantees all citizens access to hospital and medical care, regardless of ability to pay. The fact that Canada has no similar nationwide program for pharmaceuticals might come as a surprise to Canadians who have adequate private, employer-sponsored drug insurance. However, it is a problematic and at times catastrophic reality for many other Canadians who do not have private insurance, do not have sufficient insurance, or are ineligible for the patchwork of provincial drug programs that are generally targeted by age or income or both.

The lack of universal drug benefits across Canada contrasts with the country's own provincially administered but nationally universal and comprehensive public hospital and medical insurance. It also contrasts with the experience of other mature welfare states: Canada is the only country with a broad public health system that does not include drugs. Its public hospital and medical insurance is comparable in scope to national health systems in other advanced industrial democracies, such as the United Kingdom, Australia, Germany, and France. However, Canada's lack of nationwide, universal pharmaceutical insurance puts it among OECD health system laggards, such as the United States and Turkey (Jacobzone 2000).

It is the accepted wisdom that Canada lacks broad pharmaceutical insurance because it was not considered until the mid-1960s, after a therapeutic revolution in pharmaceuticals made them more effective and more expensive – in Canada, the story goes, nationwide programs were simply proposed "too late." However, this explanation is unconvincing in comparative perspective. When we consider Canada alongside similar welfare states, such as the United Kingdom and Australia,

we are led to ask why Canada did not consider pharmaceutical insurance in the 1940s and 1950s, when these other countries initiated broad
pharmaceutical programs. And if Canada *did* consider pharmaceutical
insurance early in the post-war period, as this book demonstrates, why
did it fail at that time, and how can we explain the failure of subsequent
attempts both before and after the therapeutic revolution?

This book explains why Canada lacks a broad, nationwide program
for the public provision of pharmaceuticals by comparing Canadian
policy development to that of the United Kingdom and Australia, both
of which have national, universal pharmaceutical programs as well as
public programs for hospital and medical services, although their systems developed along very different paths. Its offers an explanation
based on the pace of change – whether countries develop their health
systems all at once, in a radical "big bang" approach to policy, or take a
slower, incremental approach and adopt one health service at a time. It
argues that the pace of change has a crucial influence on the way political elites and the public think about health policy, and the nature of
these ideas in turn can act as a significant barrier to later policy development and change.

## Why Does Pharmaceutical Policy Matter?

Pharmaceutical policy provides a good opportunity to study the dynamics of health system development and change because the variation
in the Canadian case is not captured by existing explanations for differences among national health systems, and because pharmaceuticals
themselves are a highly significant part of modern health policy, in
their impact on therapy and on public and private health expenditures.
The lack of nationwide, universal pharmaceutical insurance in Canada
has important practical consequences for access, equality, and efficiency, despite non-universal public drug programs administered by provincial governments and widespread private drug insurance.

The Canadian constitution gives primary jurisdiction over health to
provincial governments, and medical and hospital insurance are administered provincially, so what makes provincially administered drug
plans different? Three main factors mean provincial pharmaceutical
programs are not comparable to nationwide, provincially organized
hospital and medical insurance: the limited eligibility for benefits, the
significant interprovincial variation in benefits, and the lack of financial
participation from the federal government.

First, public hospital and medical insurance in Canada (and in practically all developed welfare states, with the notable exception of the United States) is universal, whereas provincial drug programs are generally targeted to seniors, social assistance recipients, and sometimes patients with particularly high drug needs or costs. Eligibility for provincial plans varies, but no province provides universal coverage independent of ability to pay. While coverage for social assistance recipients is fairly consistent across provinces (comprehensive coverage with minimal patient cost-sharing), coverage for seniors varies more widely and is mostly income-tested (Daw and Morgan 2012). At the time of writing, six provinces provide catastrophic (high-deductible) pharmaceutical insurance to the general, non-senior population, while two (Alberta and Quebec) offer public insurance with income-based premiums and co-payments. Two provinces (New Brunswick and Prince Edward Island) offer no public insurance to the general population (ibid.). Quebec and British Columbia both describe their public programs as universal, but since coverage in both provinces is linked to income, they are not universal in the same sense as hospital and medical insurance are in Canada. Quebec mandates pharmaceutical insurance for all residents, with the public program acting as an "insurer of last resort" for those who do not have private insurance through their employer. As noted above, the public insurance program has income-based premiums and co-payments that have been found to result in significant out-of-pocket payments for some patients (Pomey et al. 2007, 489; Morgan, Daw, and Law 2013, 9). In British Columbia, pharmaceutical insurance is voluntary and all residents are eligible for the public program, but subsidies are determined by income (Morgan, Daw, and Law 2013, 6).

Second, provincial health systems cover a fairly consistent bundle of "medically necessary" hospital and medical services in order to receive federal funding, although research has found some variation in equity of health care use across provinces (Allin 2008). In contrast, there is significant variation in the scope of coverage provided by provincial drug plans, so even those covered by public plans would receive different benefits and be responsible for a different proportion of their costs, depending on the province in which they reside (Grootendorst 2002; Pomey et al. 2010; Daw and Morgan 2012; Gagnon and Hebert 2010). In a study for the Canadian Centre for Policy Alternatives, Gagnon and Hebert (2010) translate some of these differences into typical clinical scenarios. They describe how, for instance, a sixty-five-year-old woman with an income below the Canadian average, with multiple conditions and a "pharmacy counter" drugs bill of $454 per year must spend "between $300 and $503 a year if she lives in Quebec, Manitoba, or Saskatchewan," but less than $30 in Ontario, New Brunswick, or Newfoundland and Labrador (ibid.).

Provincial variations in the types of drugs covered are often more visible and more controversial, especially when the medication in question is for a serious or life-threatening condition. For example, in 2005, there was a flurry of controversy around the breast-cancer drug trastuzumab (Herceptin). In May 2005, clinical trials showing a benefit in survival rates for patients receiving the drug were presented at a scientific conference, and these results were quickly picked up by the Canadian media (Abelson and Collins 2009). A major thread in these stories was the disparity in provincial funding for the drug, which meant that access depended in part on patients' place of residence (Abraham 2005; Hume 2005). This type of news story continues to be an important part of the narrative of pharmaceutical insurance in Canada, whether it is about Herceptin (Priest 2011) or other drugs with the potential to save or prolong lives (Ferguson 2013).

The final reason provincial responsibility for pharmaceuticals matters is financial. The federal government provides dedicated block grants to provincial governments for hospital and medical services, which in recent years accounted for roughly 20 per cent of the cost of provincial health programs (Fierlbeck 2011, 19). The federal government provides pharmaceutical insurance for certain populations (Aboriginal persons as defined by the constitution, members of the Canadian Forces and Royal Canadian Mounted Police, and federal inmates), which accounts for 1 to 8 per cent of prescription drug expenditures in the provinces (Canadian Institute for Health Information 2013, series B).[1] It does not contribute directly to provincial drug plans. The lack of "equalizing" federal support means that prescription drug expenditure that is funded publicly varies from about 27 per cent in New Brunswick and Prince Edward Island, to 40 to 41 per cent in Alberta, Saskatchewan, and Quebec (ibid.). Thus, compared to public hospital and medical insurance, provincial public pharmaceutical insurance covers fewer people, provides significantly different benefits to those beneficiaries it does cover, depending on the province in which they reside, and operates without the benefit of financial support from the national government.

Public funding for pharmaceutical expenditures in Canada is lower than in the two comparator countries. In 2008, 38.3 per cent of total pharmaceutical expenditures in Canada was provided publicly, in contrast with 54 per cent in Australia and 84.7 per cent in the U.K. (Canadian Institute for Health Information 2011). The Canadian Institute for Health Information updated these data in 2013 and noted that, while the percentage of public pharmaceuticals held steady at 38.3 per cent in 2010, this put Canada near the bottom of a seven-country comparator group (Australia, Canada, France, Germany, Japan, New Zealand, and the United States): only the United States had a lower share, at 31.7 per cent public expenditures (Canadian Institute for Health Information 2013, iv).

Does a lower level of public expenditure and the lack of a nationwide program mean that Canadians lack drug coverage? Although the patchwork of public and private plans in Canada does cover a high percentage of the population, it is important to ask what level of coverage it provides, and for whom. Kapur and Basu (2005) find that 85 per cent of Canadians have some drug coverage through conventional public (25 per cent) or private (60 per cent) plans. By conventional plans, they mean insurance plans where the patient's financial contribution, usually in the form of a deductible or co-payment, is "reasonably affordable" (ibid., 184). When high-deductible catastrophic plans – where coverage begins after drug costs have exceeded some percentage of household income – are included, this number jumps to 96 per cent.

It appears that there is a reasonably high level of coverage from private and provincial insurance programs. However, Kapur and Basu find that the uninsured are more likely to be young (under twenty-five years of age), to be self-employed, or to have part-time or seasonal work, and to have an income between $10,000 and $30,000 per year. They conclude that with regards to drug insurance, "the working poor … appear to be in a vulnerable situation" (Kapur and Basu 2005, 192). In terms of the quality of drug coverage for those that do have it, they found the highest out-of-pocket burden fell on seniors (who often have some public coverage but tend to have higher drug costs), people living in rural areas, and people living in certain provinces (Newfoundland, Prince Edward Island, Saskatchewan, and Alberta) (191). An alternative approach to assessing the extent and quality of drug coverage is to examine rates of cost-related non-adherence, or the number of Canadians who do not fill prescriptions or skip doses because of cost. Law et al. (2012) find that 9.6 per cent of Canadians reported forgoing prescriptions because of cost in 2007, and that being in poor health, having low income, or having no insurance made cost-related non-adherance more likely, up to 35.6 per cent in people with no insurance and low household incomes. Another recent study points out that in the event of a medical crisis, most Canadians would "bear a substantial financial burden" under existing provincial plans (Daw and Morgan 2012, 23).

In short, the distribution and type of drug insurance available across Canada, both publicly and privately, does leave some potentially vulnerable people out and imposes significant burdens on others. There are also efficiency costs to a fragmented system of drug purchasing and insurance, which forgoes opportunities to integrate pharmaceuticals with other therapies and enhance patient compliance, or to develop comprehensive cost-management policies (Morgan and Willison 2004). No broad public program means the social cost of pharmaceuticals is likely to be significantly higher than it would be otherwise (Gagnon and Hebert 2010).

The lack of a nationwide pharmaceutical program in Canada is thus a significant policy gap. The cost of drugs to individuals and societies is substantial and growing: in the 1990s, combined public and private spending on prescription drugs in Canada eclipsed spending on physician services, and pharmaceuticals are now second only to hospitals in total expenditure (Canadian Institute for Health Information 2011). Other countries struggle with expanding pharmaceuticals expenditures as well, as they seek to balance patient needs with industrial goals and health system sustainability (Harvey, Faunce, and Lokuge 2004; Maynard, Bloor, and Freemantle 2004). This makes it useful to investigate how these systems came to take their current forms, and what dynamics underlie their development and change. More generally, the empirical puzzle posed by cross-national variation in pharmaceutical policy suggests that there are advantages to disaggregating complex policy systems (like health systems or welfare states) to better understand their component parts.

## How Do Pharmaceutical Programs Differ from National Health Systems in General?

This book compares Canada to two similar liberal welfare states, the United Kingdom and Australia, both of which provide broad public coverage of hospital, medical, and pharmaceutical services.[2] The incongruence of the Canadian case demonstrates that literature on national health insurance cannot provide a full explanation for variation in pharmaceutical programs. This literature (Hacker 1998; Maioni 1998; Tuohy 1999; Immergut 1992; Boychuk 2008) suggests explanatory variables such as political and economic institutions, past policies, social forces such as political parties, and interaction with broader political processes of civil rights struggles and territorial integration. Many of these works emphasize the path-dependent, contingent nature of policy development in this area. Given how well established these explanations are, some investigation of why the specific accounts of variation in national health insurance do not provide a satisfactory answer to the puzzle of pharmaceutical programs is warranted.

For example, Hacker (1998, 83) explains variations in public health services or insurance in Canada, the United Kingdom, and the United States by examining three parallel decisions in each country: the degree and form of private insurance allowed to develop; the initial target population of government programs; and the extent of technological advancement and cost of health services before government attempts to insure or subsidize them. Hacker argues that Canada, the United Kingdom, and the United States faced similar critical junctures for health policy, and that institutions structure these rare opportunities for major change. The timing and sequence of policy development matters, as past policy choices regarding the three decisions he highlights put significant constraints on the way future health policy developed.

Although Hacker provides an incisive explanation for general health system variation in the three countries, his argument cannot extend to an explanation for variation in drug insurance. He predicts that if private insurance has time to develop, it will crowd out public insurance. There was no private insurance for pharmaceuticals in the United Kingdom or Australia before their public systems were adopted. However, private drug insurance was *also* practically non-existent in Canada until the 1970s, after a national pharmaceutical program had been rejected a number of times. A broad initial target population is meant to promote the expansion of public insurance, while a specialized or expensive set of initial beneficiaries hinders expansion, but this is also unhelpful, as the United Kingdom and Australia provided some limited public drug coverage for workers or veterans, respectively, before universal programs were implemented, and Canada had no early categorical programs. According to Hacker's hypotheses, this should have resulted in broad public drug coverage for the United Kingdom, since its pre-NHS programs had a broad target population and a program that remained limited to a "clientele that are seen ... as outside the mainstream of the economy" in Australia (Hacker 1998, 82). However, there are no predictions for cases lacking any early programs, as did Canada. Finally, the suggestion that achieving technological sophistication before attempts to expand access to health services blocks public insurance is problematic for pharmaceuticals because, of the three countries, the United Kingdom was home to the most innovative domestic pharmaceutical industry at the time, as well as early and generous prescription services (Lang 1974, 23).

Maioni (1998) similarly compares health policies in Canada and the United States and finds that the role of a social-democratic party, as shaped by institutions, provides a key explanation for the significant differences in the scope of public health insurance in these two countries. Although Maioni's account of actors' motivations informs the Canadian case in this book, the full explanation is again not transferable to pharmaceuticals. In both Australia and the United Kingdom, pharmaceutical programs were introduced under Labour (social democratic) governments, but Maioni's framework relies on the *absence* of a social democratic party in the United States. Canada, the United Kingdom and Australia all had social democratic parties at this time, and while British and Australian Labour parties actually formed governments and the Canadian Co-operative Commonwealth Federation / New Democratic Party did not, it is not clear why Canadian parties would be strong enough to put pressure on the federal government for medical and hospital insurance but not pharmaceutical insurance, or why they would be uniquely unconcerned with pharmaceuticals, compared to social democratic parties in other countries.

Boychuk (2008) provides an alternative explanation of the differing health systems in Canada and the United States, focusing on the way health policy development has interacted with broader political processes of civil rights extension and the politics of race in the United States, and national territorial integration, particularly the inclusion of Quebec in nation-building projects, in Canada. This work counters what he argues is a tendency for the national health insurance literature to be "unduly institutionalist ... while being insufficiently historical" (188). He finds that attempts to develop broader public health insurance in the United States through federal intervention after 1945 were viewed as a challenge to the racial status quo and met with powerful resistance for this reason, and that the health policies that did develop were shaped by "the imperatives of racial desegregation of health services" (185). In

Canada, Boychuk finds that the politics of territory has blocked health policy development and had an expansionary effect at different times: divided interests at the provincial level blocked national plans for health insurance on more than one occasion, while at other times the federal government was motivated to take stronger leadership in health policy as a way to "create a link with individual citizens – most importantly, in Quebec – on a pan-Canadian basis" (186–7).

The argument about the role of identity politics in shaping national health systems is compelling, but this analysis also does not explicitly consider pharmaceutical insurance, which is absent in both the United States and Canada, and which in Canada has been rejected at the same time as public hospital or medical insurance was expanded. Boychuk (2008, chapter 9) also discusses the elevation of health care to iconic and "quasi-constitutional" status in Canada since 1984. His findings raise interesting questions about why a lack of pharmaceutical coverage did not diminish Canadians' attachment to their otherwise universal access to health services, and why the extension of pharmaceutical insurance was not used as a tool for national integration in the aftermath of the 1995 Quebec sovereignty referendum. These questions will be addressed in chapter 4.

Tuohy (1999) explains variation in health policy initiation and reform in Canada, the United Kingdom, and the United States by examining the way institutions and ideas shape windows of opportunity for major policy change. However, Tuohy interprets the Canadian health policy debates in the 1940s as a time when such a window failed to open (44) and begins analysis in the 1950s, when a "warming climate" of federal-provincial relations created a new opportunity for the establishment of nationwide hospital insurance (51). In contrast, I argue that the post-war welfare moment is an appropriate starting point for the analysis of health policy development in Canada. Despite the lack of immediate program adoption, examining these debates allows us to capture both the decision on an incremental pace of change and the first consideration and rejection of broad public pharmaceutical insurance in Canada.

This earlier starting point also allows a challenge to the commonly accepted wisdom among Canadian policy observers regarding pharmaceutical insurance: that it was simply attempted "too late" and has never been adopted because it is "too expensive." When observers claim that pharmaceuticals were considered "too late" in Canada, they are referring to the proposal of the 1964 Royal Commission on Health Services that the federal government contribute 50 per cent of the cost of a prescription drug benefit to be introduced by the provinces (Royal Commission on Health Services 1964). This proposal was more public than previous internal government discussions of pharmaceutical insurance. It is argued that it was fiscally impossible to develop a comprehensive scheme after the major boom in pharmaceutical innovation in the 1960s because of "constant pharmaceutical cost-escalation" (Morgan and Willison 2004): drugs were becoming more expensive and more widely used, making the initial development of a program much more difficult. Drugs were more costly in the 1960s, but this was not the first proposal for public pharmaceutical insurance in Canada – it was recommended by two advisory reports in 1943 and was included in the federal government's 1945 proposal for national health insurance (Advisory Committee on Health Insurance 1943; Marsh 1943; Canada 1945) – and the higher cost of drugs in the 1960s does not explain why Canada failed to act on pharmaceuticals early on, as did other countries like the United Kingdom and Australia.

A related argument is that drugs were not seen as an important element of therapy when the earliest discussions of health insurance occurred in Canada. It is true that in the mid-1940s the number of effective drug therapies was limited (Quirke 2005; Rivett 1998). However, the 1940s were the beginning of the global therapeutic revolution in pharmaceuticals, and many countries recognized their present and growing importance at this time by developing policies to ensure patient access to needed drugs. While the limits of pharmaceutical therapy in the 1940s and the escalating cost of pharmaceuticals in the 1960s are undoubtedly factors in Canadian policy non-development, they alone do not provide a satisfactory explanation. They fail to explain why Canada did not develop a program at the same time as similar countries, and cannot account for attempts to expand programs after this important policy window closed.

**Case Selection and Historical Synopsis**

The advantages of comparing health policy development in Canada to that of Australia and the United Kingdom can be summarized as similar countries but different paths of policy development and different policy outcomes. First the differences: both Australia and the United Kingdom have universal public health systems that cover a comprehensive range of services, including pharmaceuticals, while Canada has broad public hospital and medical insurance and a patchwork of provincial drug programs, but no nationwide, universal pharmaceutical insurance. However, while both Australia and the United Kingdom have universal, nationwide pharmaceutical programs, they differ in the way they achieved these policies. In the United Kingdom, a radical pace of policy development meant prescription services were adopted along with all other health services, while in Australia an incremental pace of policy development led to the adoption of a standalone pharmaceutical program decades before other services.

The value of choosing Australia and the United Kingdom as comparators rather than cases with a more similar sequence of policy development is that it emphasizes that pharmaceutical programs may be achieved for different reasons – and that these reasons might not initially have much to do with the specific characteristics of pharmaceuticals, although these certainly become a factor in later reform. Instead, studying two different processes (fast and slow) that both eventually resulted in nationwide pharmaceutical programs *and* comprehensive public health care systems suggests that the choice between incremental and simultaneous policy development has a more general application to other aspects of health and social policy. It demonstrates that an incremental pace does not mean pharmaceutical programs are impossible, or even that later program expansion is impossible, but rather that subsequent policy development will be constrained in predictable ways.

In terms of their similarities, Canada, Australia, and the United Kingdom are all liberal welfare states according to Esping-Anderson's (1990) typology, which means we expect them to have similar underlying beliefs about provision of social services. This avoids a potential confounding factor and deepens the policy puzzle: since Canada's welfare state generally shares so many characteristics with Australia's, and to a lesser degree the United Kingdom's, the difference in pharmaceutical programs is all the more puzzling. The cases also have similar political institutions – all three are Westminster parliamentary systems, and the Canadian and Australian systems are in fact modelled on British institutions in a number of important respects. This allows the book to focus on one aspect of institutional differences – centralized or fragmented authority due to federal arrangements – which are discussed in more detail in subsequent chapters.

All three cases focus on policymaking at the national level. In Australia, the (national) Commonwealth government attempted to introduce a standalone national pharmaceutical benefits scheme as its first foray into universal public health insurance in 1945. In 1946, it achieved a constitutional amendment that gave the Commonwealth exclusive jurisdiction over pharmaceutical benefits, so while Australia's federal institutions affected program implementation, state governments never attempted to develop their own pharmaceutical programs.[3] In Canada, provinces retain constitutional jurisdiction over all health services, but a nationwide program has been proposed numerous times both before and after the initiation of limited provincial pharmaceutical programs in the 1970s, and as noted above, has significant policy implications. Finally, health policymaking in Britain was synonymous with policy-making in the United Kingdom during the study period, as it was not until the devolution of responsibility for health services (among many other policy areas) in 1998 that Scotland and Wales began pursuing independent pharmaceutical programs.

The study period begins at the end of the Second World War, which provided an important impetus for health policy development. It is the earliest practical time to consider government involvement in pharmaceutical provision or subsidy, since it marked the beginning of effective pharmaceutical therapies with the introduction of penicillin and later different varieties of antibiotics (Quirke 2005). The study period ends with the consolidation of broad pharmaceutical programs in the United Kingdom and Australia, and the most recent major proposals for nationwide pharmaceutical insurance in Canada. It addresses the question of major change in countries taking an incremental approach to policy development though the adoption of "later stage" health services in Canada and Australia: medical insurance in Canada in 1968, and hospital and medical insurance in Australia in 1975.

A summary of the historical sequence of policy development in the three countries demonstrates the differences in paths of policy development. Canada's path to public health insurance was slow and difficult. Although the federal government began developing plans for health insurance towards the end of the Second World War and presented its first proposals to the provinces in 1945, Canada did not achieve nationwide hospital insurance until 1957. Medical insurance followed even later, with a federal-provincial agreement in 1968, and gradual provincial implementation between 1968 and 1972. Despite the inclusion of pharmaceutical insurance in the original federal proposal and repeated calls for its development from bureaucratic and research bodies, this component of health insurance has never been implemented.

Pharmaceuticals were first discussed and removed from the inter-governmental policy agenda in 1949, and federal officials consistently rejected further consideration of pharmaceutical insurance, instead focusing on the development of nationwide public hospital insurance. In 1964, the Royal Commission on Health Services included a call for broad pharmaceutical insurance in its wide-ranging report on health reform, but most of its public reporting on pharmaceuticals focused on policies related to drug pricing, and governmental debates over the recommendations directed their attention to the controversial introduction of nationwide public medical insurance.

The federal government had begun contemplating options to control drug prices some years earlier, which resulted in major changes to the Patent Act in 1969, but surprisingly this policy was pursued on a track separate from that of health insurance deliberations. In 1972, the federal Cabinet rejected a policy proposal that attempted to link a national drug insurance program to better control over drug prices. Around this time, provincial governments began expanding public pharmaceutical programs, mainly for seniors and social assistance recipients. After 1972, pharmaceutical insurance was off the federal government's action agenda for twenty-five years, until the National Forum on Health (an advisory committee of policy experts commissioned by the prime minister) recommended a nationwide, universal public pharmaceutical program in 1997. This recommendation was not accepted, and the most recent major instance of a proposal for expanded drug insurance also failed, with the rejection of the Romanow and Kirby recommendations for nationwide catastrophic drug coverage in 2002.

In Australia, the Commonwealth government decided to begin the staged introduction of health benefits before the end of the war and to start with pharmaceutical benefits. Although the Commonwealth government lacked constitutional jurisdiction over health, it passed the first Pharmaceutical Benefits Scheme (PBS) legislation in 1944 in hopes of gaining greater powers through a constitutional amendment. Later that year, the Commonwealth government held a referendum on such a constitutional amendment, which would have given it a new jurisdiction over health.[4] The referendum failed, and this provoked a constitutional challenge of the PBS in the High Court, spearheaded by the Australian branch of the British Medical Association. Early in 1946, the PBS was ruled unconstitutional. Later in 1946, there was another, more narrow constitutional referendum: this time, the Commonwealth government gained powers over health benefits, with some limits. Specifically, the amendment gave the Commonwealth government authority over "the provision of maternity allowances, widows' pensions, child endowment, unemployment, pharmaceutical, sickness and hospital benefits, medical and dental services (but not so as to authorize any form of civil conscription), benefits to students and family allowances" (Australia 2003). This was understood to cover benefits to individuals, rather than control over hospital administration or the regulation of private medical practice. These powers remained with the states as a result of the phrase preventing "any form of civil conscription," which was intended to block any possibility of a national service (Mendelson 1999).

In 1947, the government passed new Pharmaceutical Benefits legislation, but since doctors refused to participate, the scheme did not operate. Negotiations between the government and the medical association continued until 1949, when part of the legislation was again declared unconstitutional. Shortly thereafter, the governing Labor Party lost power, and the two parties of the right, the Liberal Party and the Country Party, formed a coalition government. In 1950, the Liberal-Country government modified the PBS to make it acceptable to doctors, and the scheme finally began operating. The first major change to the program came in 1960, when the Liberal-Country government expanded the formulary and introduced patient charges for prescriptions in an effort to control the costs of the PBS – as noted below, the first reform to British prescription services was almost identical, although in the United Kingdom it was significantly more controversial.

After the successful implementation of the PBS in 1950, public health insurance policy was stalled for more than twenty years – until the next election of a national Labor government in 1972. The Whitlam Labor government introduced a public system of medical insurance called Medibank, along with grants to states that allowed for free treatment in public hospitals, but this program was short-lived. A Liberal government was elected in 1975, and despite a campaign promise to maintain Medibank, had significantly shrunk the system by the early 1980s (Gray 1991; Whitlam 1985, 349). In 1983, a Labor government won power and reinstated many of the provisions of the original, universal scheme. The new Medicare system retained an important role for private insurance, unlike the Australian PBS, the British National Health Service (NHS), and the Canadian hospital and medical insurance system.

The United Kingdom took the most rapid approach to health policy development, heavily influenced by the report on Social Insurance and Allied Services by Sir William Beveridge, published in December 1942. This report did not mention pharmaceuticals but called for "a comprehensive medical service for every citizen, covering all treatment and every form of disability" (Beveridge 1942, 48). In February 1944, the wartime coalition government tabled a White Paper (*A National Health Service*) that represented a compromise position on health policy reform, although it maintained the principles of universality and comprehensiveness. Before any policy was adopted, however, Labour won a landslide majority government in the general election of July 1945 and proceeded to prepare legislation for health reform that modified some of the compromise positions of the 1944 White Paper.

The National Health Service legislation was passed in 1946, and services, including free prescriptions, were implemented in 1948. Prescription charges were proposed the following year in response to higher-than-anticipated costs for pharmaceuticals and concerns about the cost of the NHS overall. The first prescription charges were implemented in 1952, abolished in 1964, and reinstated in 1968, and continued to be a major source of political controversy until the late 1970s, when a small annual increase to the charges was made automatic (Wordsworth, Ryan, and Donaldson 1998). The book therefore includes two countries that took a slow, incremental approach to health policy development (Canada and Australia), and one that took an abrupt, radical approach (the United Kingdom). The fact that Australia has a broad pharmaceutical program is largely a matter of order: unlike Canada, Australia chose to begin health policy development with pharmaceutical insurance, but both countries experienced barriers to the expansion of their health systems after the first priority services were adopted.

## Outline of the Book

The remainder of the book is organized as follows. Chapter 2 contains the detailed theoretical argument: that a country's pace of policy development in a given policy area is predictable on the basis of the combination of institutional, ideational, and electoral factors present at an initial critical juncture. This early approach to policy development has a crucial effect on the scope of program adoption, as it produces and maintains restricted ideas among elites and the public that limit future program expansion.

Chapter 3 explains how the pace of policy development is determined in different national contexts by examining how institutional, ideational, and electoral factors influenced each country's approach to health policy development in the 1940s, and how radical versus incremental approaches affected the adoption of health programs in the

1940s and 1950s. Chapter 4 explains the barriers to policy change posed by entrenched ideas. It focuses on Canada and the failure of three significant proposals for nationwide pharmaceutical insurance in 1972, 1997, and 2002 (the 1964 royal commission is discussed in chapter 6). It also addresses the somewhat surprising circumstances of health policy stability in Australia. In the late 1940s, a Labor government faced significant opposition in implementing its first priority for health service development and pharmaceutical benefits but saw the scheme finally function under a Liberal-Country government that was otherwise opposed to universal public health benefits.

Chapter 5 examines minor change in the early days of British and Australian pharmaceutical programs and determines that there are differences in the flexibility of programs adopted as part of a radical versus incremental process of policy development. Chapter 6 addresses the question of major reform in more detail: when and how might barriers to program expansion and reform be overcome? It provides a preliminary answer by applying the framework to two instances of major program expansion in the study countries: Canada's addition of medical insurance to its nationwide public program between 1963 and 1968, and Australia's creation of nationwide public hospital and medical insurance between 1972 and 1984. Chapter 7 concludes by reviewing the empirical findings and their implications for the study of policy development and change, and for the future of pharmaceutical policy development in Canada.

# Chapter 2

# Explaining Stability and Change

The pace of policy change matters because it has long-term implications for the scope of policy development. A country's pace of change in a given policy area is predictable on the basis of a combination of institutional, ideational, and electoral factors present at an early critical moment – in this case, the post–Second World War "welfare moment" experienced in many Western countries. Radical policy development requires centralized political institutions, elite consensus on an idea that links ideology and policy action, and a public that is both attentive to the policy domain and supportive of program adoption. In the absence of these conditions, countries tend to default to a less politically and economically demanding incremental approach to policy development. In turn, its pace affects the scope of programs adopted. Slow, incremental processes produce and maintain restricted ideas among elites and the public, and these limited ideas block program expansion. The result is that incremental policy development tends to stall, and later program expansion is difficult, taking on the characteristics of a radical reform rather than a planned progression.

Radical reform later in the policy process is rare, but not impossible. Although the theory is focused mainly on a new explanation for policy stability that helps account for empirical variation (such as Canada's lack of a universal, nationwide public pharmaceutical program), it also provides guidelines for understanding these rare cases of major change. I suggest that major change later in an incremental process of policy development requires the same three conditions necessary to prompt a radical pace of change at an early critical moment: a combination of centralized institutional authority, or a temporary reduction in institutional fragmentation, favourable policy ideas from elites, and an attentive and supportive public to provide electoral motivation.

This chapter is divided into six sections. The first deals with a need to define policy change in the wide-ranging scholarly debate over the concept. The goal is not to generate additional typologies but to provide a definition that references literature and can be applied clearly and easily to the study of health policy and other complex, multidimensional policy domains. The second and third sections provide theoretical explanations for why countries adopt an incremental versus radical pace of policy development and for the barriers to policy change presented by an incremental pace. The fourth section sets out theoretical expectations for instances of minor and major policy change by explaining how the pace of change affects these different processes of reform. The fifth and sixth sections discuss the research methods necessary to capture the influence of ideas on policy, and two of the main alternative explanations for variation in pharmaceutical programs.

## Defining Stability and Change

Accounting for institutional change has been a longstanding challenge for scholars interested in historical approaches to public policy (Baumgartner and Jones 1991; Streeck and Thelen 2005; Capoccia and Kelemen 2007; Mahoney and Thelen 2010; Tuohy 2011). I argue that the pace of change or policy development is consequential because a slow pace blocks later change. So how is change defined and measured? Peter Hall's (1993) influential work on the three orders of policy change defines change on the basis of variables in the policy process that it affects: third-order change affects the overarching goals of policy, while second- and first-order change affect the policy instruments used to achieve those goals and the instruments' settings, respectively (278). More recent work has defined change on the basis of its process and results: how quickly change occurs and how different policy outcomes are from what came before (Streeck and Thelen 2005; Mahoney and Thelen 2010; Tuohy 2011).

I follow Streeck and Thelen (2005, 9) by focusing on the process and results of change and by distinguishing between abrupt, radical processes and slow, incremental processes of change. Streeck and Thelen define results in general terms: does the process of change lead to policy continuity or discontinuity? They focus on incremental processes and discontinuous results, or gradual transformation, which is further divided into categories of displacement, layering, drift, and conversion, depending on the methods by which change (usually retrenchment) is accomplished (19).

This extensive categorization leaves questions about what change looks like in specific policy areas. I argue that change is significantly context-specific. Change is major or minor compared to previous policy in that jurisdiction, for example, or parallel developments in similar jurisdictions. I define the results of policy change in reference to the area being studied: major changes significantly expand or contract the scope of the health system. While this is specific to the current study, a simplified definition of change is more useful than broad typologies that inevitably need to be customized to deal with the complexities of actual policy, and still provides guidelines to researchers in other policy areas.

The pace of change – the process – can be observed according to policymakers' own plans. I examine initial plans for policy development and ask whether policymakers go forward with all elements of the plan at once (a fast, abrupt pace) or break the plan into steps to be adopted incrementally. This approach is helpful in policy areas that can be disaggregated into discrete components, such as the provision of health services. I identify major change by asking whether policy changes significantly expand or contract the scope of benefits provided by the health system, either by changing the groups eligible to receive them or by changing the range of services provided. This type of change is interesting in incremental processes because the language they use implies that program expansion either by adding services or groups of beneficiaries will be a minor change, a natural and expected "next step," but instead the nature of incremental processes actually promotes barriers to this type of policy change.

Minor change, in contrast, is defined as any adjustments to policies or programs that do not significantly expand or contract the scope of coverage. The introduction of co-payments or patient charges, the reorganization of methods of service delivery, and the analysis of the cost effectiveness of covered services are all examples of minor change. These might affect the scope of coverage at the margin (e.g., if the introduction of patient charges makes some services less accessible) in ways that are still theoretically interesting and empirically consequential, but that are an order of magnitude different from new coverage for a key aspect of health care such as pharmaceuticals, or a new portion of the population such as employed adults.

The line between major and minor change may become blurred if minor changes can *cumulatively and significantly* expand or restrict the scope of coverage, as Hacker (2004) and others have convincingly argued. However, the deeply puzzling case of variation in pharmaceutical coverage suggests that there is still merit in considering authoritative or formal expansion and restriction of health programs, and the lessons here may also provide some traction on subsequent studies of informal types of change.

Some examples illustrate the utility of this approach to distinguishing between types of change. In early post-war development of public health services, Canada, Australia, and the United Kingdom all initiated or significantly expanded public coverage of health services. Canada introduced nationwide universal public hospital insurance in 1957, Australia launched universal public pharmaceutical benefits in 1950, and the United Kingdom inaugurated universal public hospital, medical, pharmaceutical, and other services in 1948. These were all clearly major changes in result, but they can be distinguished by the pace of change. All three countries had similar initial goals for their public health systems, aiming for programs that were both universal in eligibility and comprehensive in services covered. However, only the United Kingdom took an abrupt approach and adopted all services at once. Policymakers in Canada and Australia used strikingly similar language about proceeding in steps or stages, and so although the first step constituted a major change in health policy, it was conceived as part of an incremental process to building a broad health system over time.

## The Pace of Change: Radical Reform or Incrementalism

Taking an incremental approach to policy development is significant because even if two jurisdictions start with similar goals, it limits elite and public ideas about the policy area. Over time, "next steps" that perhaps were not radical when they were considered at the beginning of a policy process become radical as both elites and the public adapt to a more limited understanding of the policy area. Ultimately a slower pace of change means that adopting the entire program is less likely. Here, I am attentive to Grzymala-Busse's (2011, 1270) warning against mistaking temporal dynamics for causal mechanisms. However, I argue that pace (or *tempo*, to use Gryzmala-Busse's term – "amount of change per unit of time") is a useful concept, because a slow pace favours "the unfolding of particular causal mechanisms and processes" (1273). Specifically, a slow or step-wise pace of policy development allows for the entrenchment of limited ideas that in turn cause these processes to stall in predictable ways after the first priorities for policy development are adopted.

When does the politics of radical, big-bang policy development win out over incrementalism? Agenda-setting literature, particularly on the role of "windows of opportunity," provides important lessons in initiating major policy change. Windows of opportunity open because of changes in the political landscape or the new recognition of a problem as particularly pressing, often as the result of some high-profile focusing event (Kingdon 2003). Policy entrepreneurs have an important role in manipulating these opportunities, which may be predictable. A critical juncture – a closely related concept – has been defined as a point at which particular institutional arrangements are adopted, closing off other options in the future (Mahoney 2000, 513) or a period when there is a wide range of plausible choices for institutional development and the structural influences of political action are relaxed temporarily, allowing a greater role for contingency and agency (Capoccia and Kelemen 2007, 343). I follow Hacker (1998, 80) and conceptualize a critical moment as a rare opportunity for change when certain conditions for policy change coincide. There may be parallel critical moments for policy change across countries in response to exogenous world-historical events: Hacker (81) refers to "the diffusion of social insurance in the early twentieth century, the Great Depression, [and] the Second World War" as creating a crucial transnational moment for health policy development. However, conditions for change during these critical moments will vary slightly between countries, and uncovering these variations helps explain different policy outcomes.

One of the most valuable contributions in this regard is Tuohy's (1999) discussion of health policy reforms in Canada, the United States, and Britain: she finds that windows of opportunity are a product of both institutional factors (consolidated authority over health) and political will (those in authority place a high priority on "substantial change") (12). I disaggregate political will and interpret it as a combination of ideational and electoral motivations. Therefore, there are three factors that influence the pace of change during a critical moment: the centralization or decentralization of a country's institutional structure, politicians' ideas about health policy, and politicians' electoral incentives to act, as provided by the public's expectations of service.

Following Parsons (2007), I see these three factors as distinct explanatory variables that have complementary causal logics. Institutional factors help explain choices based on a logic of *position* (action is a function of "position within man-made organizations and rules" [12]) and ideational factors based on a logic of *interpretation* (action is a function of "cognitive and/or affective elements that organize their own thinking ... [and] these elements [are] created by certain historical groups of people" (ibid.). However, both are particular forms of explanation, in that they are based on *human-made* causes that were at some point contingent, in this case based on much earlier constitutional choices as well as the contingent adoption of certain policy ideas. Although I discuss the distinctions between policy ideas and electoral motivations below, it is important to note that both factors are expected to affect outcomes through similar mechanisms. Policy ideas affect actors' strategies and constrain the options considered by political elites by directing elite attention to some options and not others, and by affecting their interpretation of the relevant problems and available solutions (A.M. Jacobs 2009; Béland and Waddan 2012, 172). Similarly, public expectations of a policy area "both constrain the range of politics and institutions that decision makers believe will be publicly acceptable and affect how collective actors perceive and interpret their interests" (Campbell 2004, 109). This explanation for the pace of change builds on other recent multi-causal accounts of policy stability, incremental change, and radical change (see especially Béland and Waddan 2012), and contributes a new perspective on the interaction between interests (in the form of public expectations and electoral motivations) and ideas (in the form of elites' own understanding of the relevant problems and solutions in the policy area).

## Institutional Constraints on Radical Change

Countries with institutions that centralize authority are more likely to take a radical approach to policy than are countries where institutional authority over that policy is fragmented. Fragmented authority means more veto players with opportunities to block radical change. The main institutional difference discussed in this book is federal versus unitary government, but the theory may also be extended to other institutional arrangements that fragment or centralize authority – for example, congressional versus parliamentary systems (Tsebelis 1995). The federalism literature offers a rich and often conflicting set of predictions for when and how federal institutions might affect public policy, from creating opportunities for subnational innovation to creating an "unnecessary multiplication of fixed costs that undercut the economies of scale" (Erk 2006, 110). However, for my purposes the key concern is whether federal institutions contribute to incremental policy development. Federalism could contribute to a slow pace of change if constituent units pre-empt policy space and block radical national initiatives (Pierson 1995, 456) or more generally increase the number of veto players and constrain policies requiring intergovernmental coordination and agreement (Pierson 1995; Jordan 2009).

Treating subnational governments as veto players brings in a role for their motives, since they must determine whether or not to use their veto over health policy. This implies that we cannot make claims about the effects of institutions in isolation from the policy preferences of actors at key institutional locations. Harrison (1996) has found that the distribution of costs and benefits of a policy is likely to affect intergovernmental politics, and that "federalism has the potential to create a dynamic of competitive credit claiming in some cases and blame avoidance in others" (20). Interpreting these findings in the context of health insurance, subnational governments may conclude that health insurance or benefits provides an opportunity to claim credit with voters, since it is generally a popular policy when people are asked about it directly. However, if health policy is not a top-of-mind issue for voters, subnational governments may decide that the financial risks and potential for national control and credit claiming at their expense outweigh these incentives to act, and they will therefore block radical action by the national government.

This does not preclude subnational governments from taking action on health unilaterally, and this is what a number of Canadian provinces did between 1945 and 1966. Prior unilateral action by subnational governments would also affect their assessments of whether or not to veto national action, since a perceived national "takeover" of provincial or state health insurance programs would be a lost credit-claiming opportunity, but attempting to maintain a program beyond their financial capacity might prompt some subnational governments to prefer national contributions.

In addition, the nature of federalism places unique constraints on subnational governments as veto players. Since national and subnational governments face an overlapping constituency, a sufficiently motivated national government may bypass lower levels of government to appeal to directly to the shared public and thus effectively make subnational governments an offer they cannot refuse. States' or provinces' institutional veto power still exists, but they may make a political decision that blocking a popular national policy is simply too costly.

Thus, federalism and other institutional arrangements that fragment authority can contribute to an incremental pace of change by vetoing more radical approaches that require coordinated action from a number of actors in the political system. However, this is not an automatic result. The actual influence of federalism in a given country will depend on the particular federal arrangements, the policy in the area of interest, and the motives of potential subnational veto players. The characteristics of federalism that are expected to contribute to incremental policy development are, first, subnational governments with both constitutional and fiscal authority over health policy, determined by examining constitutional documents, intergovernmental fiscal arrangements, and secondary literature on the balance of power between levels of government. Second, subnational governments' early statements about health policy, especially at intergovernmental conferences or negotiations, should provide evidence that they are concerned with health as a fiscal cost or risk versus a credit-claiming opportunity. This need not be a unanimous position – for example, in Canada, the Saskatchewan government's position on health policy was consistently more progressive than its neighbours' – but it should be held by actors with a plausible veto power over unified, radical action by national and subnational governments.

## Policy Ideas

Ideas are a crucial factor in both the determination of a country's pace of change and in subsequent policy development: slow change matters because of the way an incremental policy process conditions and restricts elite ideas and public expectations. Ideas are not necessarily a straightforward causal factor, however, and so we need clear and testable definitions of what ideas are, whose ideas matter, and how ideas might be distinguished from other, related factors like interests.

The study of the role of ideas in politics is diverse, drawing on traditions in political sociology and cultural analysis, constructivist international relations, and the "new institutionalism" of the 1980s, among others (Béland and Cox 2011, 6). Ideas can help explain what motivates the state, if it is at least partly autonomous from societal interests, by explaining how the "national interest" is defined, and why the legacy of some past choices is more influential than others' (Hall 1993, 275). Ideas provide foundations for institutions and in turn are reproduced by institutions as they become embedded and shape the actions the organization views as "desirable and feasible" (Berman et al. 2001, 238). They provide an opportunity to critically examine the strictly objective, material view of interests by asking what political actors *think* they want, and how their interpretation of their situation affects their interests over time (Hay 2011, 70). Finally, ideas can help us understand both incremental and radical change by providing an agency-centred account of change and a rich explanation of how people make choices about political change (Béland and Cox 2011, 12).

This book contributes to a stream of ideational research that defines ideas as causal beliefs that provide "connections between things and between people in the world" and that influence the goals, choices, and actions of political actors (Berman 1998, 29; Béland and Cox 2011, 3; Mehta 2011, 24). I focus on policy ideas, which concern the substantive outcomes of policy choices: they tell actors what various options might achieve and link goals and outcomes to various ideological or normative positions. This definition of policy ideas builds on concepts of programmatic beliefs, mental models, and policy paradigms. Programmatic beliefs fall in a mid-range of generality between ideologies and policy positions, which "provide guidelines for practical activity and for the formulation of solutions to everyday problems ... [and] a relatively clear and distinctive connection between theory and praxis" (Berman 1998, 21). Similarly, paradigms are described as "more or less coherent interpretative frameworks that consist of beliefs about how the world works and should work in a policy domain" (Skogstad and Schmidt 2011). These types of ideas give actors guidelines relevant to a broad policy area (health) that provide solutions for how a theory (e.g., socialism) should be applied to particular problems (e.g., the degree of government involvement in the financing and delivery of health services).

Policy ideas may still be at a relatively high level of generality. In this way they are distinguished from specific policy instruments dictating the role of organizations in the provision of services, the determination of eligibility for benefits, or mechanisms for controlling costs and measuring cost efficiency. However, they provide a cohesive response to a policy problem and therefore a specific motivation for radical action. For example, a politician might believe that universal and comprehensive health insurance or benefits is desirable for social equality and that the direct provision of health services is the cheapest and most effective way to achieve this goal. This would constitute a cohesive policy idea about health services. A policy idea need not be particularly detailed (how should government services be organized at the local level?) or even technically correct (is the direct provision of services generally more efficient than government funding for private providers?) but it has both causal and normative content that provides guidelines for action within a policy area.

Policy ideas also filter information about a policy area, allowing policymakers to make causal propositions about the effects of certain choices and directing attention towards or away from certain information. In this way, policy ideas serve as a guide that helps elites deal with the complexity and volume of new information about a particular policy area. As A.M. Jacobs (2009, 256) argues, elites deal with an overwhelming amount of information about policy choices by using mental models that structure the types of information they need to pay attention to and bias the way they deal with new or disconfirming information. Mental models provide a "simplified representation of a domain or situation ... that allow reasoning about cause and effect" and which filter information and direct actors' attention towards particular policy options and away from others (257–8).

Policy ideas tend to be most influential when they are shared among a variety of policy elites. Denzau, North, and their co-authors write about the significance of shared mental models in helping decision-makers learn about the choices they face (Denzau and North 1994; Denzau, North, and Roy 2007), and Tuohy's (1999, 12) discussion of political will emphasizes the need for "key political actors" to be committed to policy change. In this book, *policy elites* refers to elected policymakers. State agencies, regulators, and bureaucrats are important sources of new ideas about policy and its goals (Carpenter 2010).[5] Similarly, non-governmental actors and other experts are also valuable sources of policy information. However, politicians ultimately decide which items reach the government's action agenda (Kingdon 2003, 30–2). Bureaucrats' ideas may change at a different pace or even in different directions from those of political elites, since they "have the necessary expertise, the dedication to the principles embodied in their programs" (30), and the time and resources to process the large amounts of disconfirming data necessary for ideational change (A.M. Jacobs 2009, 259). But there is no guarantee that this ideational change can be translated to political elites, and politicians are more likely to accept bureaucratic ideas if these ideas fit with their own beliefs about the policy area. As A.M. Jacobs (258) argues, "One of the most robust findings in all of cognitive psychology is that individuals display powerful tendencies both to seek and to take into account information confirming prior beliefs, and to avoid and to discount information contradicting them." Thus bureaucrats or experts may influence change when it occurs but cannot usually independently get change on the agenda – hence the focus on consensus on ideas among political elites.

Policy ideas contribute to a radical pace of policy development when they make broad links between a theory or ideology and the program in question (here, a universal and comprehensive health system), when they help filter information that might delay or derail policy development (such as projections of unmanageable cost increases), and when they are widely shared among politicians within the governing party and often across opposition lines as well. When there is no consensus on a broad idea linking theory to practice during an initial critical moment, policy development is still possible but tends to default to a slower, less risky incremental approach.

The basic characteristics of ideas in countries adopting an incremental pace of policy development are quite similar to policy ideas that contribute to a radical pace of change, in terms of mid-level causal propositions, acting as a filter for new information, and the need for consensus among key policymakers. Like "radical" policy ideas, they include causal content about the likely outcomes of certain policy choices, help define what is possible or desirable in a policy area, filter new information that elites receive, and are most influential when they are widely shared. However, the content and timing of the ideas differ. Here, ideas grow up around early practice and experience and tend to be more pragmatic than ideological in their content. Both radical and limited ideas share a tendency to become sticky: early ideas become entrenched and difficult to change over time, whether they contain broad moral or theoretical guidelines or more limited pragmatic models.

"Radical" policy ideas about health should be observable in a variety of elite statements and communications. If there is consensus on an idea about health policy that links program development to ideology in the minds of politicians, it will be the subject of public rhetoric (in election platforms and speeches and speeches to the legislature), but will also be present in more private discussions (archival records of Cabinet meetings, internal memoranda, and correspondence). I determine whether health reform is a high priority by looking for specific mentions of health (as opposed to social policy in general) in political parties' platforms and election materials. In addition, I look for sources of policy ideas in major health reports or commissions of the time, evaluating the degree to which they appear in the policy discussions noted above, and the variety of rival reports or commissions that existed at the same time. These reports can provide a public and influential statement of policy ideas and may be more influential in the absence of competing expert viewpoints. The absence of big policy ideas about health should be equally apparent in elites' statements regarding the policy area. If health policy ideas overall are limited and pragmatic, I expect to observe health services discussed most often as a trade-off between financial risk and electoral benefits rather than the principled fulfilment of some ideological goal, and to observe some initial disagreement between key political elites over the goals of health policy.

## Public Expectations and Electoral Motivations

If political elites make policy choices based on the ideas they hold, they are also expected to be strongly motivated by electoral incentives – a material interest in winning votes and being re-elected (Downs 1957). Politicians are assumed to be both office seeking and policy seeking,[6] but how can we tell whether a politician is making a decision based on policy ideas rather than a strategic calculation about votes? Demonstrating that ideas are not simply reducible to material interests has been sometimes been a preoccupation in the literature (see, for example, Blyth 2002, 2003), but I argue that there are two issues to address when attempting to distinguish policymakers' ideas and interests. First, we should acknowledge that policy motives and electoral motives might frequently point in the same direction, where "good" policies also tend to benefit large numbers of voters. For example, a politician may have an idea that free and universal health insurance lowers the social cost of health care, reduces the burden of morbidity and mortality on the national economy, or is in some sense morally desirable. These are all principled, ideational reasons to support the adoption of a broad system of public health insurance. However, since free and universal health services benefit large numbers of voters, we could also imagine a politician supporting such a policy for purely strategic reasons – because she or he has made a rational prediction that such a policy will win votes.

Second, there is likely to be an important ideational component to material interests: what do politicians *think* will improve their electoral prospects, versus objective factors that actually *do*? Hay (2011, 74) goes so far as to argue that "interests do not exist, but constructions of interests do." Blyth (1997, 246) suggests that ideas can be studied as a factor that helps "in the redefinition of existing interests and the creation of new ones" and in a later work, that interests are "necessarily ideationally bound," especially in crisis situations with significant levels of uncertainty that may make it impossible for actors to know what their objective interests are (Blyth 2002, 34). The real world is too complex and uncertain for actors to know their "true" or "real" material interests, and so interests are necessarily interpreted, perceived, and constructed. This means that the study of ideas cannot be reduced to interests, and this book accounts for both policy ideas and electoral interests, while acknowledging that they are often closely intertwined.

Public expectations of health policy contribute to a faster pace of change, because when there is evidence of public awareness of and support for a policy, politicians will be more likely to support a radical approach to policy development. Public opinion researchers have found that "elected officials [are] particularly responsive on highly salient issues" (Burstein 2003, 30). They also find that salience is "almost universally linked to dissatisfaction, particularly with government performance" (Cutler 2010, 499) and is thus a reasonable measure of demand for policy action or change. When public interest and support are lacking or are more difficult to anticipate, politicians prefer the less risky incremental approach.

This book uses different measures of salience to capture both what the public was concerned about *and* politicians' assessment of what the public was concerned about. Conventional measures of salience such as polls that ask voters to identify the country's "most important problem" are included, along with evidence of elite perceptions of the strategic costs and benefits of supporting particular proposals, as expressed in private deliberations such as Cabinet discussions and departmental memoranda. The book also references polls on the popularity of health policies, but I argue that public *support* for a policy, when voters are questioned about it directly, differs from *salience*, or where a policy fits in voters' unprompted lists of government priorities. Although support for a policy is an important element of its ultimate success, salience helps it move up the policy agenda and is especially important in providing politicians with the incentives to take a risky, radical approach to policy development.

## Explaining Stability: Entrenched Ideas and Barriers to Policy Change

The institutional, ideational, and electoral conditions present at an initial critical moment for policy development can help us understand why a country adopts a radical versus incremental pace of policy development. We still need to know why – and how – the pace of policy development matters for policy outcomes. Why does policy development tend to stall in countries taking an incremental approach? Even if "later stages" or additional services were conceived as part of an initial plan, expanding a health system, by this book's definition, constitutes major change.

The path-dependence literature sets out a number of features of the policy process that make it self-reinforcing and difficult to change, including large setup costs, learning and coordination effects, and adaptive expectations (Pierson 2000). We can see these factors at work in the way alternative institutional arrangements for service delivery arise in the absence of government programs. Private actors make investments (pay set-up costs) and create networks (develop expertise and coordinate actors), essentially staking a claim on the service area, making it difficult to displace them with later public policy development. This is an important factor in blocking the development of public health insurance in the United States and one reason that the introduction of public medical insurance in Canada was more difficult than hospital insurance (Hacker 1998; Shillington 1972).

Canadian pharmaceutical policy presents a challenge to this mechanism, since both public and private policy development was late (Grootendorst 2002; Commission on Pharmaceutical Services 1971): there were no alternative institutional arrangements for pharmaceutical insurance when the first proposals for a nationwide program were rejected. This suggests a need for new mechanisms to explain why this major change – the addition of new services rather than the modification of existing programs – becomes more difficult over time. The mechanism proposed here addresses this need and is also applicable to more general problems of policy stability. It builds on the idea of adaptive expectations: that people base their expectations for the future on what has happened in the past. Cross-national differences in expectations are driven by differences in the pace of policy change, and there is a particularly strong effect of adaptive expectations when we consider the relationship between elite ideas and public expectations. There is still a role for institutional fragmentation in explaining policy stability in incremental processes, as will be demonstrated in the empirical accounts in chapter 4. However, I argue that the role of adaptive expectations is both necessary and innovative, and thus merits a detailed explanation of its logic.

Ideas influence policy development as actors adapt their expectations regarding a policy area on the basis of what has happened in the past, and these adaptive expectations influence their preferences and choices. Pierson (2000) has written about adaptive expectations in terms of political mobilization, pointing out that the self-fulfilling characteristics of expectations help explain how people choose outlets for collective action. I focus on expectations about policy and extend these applications to include more explicitly the reciprocal causal relationship between elite ideas and public expectations. Early elite consensus on "big" policy ideas (e.g., that the government should provide free, universal coverage for most or all health services) influences public expectations for service by increasing awareness of the potential benefits, and this public awareness in turn promotes greater commitment from policymakers.

A slow pace of policy development also has a significant impact on the development of public expectations for service. Incremental approaches to policy development are characterized by a lack of consensus on such big policy ideas among elites, and the public will not necessarily form independent expectations for a complex and multidimensional policy area. If the public is not prompted to expect additional services by politicians making policy promises, by high-profile expert reports or recommendations, or by media coverage of such ideas (Noelle-Neumann 1999, 68), there will be limited electoral motivations for expansion. Internal policy documents can provide evidence of plans for a broader program, but public discussion tends to be limited to the first priorities for service adoption – in Canada, hospital and medical insurance; in Australia, pharmaceutical benefits. The public may become attached to this promise of service, but without elite prompting, does not develop expectations for additional services. This dynamic affects subsequent reforms, as elites and the public focus on the service that was initially adopted, rather than the broader program envisioned as the goal of an incremental process. Over time, both elites and the public maintain limited ideas about the range of relevant policy problems and solutions, the types of services they want or deserve, and the nature of additional services themselves, and this makes it difficult to expand the system.

The alternative is a learning model of ideational effects on policy over time, where elites and the public learn from the positive experiences of the initial service or services that are adopted, and see them as a desirable and viable model for additional services. The question of whether people adapt their expectations in a limiting or expansionary fashion is mainly empirical, and as I shall argue in chapter 4, based on whether elites view two policy problems as analogous *and* whether they draw positive lessons from the initial policy. Chapter 4 does not find evidence of this type of learning in the Canadian case.

It should be possible to observe a process of adaptive expectations in both elite's policy deliberations (captured in archival documents and interviews) and in measures of the public salience of reform options (captured in media reports and opinion polls, as well as elite interpretations of public opinion). If elites' ideas about health policy reform become more limited over time and present barriers to the adoption of additional services, we should observe early (before any health programs are adopted) policy discussions about a range of services and subsequent (post-adoption) policy discussions about existing services only. We should observe statements by policy elites about the necessity of "fixing what we have" versus "adding something new." With regards to elites' ideas about specific reform options, such as adding pharmaceutical insurance in Canada, issues that made the program a low priority initially should persist and intensify. Politicians should make "explicit, consistent reference" (A.M. Jacobs 2009, 262) to dominant understandings of additional services as unfeasible or too expensive. Policy development in the domain should be limited to programs that fit these dominant understandings. In the case of pharmaceutical policy, this means focusing on issues of pharmaceutical management such as prices, patents, and drug cost-effectiveness rather than insurance.

The theory predicts a reciprocal causal relationship between elite ideas and public expectations: as elite ideas about a policy area become more restricted, so does the public salience and popularity of certain reform options. This lack of public expectations then reinforces elites' restricted ideas about the policy area. Therefore, public opinion should reflect elites' focus on "fixing what we have": voters should be most concerned with the perceived deterioration of existing services and much less concerned about perceived gaps or services that they currently do not receive. The low salience of additional services should be reflected by their lack of coverage in opinion polls, compared to existing services. For example, it is expected that "restoring cuts to health funding" will be a greater concern to the public than "expanding public coverage to pharmaceuticals." Opinion polls will not necessarily have specific questions on a non-issue, but after a major proposal for pharmaceutical insurance is made public there will be opportunities to measure salience either through indirect questions or elite perceptions.

## Explaining Minor Change: Adjustments in Incremental versus Radical Approaches

The main goal of the theory is to provide a more complete explanation for significant instances of stability, such as the continued lack of a public, universal, and nationwide program for pharmaceutical insurance in Canada, despite the early plans for such a program, the existence of analogous programs for hospital and medical insurance, and the presence of broad public pharmaceutical programs in most other developed welfare states. However, a theory of policy stability is more useful and convincing if it can also account for change. I argue that paying attention to the pace of policy development and the role of policy ideas also provides an opportunity to understand change. When politicians take a radical approach to policy development, their commitment to a cohesive idea of health services will limit the scope for later changes that are seen to detract from this original model or plan. At least some politicians will be committed to a certain type of health system for principled reasons and will oppose changes that they perceive as threatening these principles. Furthermore, a radical pace of change initially is linked to high levels of electoral support, which means the public will have reasonably well-defined expectations about the type of service they should receive. This makes it politically difficult for politicians to introduce cost controls that threaten key aspects of the system as dictated by the original policy idea, such as universality or comprehensiveness.

The corollary is that in countries where health services are adopted in an incremental, negotiated process, without the pressure to act provided by broad policy ideas linked to ideology or strong electoral incentives, there should be greater flexibility to introduce minor changes, such as cost controls that affect existing services. In countries taking a radical approach, minor changes or retrenchments might easily be seen as a challenge to the broad idea about what a health system should be and do. In countries taking an incremental approach, there are fewer ideational constraints on policy change, since services were not adopted under a national consensus about a particular idea of health policy. I expect that similar minor changes to existing policies (particularly those that impose costs on beneficiaries) should be more publicly controversial and more difficult to accomplish in countries taking a radical approach, versus countries taking an incremental approach to policy development.

## Explaining Major Change: Rare Conditions
## for Program Expansion and Contraction

If an incremental pace of change emerges, what are the prospects for subsequent major changes, such as program expansion? I have argued that this type of change will be very difficult, far from the automatic "staged" policy development that early incremental plans often suggest. However, most barriers to change can be overcome under certain conditions, and major change is not impossible. In countries adopting an incremental pace of policy development, taking these later steps is analogous to the decision to take a radical approach to health policy initially, in that it requires a combination of institutional authority, consensus on policy ideas, and electoral motivations to overcome barriers to additional services that develop over time.

As was the case in early decisions to pursue a radical approach to policy development, policy ideas and their effect on public expectations are the key to understanding how major change occurs. If politicians are motivated by a new idea about health policy or pressured by a new wave of public expectations for service, they are more likely to find ways to overcome or circumvent institutional barriers to radical action. As noted earlier, a national government may decide to appeal to the electorate over the objections of subnational governments, making it difficult for subnational governments to exercise their veto over major change. Or one level of government may choose to overcome the institutional barriers presented by federalism by attempting to placate another level financially or subdue it constitutionally. Institutional stars do align for major change, even in systems where authority is normally fragmented. They are more likely to do so when the ideational and electoral components are also in place.

Thus, it is necessary to explain how elites change their policy ideas and the public develops new expectations. This may be an endogenous process: A.M. Jacobs (2009, 263) describes change in elites' mental models of a policy area occurring when there are "multiple clear and dramatic outcomes that depart from the model." In A.M. Jacobs's study of German pension policy, this happened when the mental model of public pensions as essentially similar to private life insurance directed attention away from the policy problems of inflation and the possibility of pension funds being raided by future governments. These problems led to not one but two collapses of the public pension scheme in the interwar period and after the Second World War. Skogstad (2011a, 241) notes that "changing material and normative circumstances" can lead to policy change, but their ability to do so depends on "the capacity of strategic actors to interpret them" and convince other actors, perhaps particularly the public, "that new ways of thinking are needed and/or desirable." We could also imagine public expectations changing in the face of changing policy circumstances – for example, if private drug insurance schemes were to repeatedly raise premiums and restrict coverage in the face of rising drug costs, the public might become more aware of their vulnerability to pharmaceutical expenses and demand government assistance, prompting elites to re-examine their ideas about pharmaceuticals in light of new electoral risks.

It should be stressed that while ideational change may be endogenous, it is still expected to be extraordinary. The role of ideas in filtering information and directing attention means that it is difficult for new or disconfirming evidence to get through, and so change requires a high volume of new information and potentially an intervention from a persistent and well-placed policy entrepreneur or interest group that increases issue salience. The rarity of such major changes means there are only two examples in the time period studied: Canada's adoption of nationwide, public medical insurance in the 1960s, and Australia's adoption of nationwide, public hospital and medical insurance in the 1970s. These cases provide an opportunity to demonstrate the plausibility of the proposed mechanisms for major change in countries taking an incremental approach to policy development and set the agenda for future research into the pace of policy development and its effect on policy stability and change. They also help provide an answer to the practical policy question that stems from the research's empirical puzzle: what are the prospects for broad pharmaceutical insurance in Canada today?

**Methods**

This book takes the ideas of political elites and the public as key elements in explaining differences in health policy across countries and across time. However, there are particular methodological problems with studying ideas, and the need to address these challenges has shaped the research approach. As Berman (1998, 16–19) argues, in order to use ideas to explain political outcomes, scholars must demonstrate that ideas are not merely epiphenomenal but they have an impact independent of material factors, and that ideas are not "too fuzzy to study." This book deals with the latter problem by setting out a clear, testable definition of policy ideas. It deals with the former by using a set of methods designed to differentiate between ideational and material factors that contribute to politicians' choices.

The method involves measuring policymakers' electoral motivations with a combination of evidence regarding what voters knew about and wanted (represented in opinion polls, constituent letters, and media reports) and what policymakers thought voters wanted (represented in statements about the electoral feasibility of different policy options, or speculations about how certain choices would play with voters). It traces when policymakers' motivations are *primarily* about policy outcomes versus electoral consequences by focusing on the sequence of various ideational or interest-based statements by policymakers, the context of these statements, and their relation to other actors' statements and responses.

This process-tracing approach allows me to "unpack" the different variables in what might otherwise be an indeterminate causal relationship (George and Bennett 2005). Subsequent chapters build detailed, chronological accounts of the policy process in the three countries using archival and published primary documents, secondary historical sources, and in the Canadian case, a series of expert interviews. Instead of "assessing the ability of a theory to predict outcomes," process tracing assesses a theory's ability to "predict the intervening causal process" implied by the hypothesis (ibid.). In other words, process tracing evaluates evidence for a hypothesized set of causal mechanisms instead of evidence of correlation between independent and dependent variables.

There is a risk of treating ideas as a residual category (Blyth 1997). They do not provide much analytical traction if anything that cannot be clearly explained by institutional structures or pressure from various actors' self-interested behaviour is attributed to ideas. However, process tracing provides a useful tool for distinguishing elites' policy ideas from their electoral motivations. Archival documents provide records of both public and private policy discussions, and the sequence of different types of ideas can be determined. Statements of policy ideas may be more common in public fora, such as election platforms or manifestos and speeches in parliament. Process tracing allows for a comparison of when these public statements of policy ideas were made, relative to both private statements and the collection of information about electoral incentives, such as the publication of opinion polls. Furthermore, when politicians discuss policy in more private settings, such as Cabinet meetings or departmental memos, they have an opportunity to be more frank about electoral motivations. If they still reference policy ideas, there is more evidence for the fact that their support for a policy is genuinely motivated by "good policy" thinking.

The U.K. case provides an example of how this technique can disentangle policy ideas and electoral motivations for supporting a radical approach to policy development. The British Labour Party made radical action on social services part of its platform by 1937 (Attlee 1937, 176 and 192; Bealey 1970, 17). This policy approach coincides with the recommendations of many of the interwar reports on a broad public health service (Klein 2010, 2). The interwar reports provided an idea about how a health service should work, which in turn helped form public opinion, so that when the Beveridge Report was published in 1942 it became, as L.R. Jacobs (1993, 113) argues, "a lightning rod, serving as a focus and indisputable symbol of existing public attitudes." This is an example of elite ideas prompting public expectations, and the wartime coalition government responded to these electoral motivations when they agreed on the 1944 White Paper, which set out a plan for a national health service.

The ideas of politicians doubtless played a role in the White Paper as well, but the influence of ideas can be most clearly distinguished by examining the 1946 decision by a new Labour majority government to adopt a more radical version of the NHS than contemplated by the White Paper. In the timing of the decision, there was both a clear, cohesive idea (that health services should be universal in coverage, comprehensive in scope, and free at the point of use) and electoral motivations (broad public support for the Beveridge Report). However, the candour with which Labour politicians supported a radical NHS for policy reasons in Cabinet suggests that it was not a purely electoral decision. There would be limited electoral incentive to reference these ideas in a setting that was presumed to be permanently out of the public view *unless* the speaker was committed to them for policy reasons. Thus, policy ideas in the United Kingdom appear to have existed before widespread public support and were expressed in forums where electoral motivations were moot. A process-tracing approach can make these distinctions by focusing on the sequence and the nature of the evidence it considers.

### Alternative Explanations: Why This Is Not a Book about Federalism or the Pharmaceutical Industry

This book addresses a puzzling and understudied element of cross-national variation in health policy: why does Canada, alone among mature public health systems, lack a broad public program for pharmaceutical insurance? This chapter has provided a theoretical framework for answering the question that has a more general application to problems of policy stability and change, but in doing so it dismisses two theoretical perspectives that might seem to be obvious candidates for explaining the puzzle, given both the countries and the policy area involved. The chapter therefore concludes with a review of why theories of federalism and theories of societal interests and power cannot explain the Canadian variation, and why the focus on the pace of change and policy ideas is a fruitful alternative.

First, why not use federalism alone as an explanation for why Canada lacks a broad pharmaceutical program, or more generally, why federal countries like Canada and Australia do not attempt a radical, abrupt pace of policy development? As noted above, it is not only the presence of federalism that matters, but the type of federalism and the way in functions in the policy area under study. Chapter 3 will demonstrate that although both Canada and Australia give constitutional jurisdiction over health to subnational governments, federal institutions posed a much greater barrier to a radical pace of health policy development in Canada compared to Australia. In Australia, the national government assumed that the fiscally dependent states would go along with national health policy development, and in fact the main contributors to an incremental pace were the ideas held by elites and the public. In Canada anticipation of provincial opposition was clearly part of federal politicians' reluctance to seriously consider a radical approach to policy development and later, to engage the issue of nationwide pharmaceutical insurance. However, I argue that the typical story of inertia caused by federal institutions and the challenges of intergovernmental bargaining is not wholly satisfactory, because of the barriers to the adoption of additional services that existed *at the national level, prior to any attempts to reach intergovernmental agreement.*

To clarify this argument, consider one possible counterfactual situation: if Canada had been a unitary country, or if the national government had jurisdiction over health policy, would it also have a national pharmaceutical program? I argue that, if all other factors remained constant, it would not. If the post-war welfare moment was still characterized by a lack of consensus about big health-policy ideas by elites, and by a corresponding lack of public expectations and electoral motivations, Canada still would have taken an incremental approach to health policy development. The Australian experience supports this assumption, since there the primary barrier to a radical approach to early health policy development was not institutional, but ideational.

If Canada took an incremental approach, even in the absence of fragmented authority over health, the theory predicts that over time, limited elite ideas and public expectations would continue to reinforce one another and maintain a health system restricted to initial service priorities, as ideas about the need to "fix what we have" and avoid the presumably uncontrollable costs of pharmaceuticals became entrenched. Provincial opposition surely contributed to these ideas at various points, but provincial experiments with segmented public pharmaceutical programs could also have provided opportunities to challenge restricted ideas about pharmaceuticals. Furthermore, there is no reason to expect that provincial opposition would be uniform or consistent over time. The nature and cost of programs has varied significantly among provinces (Grootendorst 2002; Kapur and Basu 2005), which would affect their calculation of the costs and benefits of national action.

Finally, the order and timing of policy proposals and rejections matters. The Canadian policy proposals studied in this book were rejected at the federal level *before* they were an item of serious intergovernmental contention. The question of why nationwide pharmacare failed to gain a place on the federal government's action agenda is therefore prior to the question of how proposals were blocked by federal institutions. Even if expectations about how these institutions would play out contributed to pharmacare's low place on the federal agenda, provincial opposition was not the only – or even the most frequently cited – reason for federal elites to oppose the development of pharmaceutical insurance.

A second alternative explanation for cross-national variation in the pace of change or the nature of pharmaceutical programs is the influence of organized societal interests. Political scientists have long been instructed to be attentive to the role of groups in determining which issues become matters of political contention (Bachrach and Baratz 1962, 949) and to recognize the importance of business in influencing policy choices though the use of an "automatic punishing recoil" where any policy decision harmful to business interests results in natural and inevitable economic consequences (Lindblom 1982). Interest groups such as the medical profession, the private insurance industry, and the pharmaceutical industry might wish to block a radical pace of health policy development initially, and/or block specific proposals for program expansion in countries taking an incremental approach, such as the various proposals for nationwide pharmaceutical insurance in Canada that were made between 1949 and 2002. However, an examination of both the predicted preferences of different groups and their actual role in the policy episodes studied demonstrates that societal interests cannot provide a cohesive explanation of either Canada's lack of a universal, nationwide pharmaceutical program, or the cross-national variation in the pace of health policy development.

The medical profession, private insurance industry, and pharmaceutical industry are the most powerful and well-organized groups involved in health policy development (Hacker 1998, 67; Immergut 1992, 59; Abraham 2002) and might all have an interest in more limited public health insurance. The medical profession is concerned with protecting its professional autonomy and physicians' incomes, the private insurance industry with preserving a market for its products in health insurance, and the pharmaceutical industry, insofar as it has a typical business interest in profitability, would like to sell as many drugs as possible with as few regulations on prices and distribution as possible. However, the relevant groups do not necessarily have consistent preferences over time and across different options for broad health insurance or pharmaceutical insurance programs.

In blocking a radical pace of health policy development initially, the expressed interests of groups in Canada, Australia, and the United Kingdom do not match the policy outcomes. The medical profession in Canada was surprisingly quite supportive of broad health insurance in the 1930s and early 1940s, and moved to oppose nationwide hospital insurance only in the early 1950s (Hacker 1998; Taylor 1987, 29), after a radical pace of policy development had been rejected by federal politicians. The British Medical Association was ambivalent about the advent of the National Health Service in the 1940s (Hacker 1998, 66): although they were not wholly unsupportive, it does not seem plausible that tepid support from physicians would be enough to launch a truly radical new health service. Australia is the only case where medical preferences seem to align with the pace of change that was adopted. The medical professional was fiercely protective of its professional autonomy and likely contributed to the decision to pursue an incremental pace of policy development. However, even though the Australian branch of the British Medical Association was an important actor in the subsequent battle over the implementation of the Pharmaceutical Benefits Scheme, the organization's preferences are not mentioned often in government deliberations on health policy in the 1930s and early 1940s, which focused more on questions of adequate medical resources, given the large proportion of Australian doctors serving overseas during the Second World War (Crowley 1973).

The interests and actions of private insurance are also insufficient to explain the policy outcomes of interest. Hacker (1998, 67) finds that the presence of "physician-dominated private insurance plans" helps predict when medical opposition to public health insurance will be strongest, since private insurance offers an alternative to government funding of physician services. He predicts private insurance will crowd out public insurance if it is in place before attempts to adopt government-sponsored health programs (82). However, this cannot explain the early adoption of an incremental versus a radical pace of policy development, since none of the three countries had significant private, physician-dominated health insurance markets in the immediate post-war period.

There were some municipal doctor systems in Canada before the Second World War, where communities paid a doctor a salary to attend to residents (Hacker 1998, 97), but physician-sponsored voluntary insurance schemes were not well established until after the failure of the 1945 proposals (98; Shillington 1972, 51), and the national commercial life insurance association actually endorsed national health insurance in 1945 (Taylor 1987, 31). The United Kingdom and Australia both had friendly societies, voluntary associations that contracted for medical services and provided sickness benefits to their subscribers, mainly the working class who could not afford private fee-for-service care, but the societies or lodges had a complicated and often conflictual relationship with physicians. In the United Kingdom, the friendly societies were brought under government regulation with the limited National Health Insurance legislation of 1911 and were replaced by state bureaucracy with the advent of the NHS (Eder 1982).

Like in the United Kingdom, Australian medical care in the early 1900s was dominated by friendly societies. Although by 1920, the Australian branch of the British Medical Association had gained some control over who had access to "lodge services," physicians still strove to maintain their fee-for-service (essentially, non-insured) practice (Gillespie 1991, 8). As noted above, the potential "crowding out" effect of private insurance is also unhelpful with regards to the lack of pharmaceutical insurance in Canada: private insurance for pharmaceuticals developed quite late, as did public programs at the provincial level. Provinces began adopting limited pharmaceutical programs in the 1970s, the same time as private companies began offering commercial drug insurance (Commission on Pharmaceutical Services 1971; Grootendorst 2002).

The final relevant societal interest is the pharmaceutical industry, and given how large the global pharmaceutical industry looms in most contemporary discussions of pharmaceutical access, pricing, and regulation, it may be surprising that it is not a major player in the puzzle of Canadian pharmaceutical insurance. However, the interests of the pharmaceutical industry in expanded pharmaceutical insurance are not obvious: industry strategy changes in response to new regulation, technological advances, and evolving provincial policies (see, for example, Vandergrift and Kanavos 1997; Morgan, McMahon, and Greyson 2008). Broad public insurance could increase the market for the industry's product, if patients who were previously unable to afford certain pharmaceutical therapies could now have them provided or subsidized by government. The industry would also be interested in avoiding restrictions on prices and the types of drugs covered by public plans, and the interests of generic manufacturers might differ from research-based pharmaceutical companies that sell mainly "brand-name," patent-protected drugs.

The pharmaceutical industry has played an important role in the reform of the Australian PBS since the late 1980s (Lofgren and de Boer 2004), in British prescription services starting as early as 1957 (Lang 1974, 66–7), and in conflicts over Canadian drug patent law (Gorecki and Henderson 1981; Lexchin 1997). However, there is no clear evidence that the industry was involved in the rejection of specific proposals for nationwide pharmaceutical insurance in Canada, likely because these proposals did not contain enough details on formularies and pricing to determine the potential costs to the industry.

The nascent Canadian pharmaceutical industry did not play a role in the internal federal decisions to take pharmaceutical insurance off the health policy agenda in the 1940s and early 1950s. As is argued in chapter 3, public discussion focused almost entirely on hospital and to a lesser extent medical insurance, and even if the pharmaceutical industry had chosen to involve itself in health insurance debates at this time, its relative lack of cohesion and weak contribution to the Canadian economy meant it would have been unlikely to have a significant impact on policy debates (Lang 1974, 294–5).

The Canadian pharmaceutical industry was arguably in a better position by the time the 1972 proposals for universal pharmaceutical insurance reached the federal Cabinet, as indicated by Cabinet ministers' concerns that the program would irritate an industry already on edge from the new patent controls (LAC 1971). However, at this time politicians were anticipating opposition, rather than reacting to it, and these concerns were expressed as secondary to their ideas about the cost of pharmaceuticals and priorities in the health system.

Finally, the most recent proposals for expanded pharmaceutical insurance, in 1997 and 2002, differed significantly in their scope, and so we might expect that the reaction of industry would differ as well. There is every reason to expect that the research-based pharmaceutical industry would be opposed to the 1997 proposals, which combined recommendations for nationwide, first-dollar insurance with reference-based pricing (where public plans subsidize only the lowest-cost drug in a class) (Lindsey and West 1999). However, while industry groups participated in a stakeholder conference following the release of the proposal, the conference proceedings do not identify the positions of various groups (Graham 1998), and the proposal was dropped by the federal government before further policy development could occur. The more limited catastrophic drug coverage recommended in 2002 seems more appealing to industry, as it would mainly target patients who might previously have had to forgo drug treatment for financial reasons.

Opposition from societal interests cannot therefore provide a cohesive explanation for either the pace of change or the failure of specific proposals for program expansion because, like opposition from provincial governments in Canada, expected and actual group opposition varied from one policy episode to another, while the policy outcomes did not. Furthermore, in evaluating interests as a competing explanation for the lack of nationwide pharmaceutical insurance, we should be sure that we are not confronting ideational explanations with "unusual and perhaps insurmountable obstacles" (Berman 1998, 17). As Berman argues, to study ideas as independent variables, it is unreasonable to require proof that ideas were never influenced by structural or material variables. Instead, it is necessary to show that ideas "cannot be reduced to some other (structural) factor in the *contemporary* system" (18). Therefore, in each policy episode I seek to demonstrate that the ideas of elites and the public posed barriers to policy development *before* significant opposition from organized interests, supporting the theory that politicians' own ideas about the policy area had a key role.

The next chapter contrasts politicians' ideas about health policy in the immediate post-war period in the United Kingdom, Canada, and Australia, and finds marked differences in the way elites spoke about health policy in public and private in the United Kingdom, where a radical pace of policy change was adopted, versus Canada and Australia, which took an incremental approach to policy development. In combination with institutional and electoral factors, these different ideas about health policy help explain why countries adopt a fast or slow pace of health policy development, and how this affected the early implementation of health services in the three countries.

# Radical Reform or Incrementalism

As the Second World War was ending, many of the mature democracies we now call liberal welfare states were debating health policies. The idea of broader government involvement in the provision of health services or insurance was not new: each study country was involved in some level of organizing, regulating, or funding health programs in the first half of the twentieth century. In the United Kingdom, Liberal chancellor of the exchequer Lloyd George introduced a National Health Insurance program in 1911 that covered a limited range of services for workers (Klein 2010; Hacker 1998). In Canada in the 1920s and 1930s, municipal doctor schemes developed in some western provinces, first in Saskatchewan and then in parts of Alberta and Manitoba. There were also proposals for government-sponsored insurance in the western provinces at this time, although none were implemented (Taylor 1987, 72; Gray 1991, 29). In Australia, there was a longstanding interest in public health and sanitation programs or "national hygiene" at the Commonwealth level, various state programs for public hospitals and medical income support, and in 1938 a failed attempt at a British-style National Health Insurance program to provide medical services to workers (Gillespie 1991, chapters 2–4).

However, the 1940s marked a change in the intensity and focus of social welfare and health policy debates. There was a growing sense in these countries that after the war, or even shortly before it ended, the government would need to make a new sort of contribution to a basic standard of well-being for its citizens. The privations of the Great Depression and the war years were coming to an end, and governments were preparing to take a more active role in a range of social services. Scholars have pointed to the experiences of depression and war as creating national solidarity and a greater acceptance of market control and income redistribution (T.H. Marshall cited in Flora and Heidenheimer 1981, 20); "a greater willingness to share risks under circumstances of uncertainty" (Castles 1998, 28, citing Goodin and Dryzek 1987); and "a broad consensus on the need to construct ... the Keynesian welfare state" (Simeon and Robinson 1990, 125). This post-war period has been called the beginning of a Golden Age for welfare state development, characterized by "stable, predictable and moderate" demand for bene-fits and services, and governments' confident assumptions about their control over their own economies (Taylor-Gooby 2002, 597).

These factors contributed to a critical moment for health policy, a trans-national opportunity for the development of new approaches, but the United Kingdom, Canada, and Australia all responded differently to the promise and challenge of this opportunity. In particular, each country adopted policy changes at a different pace. The United Kingdom pro-ceeded quickly, taking a radical approach and adopting a universal and comprehensive set of health services with a single piece of legislation in 1946. In contrast, Canada and Australia adopted a slower pace of change. While they both considered a universal and comprehensive health sys-tem, they chose to proceed incrementally, adopting one service at a time.

We can explain why countries adopt a radical versus incremental pace of policy development by examining the different institutional, ideational, and electoral conditions present in this critical moment for change. Certain factors rule out the radical, simultaneous adoption of a full range of services and contribute to an incremental pace of change: fragmented institutional authority, a lack of elite consensus on a broad policy idea linking theory to practice, and health policy's lack of sali-ence and/or popularity with voters. The factors that produce an incre-mental pace of change also affect the way priorities are set among health services, as they mean that certain services are deemed less de-sirable or unfeasible, and this varies by country. This initial priority setting limits the scope of health policy development, regardless of how ambitious initial plans might be. Since incremental processes are char-acterized by increasing barriers to the adoption of additional services over time, an incremental pace of change often means that where a country starts in health services is where it ends up.

### The United Kingdom: Radical, Abrupt Health Policy Development

The National Health Service (NHS) was a groundbreaking achieve-ment in welfare state development, providing universal coverage for a comprehensive range of health services that was "free at the point of use." There were important elements of continuity with previous policies, such as the 1911 National Health Insurance scheme that provided medical insurance and sickness benefits to workers (Hacker 1998, 84). The 1944 NHS White Paper (Great Britain 1944) acknowledges the legacy of past policy development when it notes that establishing a universal and comprehensive service would not be "a question of a wholly new service, but of one with many roots already well-established." However, the NHS represented a significant innovation in the population covered, the range of services included, and the mechanism for coverage, moving from an insurance principle to a nationalized service.

Even though decades of health policy and planning contributed to the creation of the NHS, actual program adoption happened relatively quickly, between the wartime coalition government's White Paper in 1944 and the first delivery of services in 1948. To explain this radical development in health policy, authors have pointed to the legacy of past policies, which created a growing health bureaucracy and contributed to increasing public discontent with the state of both medical services and the voluntary hospital system (Hacker 1998; Klein 2010); to the centralization of policy power in the national government, particularly after the Labour Party won a majority government in 1945 (Hacker 1998; Tuohy 1999); and to the importance of consensus on overarching goals for health services (Klein 2010; Tuohy 1999).

This chapter builds on these explanations but emphasizes the particular conditions that meant the NHS was adopted and implemented abruptly rather than incrementally, and then contrasts these conditions with markedly different institutional, ideational, and electoral conditions in Canada and Australia. In anticipation of the different ideas about pharmaceuticals expressed in early policy discussions in Canada and Australia, the chapter demonstrates that the specific politics of pharmaceuticals was not a factor in their inclusion in the NHS. Instead, they were part of a broad effort to provide comprehensive health services, and the particular challenges of prescription services became apparent to British policymakers only after the NHS had been introduced.

## Centralized Authority over Health

Unlike Canada and Australia, policymakers in the United Kingdom did not have to contend with the health policy preferences of other levels of government. The unitary system ensured that the national government had the final say over health policy development. Although local authorities opposed some of the nationalization entailed by the new health system, they were subordinate to the central government, without the separate constitutional source of sovereignty of provincial governments in Canada and state governments in Australia. In addition to the centralization of authority provided by a unitary system, there was the centralization of power inherent in the United Kingdom's Westminster parliamentary system, where responsible government and strong party discipline provides Cabinet with a high degree of policy control (Weaver and Rockman 1993, 12–15). This effect was heightened in the U.K. after 1945, when a "landslide upset" election moved the country from the wartime coalition government to a Labour majority government (L.R. Jacobs 1993, 168).

The national government faced no institutional vetoes over the passage of legislation, and the concentrated power of the government at this time also had implications for how it dealt with societal interests. Hacker (1998, 94–5) argues that the Labour government's strong institutional and electoral position after 1945 meant that it did not have to dilute its plans for radical health policy development to appease the medical profession. This allowed health minister Anuerin Bevan to decline negotiation with the British Medical Association (BMA) before the legislation was passed, and afterwards to grant concessions that were relatively limited, given the sweeping nature of the bill.

The role of centralized authority becomes apparent when comparing the language of the Canadian federal government in the early days of health policy development with the United Kingdom's Ministry of Health. In 1946, Canada's Cabinet Working Committee on Health Insurance recommended that "further consideration of the second stage of the Health Insurance Proposals be deferred pending the outcome of the reports from the provinces regarding planning and organization" (LAC 1946). This deference to other levels of government was not present in the United Kingdom. The ministry's 1944 White Paper recognized the risks of a single, national health service when it discussed "the danger of over-organisation" but argued that a nationalized service was necessary because "medical resources must be better marshaled for the full and equal service of the public, and this must involve organisation – with public responsibility behind it" (Great Britain 1944, 8). A year later, the minister of health noted that when the nationalization of hospitals was approved, there were some concerns about "the risk of losing from the health service the benefits of local interest and local knowledge in day-to-day administration" (TNA

1945), but it was determined that the benefits of a single national service outweighed these risks.

The centralization of authority did not prevent opposition to parts of the NHS proposals. During the design and adoption of the NHS, national policymakers recognized that certain elements of its organization would be contrary to the interests of local authorities but were able to easily overcome this resistance and to introduce the type of program favoured by the central government. The power of the central government on health policy development can be seen in the controversy over the nationalization of hospitals, which were previously the responsibility of local authorities.

The first design for the NHS was put forward in the 1944 White Paper by the wartime coalition government. Klein notes that this plan involved significant compromises that did not please Conservatives or Labour, or the medical profession or local governments completely (Klein 2010, 11). For example, the White Paper called for joint authorities (made up of counties and county boroughs) to be responsible for "securing all the hospital and consultant services covered by it," where previously this had been the responsibility of smaller local authorities (Great Britain 1944, 11). When Labour took power, they abandoned some of the compromise positions of the 1944 White Paper and nationalized hospitals, which "flew against the interests of local authorities" but was supported by the powerful consultants, specialist physicians who staffed these hospitals (Tuohy 1999, 39).

The United Kingdom's unitary system allowed the central government to disregard certain local government opposition to a radical approach to health policy development, but this possibility existed before Labour came to power in 1945: the coalition government was simply not willing or able to act on it. Institutional authority provides a crucial prerequisite for radical policy development, but it remains to explain why the post-war Labour government took this path. Institutions suggest that they *could*, but ideas and electoral incentives help explain why they *did*.

## Consensus on Health Policy Ideas

There was a mixture of strategic and principled reasons for the postwar government to place a high priority on the adoption of the NHS, and although these factors reinforced one another over time, it is possible to trace the sequence of elite policy ideas and public response in the course of policy development and thus distinguish between them.

Chapter 2 suggested that a radical pace of policy development would be prompted by broad policy ideas that link program development to ideology, that filter information to emphasize potential benefits and downplay risks, and that enjoy a high degree of consensus among politicians of the day. All of these factors were evident in the British Labour Party's commitment to a national health service in the 1930s and 1940s.

Support for bold policy development in social services has some history in British Labour ideology. In 1937, future prime minister Clement Attlee wrote about the Labour Party's preference for radical action, saying, "The Labour Government will not dissipate its strength when returned to power by dealing only with minor matters. It will proceed at once with major measures while its mandate is fresh" (Attlee 1937, 176). He added that, in priorities for action, "Labour does not intend to delay the introduction of measures calculated to effect an immediate improvement of a far-reaching character in the social services" (192). A review of Labour thought highlights the party's longstanding commitment to "universality in social services," which was repeated throughout the 1930s with calls for a national health service and other social programs such as free secondary education and family allowances (Bealey 1970, 11).

During this time, a more specific elite consensus about health policy developed, with broad agreement across party lines that the existing provisions for health services were inadequate, and that a service-based, versus insurance-based, scheme was the most appropriate solution (Klein 2010, 4–5). Health services reports published between 1918 and 1939 shared the view that universal and comprehensive services were necessary. The government's 1944 White Paper reflected on this consensus and summarized it by saying "that there should be made available to every individual in the community whatever type of medical care and treatment he may need; [and] that the scheme of services should be a fully integrated scheme," that is, it would cover a comprehensive range of services (Great Britain 1944, 76). Klein (2010, 24) notes that even after the wartime coalition government lost power, there was a "remarkable ... shared assumption that the health service should be both free and comprehensive," both within the Labour government and the Conservative opposition.

These principles of universality and comprehensiveness were most prominently and powerfully articulated in the 1942 *Report of the Interdepartmental Committee on Social Insurance and Allied Services*, known by the name of its chair, Lord Beveridge. The Beveridge Report described "comprehensive health and rehabilitation services" as key for its proposed program of social security (Beveridge 1942, 158). Although it did not describe the specific instruments that should be used to achieve these principles, it helped define politicians' ideas on the scope of action required in health policy and to galvanize the public to demand new services. The combination of a cohesive policy idea and public support led to the coalition government announcement in February 1943 that it accepted Beveridge's assumption "that a comprehensive national health service, for all purposes and for all people, would be established" (Great Britain 1944, 76). However, the coalition government had some difficulty agreeing on the precise form this action should take. There was a consensus on the need for a new approach to health services, but "not on the method of achieving it" (8).

This disagreement on methods became moot after the 1945 election. The Labour Party's landslide win meant that "the way was open for the politics of ideology to take over from the politics of compromise" (Klein 2010, 12), and Labour was free to take the consensus on certain elements of health services (such as universality and comprehensiveness) and apply their own ideological preferences to the design of services. Some of these preferences were expressed by individual politicians. Authors emphasize the values and charisma of the Labour minister of health, Anuerin Bevan, who was a powerful Cabinet member and key decision-maker in health policy (Klein 2010, 13; Webster 2002, 13), and argue that for Bevan "and for many others," the idea of a free health service "represented the embodiments of a pure Socialist ideal" (Ryan 1973, 219). Certainly the 1945 Labour election manifesto emphasized health, saying, "The best health services should be available to all. Money must no longer be the passport to the best treatment" (Craig 1975, 129).

There is also evidence of commitment and consensus in non-electoral forums. In a 1945 memorandum to Cabinet, Bevan argued for major reforms: "As I see it, the undertaking to provide all people with all kinds of health care ... creates an entirely new situation and calls for something bolder than a mere extension and adaptation of existing services" (TNA 1945). Bevan further demonstrated his commitment to the NHS's founding principles in 1949 by opposing the new legislative powers to impose charges for certain services (TNA 1949b; Ryan 1973, 223) and in 1951 by resigning from Cabinet temporarily when prescription charges were first introduced, arguing that this represented "the beginning of an avalanche" eroding NHS principles (225).

The health policy ideas contained in the interwar studies and Beveridge Report enjoyed a high degree of consensus among politicians of both Conservative and Labour Parties. The Labour Party victory in 1945 gave policymakers the opportunity to put those ideas into action, which responded to public demands but also personal ideological impera- tives, as evidenced by the statements that leading health policymakers like Bevan made in forums where there was no expectation of electoral payoff. The type of information and debate that these ideas filtered out, however, was also highly significant for the development of the NHS.

First was the surprising lack of focus on financial questions, espe- cially compared to Canada and to a lesser extent Australia. Klein (2010, 26) notes that "nothing is more striking" in the extensive pre-NHS dis- cussions preserved in the National Archives than the fact that so few of these discussions were focused on financial matters: "Even the Treasury dog did not bark." Even what limited attempts there were to predict the cost of the NHS appear to have been significantly optimistic and in- accurate. Only four months after the service launched, Bevan explained to his Cabinet colleagues that the NHS would cost £225 million in 1948– 9 instead of the predicted £176 million, saying, "That, then, is the cost of social innovation. The justification of the cost will depend upon how far we get full value for our money" (TNA 1948).

The second important filter on British health policy ideas was the limited discussion of the need for prescription and other auxiliary ser- vices. Most of the conflict focused on hospital nationalization and the work of general practitioners, but these debates occurred in a situa- tion where a comprehensive range of health services was taken for granted by everyone. This meant that the earliest archival records of pharmaceutical policy discussions, from 1943 and 1944, focus on questions of *how* prescription services were to be delivered, not *wheth- er* they should be included or where they fell in the order of priority for services, as was the case in Canada and Australia. For example, a series of Ministry of Health memos from 1943 debate dispensing drugs from central clinics rather than existing chemist shops: one of- ficial argued that this would curb "the excessive cost of a practition- er's prescribing habits" in some cases, while another was "doubtful whether it would be convenient or economical to supply drugs through dispensaries attached to the clinics" (TNA 1943). In 1944, a ministry memo estimated the potential annual drugs bill to be "some- where about £10,000,000 and it will, therefore, be worth while to set up some considerable machinery to ensure that we get what we are paying for" in quality products (TNA 1944). The place of pharmaceut- icals in the new, radical health scheme was not questioned until *after* the program had been implemented and the challenges of an open-ended commitment to free prescriptions became apparent – a subject taken up when chapter 5 discusses opportunities for minor policy change to existing programs.

Health policy ideas in the United Kingdom during the 1940s therefore conform to our theoretical expectations of the type of ideas that promote a radical pace of change. They were programmatic, providing a clear link between socialist ideology and a national public health service that was both universal and comprehensive. They filtered information and constrained the debate, so the option of prioritizing services or adopting services one at a time for practical or financial reasons was not discussed. Finally, they enjoyed a high degree of consensus among the political elite, with the main tenets of comprehensive health services shared across party lines. Institutions allowed for a radical pace of change, and ideas inclined politicians towards this approach to health policy. The final piece of the puzzle is public demand and electoral motivations.

## Electoral Motivations for a Radical Pace of Change

Elite consensus on health policy ideas was an important motivator of radical change, but politicians must win elections to implement their ideas. Labour was, in part, elected in 1945 because of their ideas, since the public found Labour more credible on health policy than the Conservative Party (L.R. Jacobs 1993, 169). A positive public response to health policy ideas reinforced these ideas in the minds of political elites.

The principled nature of Labour's actions on health services was closely linked to electoral incentives. Longstanding Labour ideology favoured radical action and a broad, universal approach to social services. Public dissatisfaction with the limited National Health Insurance arrangements of 1911 and support for the Beveridge proposals also likely helped make health policy a higher priority in the minds of most politicians. The National Health Insurance Act provided coverage only for general practitioner services, and only to manual workers – even their dependents were excluded – and by the mid-1930s voluntary hospitals, which were supported mainly by charitable contributions, faced serious financial difficulties in providing services (Klein 2010, 2–3). These deficiencies promoted a high degree of public support for "free and universal health care" (Hacker 1998, 93), and when combined with high levels of public support for the Beveridge Report, resulted in a fairly clear public demand for change.

The Beveridge Report was both very prominent and broadly supported by the British public. A special Gallup poll conducted during the month of its release found that 95 per cent of respondents had heard of the report and 88 per cent wished to see it implemented (L.R. Jacobs 1993, 113). This high degree of public attention and support provided incentives for government action on health policy, although the wartime coalition government had difficulty in reaching the necessary compromises to implement policy. This changed after the 1945 election, which L.R. Jacobs argues "provided indisputable evidence of public support for innovative legislation; this perception created nearly irresistible incentives for policymakers to pursue reform" (167). Although the Conservative election promises also included "a comprehensive health service covering the whole range of medical treatment" (Craig 1975, 118), L.R. Jacobs notes the perception that the Conservatives were "lukewarm" on the recommendations of the Beveridge Report and cites analysis of polls and election results that "suggests that Labour was uniquely identified with social welfare reform and greater state involvement" (L.R. Jacobs 1993, 169).

Public interest in and support for radical health policy development continued after the crucial 1945 election. In 1948, the Gallup Poll of Britain noted, "The Health Service is scheduled to start July 15 next, and [pollsters] ascertained that over six in every ten adult Britons were sufficiently interested in the service to know this date," and 61 per cent reported that they felt the new health service was a "good thing" (BIPO/Gallup Poll 1948), so the polls continued to supply electoral motivation for rapid policy implementation.

In the 1940s, the United Kingdom had three factors that were completely or partially missing in Canada and Australia. The government had centralized authority over health, consensus on a clearly defined idea of universal and comprehensive health services, and strong support from an attentive public. This resulted in the simultaneous adoption of hospital, medical, pharmaceutical, and other auxiliary services (notably dental and ophthalmic) in 1946, and their implementation in 1948. Institutional, ideational, and electoral factors in Canada were quite different, and so were decisions about the pace of health policy development.

## Canada: Health Insurance in Stages

To explain Canada's puzzling lack of pharmaceutical coverage, we must turn to its first proposals for health insurance. There were two early versions: a comprehensive scheme developed by federal experts between

1942 and 1944, and a less radical proposal that went to the Dominion-Provincial Conference on Post-war Reconstruction in 1945. The idea that health services should be adopted incrementally was first suggested in the 1945 Green Book (the *Health, Welfare and Labour Reference Book for Dominion-Provincial Conference on Reconstruction*), which called for a comprehensive national plan but specified it should be "capable of being introduced in any province by several stages" (Canada 1945). The choice to implement health policies incrementally had far-reaching implications for the way Canadian health insurance developed and is a crucial factor in explaining the lack of pharmaceutical benefits. But why did the federal government decide to proceed this way?

In Canada the national government lacked the relatively centralized, unitary control over health policy present in Britain: Canada is a federal country, and the constitution gave jurisdiction over health to provincial governments (Canada 1867). The British Beveridge report on universal and comprehensive social services made a significant impression on some Canadian experts (Marsh 1943; Simeon and Robinson 1990, 107; Taylor 1987, 34), and some of the first studies and proposals from the Department of National Health and Welfare (DHW) emphasized the benefits of a program covering a comprehensive range of services (Marsh 1943; Advisory Committee on Health Insurance 1943). However, the effect of these ideas was limited, as they did not enjoy anything like a consensus among national political elites.

In Canada, provincial governments had the veto power necessary to block radical health policy development. There was no consensus among federal politicians on health policy ideas and correspondingly low public expectations for services. These factors made the incremental introduction of health insurance a seeming inevitability to most elites. They also had a long-term impact on the shape of Canadian health systems though their influence over the order of priorities. The preferences of institutional veto players – provincial governments – and the limited, pragmatic ideas about pharmaceutical services held by federal politicians had a crucial influence on which services would be adopted first, and, over time, these services came to represent the totality of feasible health services in the minds of both elites and the public.

## Institutional Constraints on Radical Change

Federal institutions potentially allow subnational governments to block a radical pace of health policy development, which requires an extraordinary degree of intergovernmental coordination and consensus. Provincial governments have tended to be protective of their jurisdiction, at least over policies that allow them to claim credit with voters, such as health benefits (Harrison 1996; Cairns 1977). Although federal and provincial governments can and do cooperate on policy initiatives, levels of cooperation ebb and flow, and during the late 1940s they were low. Tuohy (1999, 44) refers to "the inauspicious climate of federal-provincial relations" immediately after the Second World War and argues this made agreement on a federal-provincial health policy impossible.

The federal fragmentation of authority in Canada is accentuated, compared to Australia, by the unique position of the province of Quebec. Unlike any Australian states, Quebec protects its jurisdiction for reasons of cultural and linguistic distinctiveness. A second difference from Australian federalism is greater limitations on the power of the federal government to spend in areas of provincial jurisdiction in Canada. The Canadian federal government can and does spend money on programs such as health that are not within its constitutional jurisdiction. However, Smiley (1962, 62) argues that its ability to do so was limited by the "unchallenged right" of provincial governments to chose whether or not they wished to participate in joint federal-provincial programs, the fact that provinces retain "primary administrative responsibilities," and the fact that at this time the constitution was interpreted to prevent the federal government from making specific levies for a provincial activity. This can be contrasted with the constitutional situation in Australia, where the Commonwealth Parliament is empowered to "grant financial assistance to any State on such terms and conditions as the Parliament thinks fit" (Australia 2003, section 51 xxiiiA).

The exigencies of Canadian federalism were a significant factor in the decision to rule out a radical, simultaneous approach to health policy development, although the first Canadian proposals were quite radical in their scope. The federal Interdepartmental Advisory Committee on Health Insurance, headed by J.J. Heagerty, presented a first-draft health insurance bill in Cabinet in 1943. This bill outlined a comprehensive, universal, national system to be achieved through conditional grants to the provinces: the proposal also included a draft bill for adoption by provincial governments to coordinate these functions (Taylor 1987, 18). Cabinet, and particularly the Economic Advisory Committee, raised concerns about provinces' ability to make the necessary financial contributions and in 1944 referred the plan to a special committee of the House of Commons. The House committee held hearings and approved the draft bill but pointed out that agreement on the financial arrangements would require a federal-provincial conference (38).

In the intervening months, a new federal department of health was formed and a new minister was appointed. The proposals for health insurance were modified from a standalone program with significant federal control to one part of a broader program of post-war reconstruction, which included less federal intervention in provincial decisions and a plan to introduce health services in two stages. Taylor (1987, 46) finds that these adjustments came about for two reasons. First, the proposals were modified because of Prime Minister Mackenzie King's decision to prioritize family allowances as the best use of limited financial and political resources. The second reason for less ambitious proposals was King's calculation that greater flexibility in the health proposals would be more likely to garner agreement from the provinces. Therefore, the fact of limited federal jurisdiction over health may have modified health plans even before they faced the test of provincial agreement.

The 1945 Green Book proposals that went to the Dominion-Provincial Conference on Post-War Reconstruction were thus not the most radical proposals considered by the federal government, although they were more radical than subsequent policy development. They envisaged a complete health insurance program that provinces would "have to take, in its entirety, and in a fixed order, within a certain time limit," although health services could be introduced one at a time (LAC 1949e).

This proposal failed after being linked to tax rental agreements that the provincial governments would not accept. The federal government proposed a continuation of the wartime arrangement where provinces gave up certain powers of direct taxation in return for a fixed payment from the federal government, and when Ontario and Quebec vetoed this plan, the entire package of proposals for taxation arrangements, social security, and health insurance collapsed (Taylor 1987, 66; Maioni 1998, 76). The provincial veto during the 1945 negotiations was not primarily about their objections to health insurance: the western provinces were in favour of the plan, although Ontario remained quite sceptical (Taylor 1987, 56). However, the decision to link health insurance negotiations to a complex package of federal-provincial arrangements, and the need to secure provincial consent and financial participation, meant that any future policy development would necessarily be contingent on provinces' priorities and preferences for health insurance. It would be unlikely to resemble the fairly radical plan first proposed by the federal interdepartmental committee in 1943.

In 1946 the Cabinet Working Committee on Health Insurance recommended postponing any further planning of health insurance until provinces had made their reports on planning and organization (LAC 1946). In 1949, the DHW was asked "to arrange the various features of an over-all Health Insurance program into related parts which might be treated as separate units for introduction at different times" (LAC 1949e). In response, the DHW wrote a memo for the federal government's Interdepartmental Working Committee on Health Insurance. This memo outlined two additional options for a comprehensive health policy with more flexibility for provincial governments, who were presumably wary of a major new health program with federal direction and provincial funds. The first option was to propose a program provinces could take up as they liked, and the second was to offer a program starting with one basic service (either general practitioner services or hospital care), with the rest "following in a related order of priority, possibly within a fixed period of time" (LAC 1949b).

When health insurance proposals were next discussed at the prime minister and premiers' level, at the 1955 Federal-Provincial Conference, Prime Minister Louis St Laurent's opening statement demonstrated both deference to provincial governments and acceptance of the principle of incremental policy development: he noted that the federal government would not "wish to be party to a plan for health insurance which would require a constitutional change or federal interference in matters which are essentially of provincial concern" and solicited provincial input "as to the order of priority of the various services" (Canada 1955).

Preferences for a slower pace of change varied by province and over time. For example, at the 1955 conference, British Columbia called for the consideration of "health insurance embodying medical, hospital, dental and pharmaceutical services" (Taylor 1987, 209). Then, in 1964 British Columbia advocated for a program "designed in such a way so as to permit step-by-step implementation" (LAC 1964a). A survey of provincial departments of health in 1965 noted, "The majority of the provinces stated that their ultimate aim was complete health services available to everyone, but stressed the importance of priorities, phasing and timing, which would depend to a considerable extent on federal financial participation" (LAC 1965a). However, a participant in policymaking at the time cautioned that this report overstated provinces' actual support for health insurance, since it captured the views only of professionals in the health departments, and was out of touch with politicians who were much more sceptical of the program.[7] Crucially, there was never federal-provincial consensus on a radical "big bang" approach to policy development, and standard path-dependent accounts of the process suggest this type of consensus would be increasingly unlikely the further the country travelled down the incremental path (Pierson 2004, 21).[8]

Although the institutional barriers to simultaneous policy development were considerable, it is possible elite consensus on a broad idea about health services or a high degree of electoral motivation could have overcome them. If federal politicians saw the adoption of a radical new health program as integral to the government's platform or the dictates of "good policymaking," or there was sufficient public attention to and support for the idea of universal and comprehensive health services, the federal government would be motivated to spend the necessary financial and political capital to placate provincial governments. It is typically true that every veto player has its price, as can be seen later with the federal government's concessions to provinces in order to achieve nationwide medical insurance. However, some combination of policy ideas and strong electoral incentives is required before politicians are willing to pay that price.

## Lack of Consensus on Health Policy Ideas

The lack of policy ideas in Canada can be traced back to the impetus for the first attempts to introduce health insurance. In Britain, Labour's post-war victory resulted in the party and its ideology of social reform winning its first majority government. In Canada, the Liberal Party under Prime Minister Mackenzie King had been in power for almost a decade and had included health insurance in its platform since 1919 (Bryden 2009, 319). However, the main reason that the Liberals promised action on social security, including health insurance, in 1944 was because of electoral pressure from the Co-operative Commonwealth Federation (CCF), a social democratic party that was gaining power at both the provincial and federal level (Hacker 1998, 97; Maioni 1998, 74). Pressure from the CCF meant the Liberals were forced to act on health insurance, but action was a political compromise rather than an ideological imperative for the party, and this favoured the slow, staged introduction of actual policy.

The lack of consensus on health policy or commitment to sweeping reforms within the Liberal Party is well documented in the memoirs of Paul Martin Sr, who was appointed minister of national health and welfare in December 1946 and became one of the few political champions of public health insurance within federal government. He discusses his difficulty in getting Cabinet to approve public health and hospital improvement grants to provinces after the first federal health insurance proposals failed in 1945, and his concerns that these grants would not lead to a comprehensive national insurance plan as he hoped: "I knew that some of the most powerful voices in cabinet did not share my desire to move quickly towards a national insurance plan. Although the party had proclaimed its support for such a scheme on many occasions, I had my work cut out to keep it fully committed to proceeding towards this objective" (Martin 1985, 61).

Martin struggled to get support from Prime Minister Mackenzie King, who was "uneasy about the financial ramifications of health insurance" (Naylor 1986, 131) and from King's successor, Louis St Laurent. Beyond concerns about difficult federal-provincial negotiations or expense, it seems that St Laurent simply did not perceive government health insurance to be a good policy idea. The Conservative premier of Ontario, Leslie Frost, pushed for hospital insurance's inclusion on the 1950 Federal-Provincial Conference agenda, and Martin reports that "St Laurent was taken aback. He did not believe in health insurance and was amazed that a Conservative premier would openly confess that he was for it" (Martin 1985, 220). Instead, St Laurent favoured the expansion of voluntary insurance through existing private plans. In 1951, he answered a parliamentary question about the possibility of national health insurance by making a statement in support of private, physician-sponsored plans, saying, "I think it would be a most happy solution if the medical profession would assume the administration of and the responsibility for, a scheme that would provide prepaid medical attendance to any Canadian who needed it" (Taylor 1987, 191). Two years later, in 1953, the Liberal Party's electoral platform expressed support for "a policy of contributory health insurance to be administered by the provinces" (quoted in Maioni 1998, 94), which was a significantly less ambitious policy than the universal, non-contributory scheme suggested in the 1945 Green Book.

This lack of support, especially at the highest level, made it difficult for the DHW to keep health insurance on the agenda. A 1950 memo from Martin's deputy expresses the hope that "we can keep this whole matter [of health insurance] a live issue" and advises preparing health insurance materials for the upcoming federal-provincial conference, despite St Laurent's desire to avoid the problem (LAC 1950). After the 1953 election, Martin was faced with a cabinet where "most ministers supported voluntary health insurance and opposed government involvement" (Martin 1985, 226). Although there was more support for the idea of broad government-sponsored health insurance in caucus, Martin says, "the division of opinion made it obvious that I would never get a combined hospital and medical plan into operation, so I opted for hospital insurance as the easier route" (226). Some politicians, like Martin, were committed to an idea of a broad system of public health insurance, but the lack of consensus among federal decision makers and particularly support from the prime minister were formidable barriers.

## Lack of Electoral Motivation for Radical Action

The lack of Cabinet support for a bold health policy is explained at least partly by the low salience of health insurance among the Canadian public at this time. There is a two-way relationship between elite ideas about health policy and public expectations for services. Generally, public expectations develop in reaction to some government proposals or debate about policy, and a favourable public reaction reinforces the desirability of action on these ideas. Since neither federal nor provincial governments outside Saskatchewan were providing clear proposals, there was little evidence of public enthusiasm and no clear electoral motivation at the national level for the Liberal government to act radically or quickly.

Others have argued that public opinion had an important role in prompting the first steps of health policy development in the 1940s. Taylor (1987, 7) finds that public opinion towards the end of the Second World War produced "intangible but ... persuasive" reasons for policy action, noting "the growing conviction that the sacrifice and toil of war could be justified only if the goals were positive." He notes that all national party platforms for the 1945 election mentioned health and argues that by this time, "health insurance had become a major issue of public concern, the declarations of political parties matching citizens' response in the public opinion polls," citing a 1944 poll where 80 per cent of respondents say they would contribute to a national hospital-medical insurance plan (47).

In contrast, I argue that support for a policy, when questioned about it directly, differs from salience, or where a policy fits in voters' unprompted lists of government priorities. Although support for a policy is an important element of its ultimate success, salience helps it move

up the policy agenda and is especially important in providing politicians with the incentives to take a risky, radical approach to policy development. I find less evidence for this high level of salience in Canada
in the 1940s and early 1950s.

In his memoirs, Martin reports the results of a Gallup poll mid-1947,
saying that the public wanted more funds for research, hospitals, and
free clinics, but "national health insurance unfortunately received scant
support" (Martin 1985, 45). A comprehensive review of the weekly
news service Gallup published on its polls between 1941 and 1960 re-
veals high levels of support for a national health plan between 1942 and
1945, and in 1949 when the question was asked again, but this was
when respondents were questioned directly about their support for
health insurance (CIPO/Gallup, 8 April 1942; 22 May 1943; 8 April
1944; 13 July 1949). When Canadians were asked variations of a "most
important problem" question (a standard measure of salience that provides information on the unprompted top-of-mind issues) between
1945 and 1951, the top answers were jobs, taxes, prices or price control,
housing, or threat of war. Health appeared on the "most important
problem" list for the first time in July 1949: 10 per cent of Canadians
thought "social security; old age pensions; hospitalization; national
health plans; etc." were the most important problem. However, at this
time social services including health were a lower priority than housing
(19 per cent) and "employment problems; avoiding depression" (15 per
cent) (CIPO/Gallup, 6 July 1949). Health did not appear among the
listed problems again until 1953, but at this point a much lower percentage of respondents called it a top problem. "Health and hospitalization" were listed separately from social security measures and
ranked fourth in August (3 per cent, compared to 26 per cent who
thought taxation was the top problem) and sixth in November (4 per
cent, compared to 21 per cent who were again most concerned with
taxation, reduced taxes, lower budget, and economy) (CIPO/Gallup, 1
August 1953; 14 November 1953). Thus, even though health policy was
included in party platforms at this time, it does not appear to have been
a high priority for voters.

In addition to the lack of pressing public concern about health insurance demonstrated by the "most important problem" questions, there
are other indicators that health was not a top-of-mind issue for the public when early decisions about how to approach health policy were being
made. In 1943, when the Beveridge Report was generating astonishingly
high levels of public attention and support in the United Kingdom (L.R.

Jacobs 1993, 113), only one in four Canadians could recognize the phrase "the Beveridge Report" (CIPO/Gallup, 6 February 1943).

The cohesive idea of universal and comprehensive health services contained in the Beveridge Report did not enjoy similar prominence with the Canadian public, and there was no domestic equivalent until the *Report of the Royal Commission on Health Services* (the Hall Commission) was published in 1964. Furthermore, even the compromise health policy proposals that appeared in the late 1940s failed to draw the public's attention. In 1948, only 52 per cent of Canadians had heard of the new National Health Grants, referring to a five-year program providing funds to provinces, mainly for hospital construction (CIPO/Gallup, 24 July 1948). Of those who had heard of the plan, "about four in ten ... were not able to name any specific feature of it," leading Gallup to conclude that despite the "sweeping" nature of the plan, "there are large sections of the Canadian voting public on which the proposals have made little or no impression" (ibid.). No impression or attention from the public meant there was no clear incentive for the federal government to take radical action, given the opposition from the provincial governments. This meant that health policy would follow a less risky, and ultimately less comprehensive, incremental approach.

## The Effect of Institutions and Ideas on Health Policy Priorities

Provincial governments did not veto all federal-provincial health policy development, of course. Their preferences for the way incremental policy development should proceed had a significant impact on the starting point for service adoption and therefore the long-term shape of Canadian health systems. Why were hospital and then medical insurance on the agenda, and why were pharmaceuticals emphatically off?

The conditions the federal government placed on a possible health insurance agreement – that a majority of the provinces representing a majority of the population must reach a tax rental agreement with the federal government prior to any funding for health insurance – meant that Ontario and Quebec had an effective veto over policy development. Saskatchewan's early success with public hospital insurance suggests that smaller provinces could have an influence through a demonstration effect, although this is perhaps not as strong as a veto. Provincial preferences over policy were a key determinant of the order of priority for service adoption, and these preferences in turn were shaped by the interaction of resource constraints, elites' policy ideas, and public expectations about health insurance.

Saskatchewan's smaller population meant it could not single-handedly block a federal-provincial agreement. Indeed, given that the Saskatchewan government preferred *more* federal involvement rather than a continuation of the status quo, this would not have been a helpful strategy. Saskatchewan's success as a "first mover" on heath insurance, however, did influence how the federal government thought about priorities. In 1949, the DHW noted that there were already two provincial hospital plans launched in expectation of federal support (Saskatchewan's compulsory program was implemented in 1946, and British Columbia began a similar program in 1948), and that it would be a shame to let them lapse by not providing stable funding (LAC 1949d). In fact, there is a two-way causal relationship between Saskatchewan's implementation of hospital insurance and the advent of federal support.

Saskatchewan launched its hospital insurance program in the expectation that federal cost-sharing would follow shortly (Taylor 1987, 80; Boychuk 2008). Boychuk (2008) argues that the Saskatchewan government would not have chosen to implement its hospital insurance plan if it did not expect federal funding in the very near future. The province's decision to begin with hospital insurance was likely influenced by a commissioned survey of provincial health needs in 1944 (Maioni 1998, 93), as well as concerns about doctor shortages (Taylor 1987, 78). However, its expectation that the federal government would begin the staged introduction of health policies with hospital insurance was not unreasonable, given that this was the default position of federal bureaucrats prior to their in-depth consideration of the issue (LAC 1949c). Thus, the provincial government began with hospital insurance at least in part on the basis of its expectations of federal support, and later the federal decision about where to begin supporting health insurance was influenced by Saskatchewan's success in the hospital field.

Taylor (1987, 181) and Boychuk (2008) argue that Ontario's preferences on priorities for health policy development were instrumental in the decision to begin with hospital insurance. This view is supported by Ontario's veto position in the quest for a federal-provincial agreement on health insurance and tax rental arrangements. The federal government was well aware of Ontario's preferences: a 1955 memo to health minister Paul Martin notes that hospital insurance "was the only practical possibility at this time so far as Ontario was concerned," (LAC 1955b) and this position was repeated forcefully by the Ontario premier in more formal federal-provincial settings (Canada 1955).

Boychuk (2008) argues that Ontario's preferences for hospital insurance over other priorities was shaped by an extensive system of private hospital insurance in that province in the early 1950s. Instead of crowding out the development of public insurance, as Hacker (1998) suggests, pre-existing private benefits solved potential problems of administration and increased public acceptance of the principle of collective insurance (Boychuk 2008). Taylor (1987, 113) suggests that Ontario's desire to act on hospital insurance was also motivated by the limits of voluntary insurance that had appeared by 1953, when about one-third of the population still did not have adequate private insurance to protect them from hospital costs. Furthermore, Taylor notes a change in public expectations of insurance: "In 1945 only a small proportion of the population had any direct experience with [hospital insurance], now almost everyone was aware of it," but coverage was far from universal, and even those with coverage faced significant additional out-of-pocket costs (114).

Certainly, once proposals for hospital insurance began to be discussed publicly, they were very popular with Canadians (CIPO/Gallup, 18 April 1956; 21 April 1956). The headlines of the relevant poll news service releases included "Big Majority Like the Idea of Government Hospital Plan," and "Wish for Government Hospital Plan Increases." Ontario's insistence at the 1955 Federal-Provincial Conference that "at this time, our proposals relate to hospital and diagnostic services only" appears to have trumped federal deliberations about the costs and benefits of different orders of priority (Canada 1955). Instead, it was settled between the federal and provincial governments that "the introduction of a hospital care scheme would cause less disruption of the existing order of things" (LAC 1949b). Although the choice of priority was the subject of much deliberation and intergovernmental wrangling in the early 1950s, this 1949 memo demonstrates that hospital insurance was considered a good option by some federal bureaucrats quite early.

The order of priority for health services adoption was thus influenced by provincial preferences, but the ideas of federal elites also played an important role. These elites lacked consensus on ideas that might have provided a broad outline for a nationwide health system, but they did share more limited and pragmatic ideas about the financial risks of health policy development, and, starting in the early 1950s, specific concerns about the cost of pharmaceuticals. These limited, pragmatic ideas filtered the options for policy development that were seriously considered by federal politicians. Since the first proposals were developed after the Second World War, the cost of health services was a constant concern within the DHW, the federal Cabinet, and intergovernmental discussions, despite the fact that Canada's economy recovered more quickly than anticipated after the war, and the years between 1950 and 1956 were marked by relatively high economic growth (Perry 1989, 15). The ability to fund any programs was a key consideration, with cost estimates prepared for each new proposal, and financial concerns greatly influencing policymakers' discussions.

Cost concerns stalled consideration of pharmaceutical benefits early in policy development, despite the fact that in the late 1940s and early 1950s, pharmaceuticals were clearly less expensive overall than hospital or medical care. Instead, it was policymakers' conclusions about the rate of cost increases that made a pharmaceutical program undesirable. Drugs were included as part of the "later stages" of the 1945 proposals (Canada 1945), but when the DHW reconsidered the order of priority for services in preparation for the 1950 Federal-Provincial Conference, officials recommended leaving pharmaceuticals off the agenda entirely, because "all the experience to date indicates that *it is almost impossible to control the costs in such services*, and, until something has been developed in this connection, we do not feel capable of making any suggestions at all as to cost" (LAC 1949d; emphasis added).

Why Canadian officials were more pessimistic about the possibility of controlling the costs of pharmaceutical benefits than other health services, or why they were more pessimistic than policymakers in other countries, is not clear. By 1949, higher-than-expected costs of prescription services were becoming an issue in the United Kingdom, but Canadian officials did not cite British experience explicitly at this time. However, Canadian policymakers were likely aware of the cost overruns in the British NHS. Martin (1985) mentions warnings by the general secretary of the Canadian Medical Association about the cost of following the British path of "socialized medicine" around 1948, and both the Department of National Health and Welfare and the CMA undertook studies of the NHS in 1949 (LAC 1949a). Initially, Australian policymakers were more concerned than the British about pharmaceutical costs, but they focused on designing tools that would allow some measure of cost control. However, Tom Kent, the architect of Liberal health policy in the 1960s, notes that at that time, drugs were seen as more difficult to ration than doctor's visits, and that it was easier to "want too much" in pharmaceutical products, and it seems likely that this thinking played a role at this earlier juncture as well.[9]

Whatever the reason for Canadian policymakers' reluctance to grapple with the financial implications of pharmaceuticals, it was persistent.

In 1955, a meeting of federal and provincial deputy ministers of health concluded that pharmaceutical benefits were "not considered to be feasible at this stage ... except for the necessary drugs which would be provided as part of the in-patient treatment services under a hospital care program" (LAC 1955a). In 1963, the federal Departmental Group to Study Health Insurance discussed pharmaceutical benefits in conjunction with the early work of the Royal Commission on Health Services, which had not yet made its final report. The minutes of the 28 March meeting note that while some members wished to consider pharmaceutical benefits despite the administrative difficulties, others suggested "that in view of the difficulties inherent in the control of costs and in light of the availability of drugs provided in hospitals, that pharmaceutical benefits might be excluded from any Canadian medical care program." The remainder of the discussion focused on "a variety of possibilities in connection with acquiring drugs at a reduced rate" (LAC 1963).

The decision to place a low priority on pharmaceutical insurance is a result of the somewhat inexplicable way ideas about the costs of such services manifested in the DHW in the late 1940s and 1950s, although, as will be discussed in chapter 4, federal bureaucrats took a different position on drug costs in the early 1970s, a time when the greater availability of new drugs might lead us to expect bureaucrats to be even more wary of costs. The order of priorities that won the day – hospital and diagnostic services, with medical services following after a lag of nine years – may seem logical, since these were clearly the larger programs, and particularly in the case of hospital care, were more likely to impose costs that individuals would be unable to deal with themselves. However, this "logical" sequence was not universally followed in other countries taking an incremental approach, as the Australian case will demonstrate. Furthermore, Canadian policymakers at this time were making an explicit decision to take pharmaceuticals off the agenda, rather than simply arguing that other services were comparatively more urgent. This decision had a long-term effect on politicians' ideas about the desirability and feasibility of a pharmaceutical program, particularly when the possibility of additional health services was discussed in the early 1970s.

## Australia: A Decisive Move to Stages

Like Canada's, Australia's decision to develop health policy incrementally was taken quickly. Unlike Canada, there was no lengthy debate about the order of priorities after politicians had determined that health policy should proceed in stages. In fact, the decision to begin with pharmaceutical benefits appears to have been taken at about the same time as the decision to proceed in stages, between 1942 and 1943.

Given that Australia is a federation and state governments retain constitutional authority over almost all aspects of health, we would expect fragmented authority to have been a major barrier to a radical approach to health policy in Australia. In fact, the most important barriers to the simultaneous development of health insurance in Australia were the lack of consensus on a cohesive policy idea about how health services should function, and the lack of strong electoral incentives to act. The Australian Labor Party was less reluctant to attempt health policy development than the Canadian Liberal Party. However, the lack of consensus on a policy idea and lack of public demand for services meant the Labor government was unable to overcome powerful opposition from the medical association and meant that it gave precedence to concerns about resource constraints when designing policy. The result was that the simultaneous introduction of comprehensive health services was not seriously considered.

## Centralized Authority through Fiscal Means

Although Australian states had jurisdiction over health policy, opposition from state governments was a less significant barrier to the simultaneous development of health policies in Australia than in Canada, partly as the result of a difference in the position of the governing parties in the two countries in the 1940s. While Canadian federalism became more centralized during and immediately after the Second World War (Simeon and Robinson 1990, 120), the national Liberal government remained quite conscious of a need to negotiate with provincial governments, particularly on policy that fell under provinces' constitutional jurisdiction. In contrast, the Australian Labor Party was initially opposed to federalism, preferring a unitary system. The party maintained a "lukewarm attitude to the Constitution" and a longstanding preoccupation with increasing Commonwealth (national) powers (Bennett 2003, 17). All national political parties in Australia have proposed constitutional amendments at one time or another, but Labor was most consistent in its calls for greater Commonwealth powers, even in the face of limited success in actually amending the constitution to this end (Livingston 1956, 152).

The Second World War increased Commonwealth powers in Australia, as it did in many federations. Kewley (1973, 173) argues that this "almost unlimited jurisdiction over the social and economic life of the community" had the effect of establishing new expectations in both government and citizens about the appropriate roles of federal and state governments. This, in combination with Labor's longstanding preference for centralized policymaking, may account for the Commonwealth government's willingness to consider social policies that were, strictly speaking, outside its area of jurisdiction. In 1942, the federal Labor government introduced widows' pensions, followed by an unemployment and sickness benefit in 1944, and then the Pharmaceutical Benefits Act and various other health grants to states that aimed to subsidize public hospitals, tuberculosis care, and mental health care (Mathews and Jay 1972, 170–1). According to Sackville (1973), "The Commonwealth Government was alert to the formidable constitutional difficulties posed by its social welfare innovations" during the Second World War but proceeded in hopes of gaining the necessary constitutional amendments at a later date.

The Labor government's first attempt to gain these powers came in 1944, with a proposed constitutional amendment that gave the Commonwealth new powers over fourteen policy fields, including health. This initiative was rejected in a national referendum, but the more limited 1946 social services amendment passed and "was important for establishing the Commonwealth's postwar dominance in social welfare and fiscal federalism" (Galligan 1995, 120). Therefore, Labor's early plans for social benefits to be provided by the Commonwealth government, and later attempts to achieve constitutional amendments to this end, were characteristic of the party's approach to federalism at the time. Federalism became a major barrier when a federal Labor government attempted to implement pharmaceutical benefits, but federal institutions had less impact on elites' deliberations when selecting an approach to policy development or a first priority for adoption.

Labor's centralist conception of the federation is one reason that states were a less important part of early health policy deliberations at the Commonwealth level. Another more material reason for the minor impact of federalism on the pace of change in Australia is the weak fiscal position of states vis-à-vis the Commonwealth government. In 1942, the federal government took over the income tax field in return for fixed grants that provided a lower level of revenue than states had previously received from their own taxation of income, a policy called "uniform taxation." After the war, the power was found to rest on taxation rather than defence power and was therefore made permanent (Kewley 1973, 173; Mathews and Jay 1972, 175). As a result, states were dependent on federal grants and loans for about half their revenues (Galligan 1995, 195), and this had a correspondingly significant impact on their ability to pursue independent social policies. Mathews and Jay (1972, 185) argue that in fact if states regained their income tax powers after the war, "the expansion of or otherwise of welfare benefits ... [including health benefits] would no doubt have been a matter for decision by individual States," but this was not possible without financial resources.

States retained constitutional jurisdiction over health, but they lacked fiscal resources and were constrained by the Commonwealth government's grants power under section 96 of the Constitution, which gives Parliament discretion over how financial aid to states is organized (Australia 2003, section 96). This can be contrasted with the Canadian situation, where provincial governments were more assertive and retained an effective veto over health policy: wartime tax rental agreements ended in 1947, and provinces regained some powers of direct taxation (Bélanger 2001). The power of the Canadian federal government to spend in areas of provincial jurisdiction was also more restricted (Smiley 1962, 62), and more likely to be resisted by Quebec.

Thus, although the barriers federalism posed to radical policy development were real and became increasingly important as policies reached the implementation stage, the Commonwealth government may have had the institutional authority for a radical pace of health policy development. However, this option was not seriously considered by federal Cabinet. Why was Australian health policy developed incrementally?

## Lack of Big Policy Ideas

The primary barrier to a radical pace of health policy development in the early 1940s was the lack of consensus on policy ideas about health in the governing Labor Party. While in opposition in 1938, future Labor prime minister John Curtin said, "The Labor Party believes that the time has arrived when national health services should be treated, in principle, in the same way as education. They should be free to all members of the community" (quoted in Sax 1984, 49). However, this general statement does not appear to have been supported by a programmatic idea about health policy that linked ideology and practice. Throughout the 1940s, the main expert ideas concerning health policy focused on public health and national hygiene, with the possibility of a segmented salaried medical and hospital service. These expert ideas were not accepted by political elites.

There was no elite consensus on a galvanizing vision of how health services should work. Health services were not a priority when elites debated the range of social services that might be addressed by a post-war government, and responsibility for health policymaking was delegated to Treasury, where more limited and pragmatic financial concerns were paramount and filtered out the possibility of broader health planning. The lack of big ideas about health policy development meant there were no prompts for politicians to overcome the limited institutional barriers to radical policy development, and nothing to spark the public interest and support necessary for sustained bold action in this policy area.

In Britain, the central place of comprehensive health services in the British Labour Party's platform was supported by a prominent expert report: the Beveridge Report presented a cohesive idea about the shape health services should take and prompted a high degree of public attention and popularity. In Australia, despite work from two expert bodies, the National Health and Medical Research Council and the Joint Parliamentary Committee on Social Services, no such authoritative consensus on health policy ideas affected the Labor Party, which held power 1941 to 1945, or the Liberal-Country Party coalition governments that preceded and followed it. Roskam (2001, 279) notes that there was no equivalent to the British Beveridge Report in Australia. He argues that this is evidence of Australian governments' practicality, but I argue that it was precisely this lack of consensus on a clear health policy idea that prevented the adoption of a radical, simultaneous approach to health policy development in the 1940s.

The main support for broad health policy development came from the National Health and Medical Research Council (NHMRC), an independent forum for consultation between Commonwealth and state health departments and the medical profession.[10] This body, which Gillespie (1991, 132) describes as "dominated by public health administrators," was tasked by the minister with planning a comprehensive health scheme in 1940 and worked at this "independently of other government departments and agencies" (133). In July 1941, the NHMRC presented recommendations to Cabinet for a system of public health services based on earlier ideas about "national hygiene." These ideas had developed in the interwar period among health planners and experts and were linked to eugenics and concern with "racial vitality and the strengthening of the nation" (33–5). These ideas prioritized preventative over curative health services and removed national health insurance from health policy priorities (138). The NHMRC recommendations included a national system for clinics and hospitals, either a full- or part-time salaried medical service, combined with the retention of private practice for patients who could afford it, and the assumption of Commonwealth control over health administration (132–40; Sax 1984, 52). Although the NHMRC was not clear on the question of physicians' remuneration, the Australian branch of the British Medical Association[11] found the proposals of sufficient concern that the association expanded its own health service planning, focused on a system of government subsidies that would offer minimum interference in private medical practice (Hunter 1966, 321).

The NHMRC report proposed a radical reshaping of Australian health policy, but it did not enjoy a consensus among political elites. The Liberal government, which lost power shortly after the NHMRC's recommendations were presented to Cabinet, did not champion the report, and the lack of consensus on and acceptance of the NHMRC's proposals was not solved by the change in government. When Labor took power in September 1941, it initially seemed to support the NHMRC's approach to health policy, but this approach was incongruent with the party's focus on general social security and its concerns about the country's medical capacity. In 1941 the new Commonwealth health minister, E.J. Holloway, promised there would be no changes towards a salaried medical service until after the war, because so many Australian doctors were overseas with the armed services (Gillespie 1991, 144). In October 1942, treasurer Ben Chifley requested a report from the bipartisan Joint Parliamentary Committee on Social Security (JPCSS) on health services, "with particular reference to such measures as it might be possible to introduce during the period of the war" (ibid.).[12]

The Commonwealth director-general of health, J.H.L. Cumpston, responded on behalf of the JPCSS the following month with a "radical scheme for immediate action," based on previous NHMRC reports and calling for the gradual introduction of a salaried medical service, beginning in remote areas (Gillespie 1991, 146). This plan was echoed in the JPCSS's formal *Sixth Interim Report* in July 1943, which called for centralized administration by the Commonwealth, a combination of salaried and private, fee-for-service medical services, and free treatment in the public wards of public hospitals (Sax 1984, 52). However, archival records indicate that by this time the government had already bypassed the health-planning bodies and begun consultations for the eventual Pharmaceutical Benefits Scheme with the Pharmacy Guild (NAA 1943b). The political elite had not taken up the health policy ideas of the NHMRC and JPCSS.

In December 1942, one month after Cumpston's report on the wartime development of health services, Cabinet met to discuss social security. Gillespie (1991, 145), notes that "the government's plans for the health service remained sketchy" and there was a greater focus on unemployment and sickness benefits, and widows' pensions. Although Chifley's Cabinet submission included Cumpston's cost estimates for his plan, it also included "a proposal for pharmaceutical and dental benefits, contradicting the direct service emphasis on the NHMRC's proposals" (ibid.). This was the first indication that the Labor government intended to proceed with the staged introduction of *services*, rather than the gradual introduction of salaried medical services by area, as recommended by the NHMRC.

The need to proceed in stages became a common theme in subsequent health policy development. In 1943, the federal Cabinet approved a National Welfare Fund to provide cash maternity and funeral benefits, with the understanding that a comprehensive scheme would eventually include health services, unemployment benefits, and other social services (Kewley 1973, 234). When describing the scheme, Labor Prime Minister Curtin mentioned health as a subject that "embraces many items such as medical, hospital and dental services, and children and maternal welfare," but went on to say, "It is impracticable in war-time to devise and introduce a comprehensive scheme for all these services ... but investigations are proceeding, and it is anticipated that it will be possible to give effect to some or all of these services either wholly or in part when the inquiries have been completed" (quoted in Crowley 1973, 79).

The maternity and funeral benefits, which Kewley (1973, 255) describes as "token installments" to a scheme for social services, were implemented immediately. As is discussed further below, the priorities for an incremental approach to health services were set shortly thereafter, and the first Pharmaceutical Benefits Act was passed in 1944. An internal Treasury memo from between 1943 and 1944 explains and justifies the approach, saying, "The Government intends to deal progressively with the provision of a high grade service under which the public can, at the public cost, obtain all necessary medicines, a hospital service ... and ultimately, the introduction of a system under which medical services ... also will be available to every citizen at the public expense." It goes on, "These measures for their full practical application require progress step by step, and the Government has decided that the first step, which will be immediately introduced, is the provision of a service under which necessary medicines will be made available to every citizen" (NAA 1943–4d).

In Australia, like Canada, there was a desire to undertake some health policy development in the 1940s. There was a lack of consensus on a broad approach, but Labor did wish to begin implementing new social security measures during the war, perhaps to take advantage of the "elastic" properties of the wartime defence powers under section 51 (vi) of the Australian constitution, which, beginning in the First World War, expanded beyond purely military matters to social and economic powers for the Commonwealth government as well (Gilbert 1980, 316). Chifley argued that if the government did not begin on cash benefit programs during the war, "all sorts of excuses will be found when the War ends for not passing them" (quoted in Gray 1991, 69).

Even after the Pharmaceutical Benefits Act was passed, however, it did not appear to take a central place in the Labor Party's manifesto or electoral communications. The 1946 Labor policy speech mentioned the passage of the Pharmaceutical Benefits Act and new hospital grants to states without comment (McAllister and Moore 1991, 27). Pharmaceutical benefits were the subject of intense controversy with the medical association in the subsequent years, but the 1949 speech simply alludes to the fact that legislated benefits were not functioning, saying, "The people are now dependent on the good-will of members of … [the British Medical] Association," who were refusing to comply with the legislation (37). This desire to create new benefits combined with a lack of consensus on ideas about health policy helps explain the Curtin government's decision to bypass the ambitious and often internally conflicted health-planning bodies and give Treasury the responsibility for health proposals (Gillespie 1991, 155), a decision that was to shape both the pace of change and the priorities for policy development. Thus, a lack of consensus on ideas about health policy among federal politicians was one major element of the choice to take an incremental approach to policy development; another was the lack of obvious electoral incentives to take radical action.

## Lack of Electoral Motivations

The lack of a single, prominent report on health policy or services meant that there was no real rallying point for public opinion on health policy.

During this time, there was very little public opinion polling in Australia on the importance or even popularity of health insurance with voters, which is perhaps itself an indicator of the issue's low place on the public agenda. The earliest polls on health from this period, conducted in 1943, questioned voters about their preferred method of financing social services, including medical care (from taxation or a weekly household contribution). It did not include questions about where respondents ranked health or social service among other public issues, or whether they liked the idea of government involvement in health services at all (Gallup Poll [Australia] May–June 1943, August–September 1943).

In October 1943, Gallup reported, "Three out of four Australians would favor a national medical service, irrespective of whether it were free, or cost each family 2 [shillings] a week" (Gallup Poll [Australia] October 1943). However, about ten months later Gallup found that "the proposed non-contributory national hospital and medical service is right out of step with public opinion," since 60 per cent of voters wanted to require individual or household contributions for medical services (Gallup Poll [Australia] July 1944). In 1944, Australian voters rejected a constitutional referendum that would have greatly increased the Commonwealth government's powers over health and thirteen other areas. The preference for contributory social benefits, rather than free, tax-financed services such as the Pharmaceutical Benefits Scheme, was maintained until 1947, when a slight majority (53 per cent) of Australians preferred that social services be financed "from ordinary taxes" (Gallup Poll [Australia] March 1947).[13]

At the same time, however, Australians maintained a suspicion of high rates of taxation in order to fund social services. In 1945, Gallup found that "the Federal Government's plan of post-war social services is not supported by the people, if it means maintaining the present taxation levels" (Gallup Poll [Australia] May 1945). In 1948, voters were asked whether they would prefer increased social services (the type of increase was not specified) or reduced taxes, and about 70 per cent preferred lower taxes (Gallup Poll [Australia] February–March 1948). Therefore, it appears that even after the Labor government's attempts to implement the PBS were well underway, social services were not a high priority for voters.

Perhaps the most striking contrast with the United Kingdom in electoral incentives for action is that opinion on health policy in Australia remained divided along party lines for decades longer. In the United Kingdom, both major political parties supported the idea of a free, universal, and comprehensive public health service. The original plan for a broad health service was made by the wartime coalition government of both the Labour and Conservative parties, and when a new Labour government proposed the revised plan for the NHS, the Conservative Party quickly got on board – in fact, the Conservative Party's 1945 conference included a motion welcoming "the Government's decision to make a comprehensive National Health Service available to all" (Craig 1982, 60). Therefore, there was no policy alternative of "no public health services" being offered, and British polling from the time indicates that the principles of the NHS were salient to a large majority of the *entire* electorate, not a particular partisan group (L.R. Jacobs 1993, 113).

In contrast, in Australia, compulsory public health services were the exclusive policy domain of the Labor Party and tended not to elicit high levels of support from conservative Liberal-Country Party voters, as was evident late in 1945, shortly after the High Court ruling against the constitutionality of the PBS. Gallup questioned voters about the benefits that the Commonwealth government should provide, and while both Labor and non-Labor voters were in favour of benefits that had been in place for some time, such as old-age pensions, widows' pensions, and child endowments, they were divided about pharmaceutical benefits. Overall, 64 per cent were in favour of the Commonwealth government providing free medicines, but this represented about 75 per cent of Labor voters and 50 per cent of non-Labor (Gallup Poll [Australia] December 1945–January 1946). This partisan division continued in May 1948, when voters were asked if they favoured or opposed the government's plan for free medicines – the unimplemented PBS. Gallup reported, "Public opinion is unsettled … a bare majority of 51 percent is in favor, 33 percent opposed, and 16 percent undecided" (Gallup Poll [Australia] May 1948). However, a breakdown by voting intention provides more information: 70 per cent of interviewees who planned to vote for Labor in the next election were in favour of the free medicines scheme, while only 28 per cent of Liberal-Country Party voters were in favour. This split was repeated in later polls on the PBS and other health policies (Gallup Poll [Australia] February–March 1949, May–June 1949, March–May 1969), suggesting that even though these policies might appeal to Labor voters, they did not have the broad public appeal necessary to motivate radical action by the government. There is imperfect information available on where health issues ranked on Labor and Liberal voters' agendas, but the fact that free services were actually unpopular with a significant portion of the electorate likely made them less tempting for politicians to tackle.

## The Influence of Ideas on Priorities for Health Policy Development

In Canada, the choice of initial priorities for health policy development was strongly conditioned by the preferences of provincial governments. In Australia, the choice of priorities was determined mainly by the limited, pragmatic ideas about the problems of health policy development within the Commonwealth Treasury. It was the Treasury, rather than the Department of Health or any of the pre-existing health-planning bodies, that made the decision to proceed incrementally and begin with pharmaceuticals. This meant that "control of costs began to dominate official thinking" on the initial design of the PBS (Gillespie 1991, 157) and is further evidence of the lack of broad policy ideas on health policy development in Australia at this time.

Beginning with pharmaceutical benefits is not intuitive: they are not the most obviously important service, and this decision has been something of a puzzle in Australian health policy. However, archival records indicate that, in keeping with the government's concerns about the lack of resources to implement social security measures, the decision to begin with pharmaceuticals was a pragmatic one. The choice of priorities was also supported by compliant state governments and the federal government's expectation that pharmaceutical benefits would be less controversial with the medical profession. As we shall see, the government was incorrect on this last point, which meant that the PBS did not function until a Liberal-Country Party coalition government was elected in 1949 and was able to negotiate new terms with the Australian branch of the British Medical Association for the scheme's implementation.

During the Second World War, more than one-third of Australian doctors were on active service (Crowley 1973), and military dominance of medical mobilization resulted in "major gaps in civilian services" (Gillespie 1991, 118). This had a significant impact on the federal government's priorities for health services. A 1944 Treasury memorandum explained that pharmaceutical benefits were meant to be part of a comprehensive health scheme eventually, but alone, these services "will not involve any significant additional drain on professional man power and it is this feature which enables the introduction of the scheme before the end of the war" (NAA 1943c). Another Treasury document reiterates that the government was considering medical benefits, but

"owing to the absence in the fighting services of a substantial proportion of medical men, it is expected that it will not be possible to introduce a scheme of free medical services until after the war" (NAA
1943–4c). A survey of pharmacy facilities between 1943 and 1944 concluded that they were "completely, indeed more than, adequate as regards facilities for a government scheme of pharmacy benefits," since
"mortality among dispensers has been negligible since war broke out
– pharmacists have joined the Forces, but their shops have not been
closed" (NAA 1943–4a). This suggests that the choice of pharmaceuticals as a first priority depended on fairly idiosyncratic factors.
However, the Australian government's response to these particular resource constraints is consistent with a government motivated by a
pragmatic desire to implement some policy change, without guidance
from a broad idea about goals and approaches in the policy area.

Government documents emphasize that pharmaceutical benefits
were a practical rather than principled decision. A draft speech for the
second reading of the Pharmaceutical Benefits Bill in the House of
Representatives notes that other health priorities such as hospital construction and tuberculosis treatment were important, but that they
were "subject to matters of higher policy, such as manpower, etc." The
minister went on to say, "I am quite sure that the average citizen is not
likely to object to having free medicines simply because he is not able,
at present, to get free medical advice" (NAA 1943–4b). A caucus meeting in 1944 repeats this point, with one member arguing that pharmaceuticals were going first because they were practical, not because they
were most important: "I will admit that the provision of a medical service would have a more profound effect on the public health and on the
axiom of first things first it might be argued that free medicines could
wait" (NAA 1944c). A government pamphlet published in 1945 also
deals with this issue, asking whether the money intended for the PBS
should be spent on other health services. The publication answers,
"The only justification for such a question would be some evidence that
certain important health services were being denied to the public merely because there was no money to finance such schemes. *The reason why
pharmaceutical benefits have been introduced before other urgent measures is
merely a matter of practicability* since war conditions do not hamper its
introduction, on the contrary it assists the war effort" (NAA 1945d; emphasis added).

Therefore, pharmaceutical benefits do not seem to have been introduced out of any sense of urgency by the government to ensure that

citizens had access to free drugs. Rather, pharmaceutical benefits were a starting point for other policies. For a government anxious to implement some new social security measures "before the disruption of demobilization" (Gillespie 1991, 210) but wary of straining medical resources, pharmaceutical benefits became an "obvious" first choice of priorities. Pharmaceutical benefits and hospital grants for states that fell short of providing universal access were not strongly contested by state governments, but pharmaceutical benefits encountered greater opposition than expected from physicians – an issue taken up in the next chapter.

## Conclusion

The radical, simultaneous adoption of a full range of health services in the United Kingdom required radical conditions. Institutions centralized policy authority, there was a strong elite consensus on a cohesive health policy idea, and the public was both attentive to health policy and broadly supportive of action in the area. These conditions were not present in Canada and Australia, and their absence led to slower, incremental health policy development. This was the case even though both Canada and Australia initially considered adopting more comprehensive health programs and assumed that a full range of services was the eventual goal of health policy development.

In Canada, federal institutions gave provincial governments a veto power over the intergovernmental health policy agreements that would have been necessary for a radical, simultaneous approach to policy development. The national government could have chosen to expend the necessary political and financial capital to press for provincial agreement, but it lacked consensus on a programmatic idea of what health services should do, and health lacked the high levels of public salience that might have prompted government to refine its ideas on policy development.

In Australia, the barriers posed by federal institutions were somewhat lower, as the result of the national government's assertive constitutional position and comparatively greater fiscal powers. However, Australian politicians also lacked consensus on a clear, programmatic idea that linked ideology to health policy in practice. Furthermore, the lack of electoral motivations in Australia was even more significant in Canada. Here, health issues remained partisan, and a significant portion of non-Labor voters were actually opposed to the development of government health insurance and benefits.

The lack of centralized authority, consensus on health policy ideas, and electoral motivations led to a slower pace of health policy development in Canada and Australia. This meant that there was also an initial setting of priorities among health services, since both countries planned to adopt services in steps or stages. The process of priority setting had different results in the two countries but in both cases was strongly influenced by the more limited ideas about health policy that developed in the absence of a consensus on the nature of health services overall.

In Canada, the federal government's priorities for service adoption were influenced by provincial preferences and by federal elites' own ideas about health policy. In particular, Canadian elites developed an early and not entirely explicable concern about the cost challenges posed by pharmaceuticals that led them to discount this service as a possibility for current or even future policy development.

In Australia, priority setting was also influenced by pragmatic ideas about resource constraints, especially since the Treasury, rather than the Department of Health, decided which health benefit to adopt first. However, elites in Australia had different ideas concerning the feasible costs of services, shaped by Australia's experience with the wartime mobilization of doctors. They saw pharmaceuticals as a smaller, cheaper service, compared to hospital or medical services, and one that could be initiated without engaging in the politically charged question of physician autonomy.

The difference in priorities for service adoption in Canada and Australia had a crucial effect on the scope of their health systems over time, because both countries experienced increasing barriers to the adoption of additional services after the implementation of hospital services in Canada and pharmaceutical benefits in Australia. Chapter 4 turns to the particular politics of these barriers to change, and the role that ideas played in maintaining the scope of health systems.

# Entrenched Ideas and Barriers to Major Change

The previous chapter sought to explain why countries adopted either a radical or an incremental pace of health policy development. This chapter turns to the next element of the theoretical story. Why and how does the pace of change matter for policy outcomes? This chapter argues that the limited ideas and public expectations that help initiate an incremental pace of change also have a long-term effect on policy outcomes because they increase the barriers to major change, such as the adoption of additional public health services. Actors adapt their expectations for policy on the basis of what has happened in the past. However, an incremental process is characterized by a limited idea of what health services should do, and by specific ideas concerning the unfeasibility or undesirability of certain services. This results in lower expectations for services over time, as both policy elites and the public focus on existing services.

This theoretical expectation is based on policy ideas acting as a filter, to direct the attention of actors (and particularly elites) towards some aspects of a policy problem and away from others. This affects their choices and therefore the path of policy development. Another theoretically plausible expectation is that actors will learn from past policies (drawing either positive or negative lessons), and this will affect their choices and the path of policy development. For example, Heclo (1974, 315) describes a process of "classic conditioning" of elites, where "once implemented, a technique such as social insurance has tended to be readopted, to be considered the 'natural' policy response for other types of income risk." If this was the case, we might expect that experience with hospital and medical insurance in Canada would lead to the application of these policy models to other services, such as pharmaceuticals. However, in order for this type of learning to lead to policy

adoption, political elites must first see two policy problems as analogous (i.e., pharmaceutical services present basically the same type of
problem as hospital and medical services). Second, they must draw
positive lessons from the initial policy. This chapter will document the
lack of evidence that either of these conditions is met in the Canadian
case. For reasons that are not entirely clear, Canadian political elites
throughout the study period considered pharmaceutical services to be
substantively different from hospital and medical services, in some
cases explicitly rejecting expert attempts to "teach" them about the parallels and therefore prompt policy expansion. Furthermore, despite the
partisan consensus and public attachment to public health insurance in
Canada, the longstanding narrative of reform has tended to be framed
as a need to "fix what we have" rather than "build on our success,"
limiting the opportunities for positive lesson-drawing by elites.

In Canada and Australia, the development of health policy provides
an opportunity to observe the way limited ideas about the health system and pharmaceutical policy become entrenched in the minds of
elites and the public. These entrenched ideas become significant barriers to major policy change and help explain policy stability, even when
we might expect institutional or economic barriers to change to be less
problematic.

## Canada

In 1957, after years of negotiation, Canada adopted a program of nationwide public insurance for in-patient hospital care and diagnostic
services, with half the funds provided by the federal government. It
required compromise both within the federal government, where
health minister Paul Martin and his department continued to advocate
for health insurance, despite the scepticism of Prime Minister St
Laurent, and between federal and provincial governments (Taylor 1987,
chapter 4). The final implementation of the policy was actually undertaken by a Conservative government after the Liberals lost power in the
June 1957 election, and after hospital insurance was in place, the slow,
cautious process of nationwide health policy development stalled.

At the time, medical insurance had received substantial attention
from both elites and the public as the next step in policy development,
but as will be detailed in chapter 6, its eventual adoption was far from
automatic. The barriers posed by alternative institutional development in the provinces and the greater organization of the Canadian

Medical Association and its physician-sponsored insurance plans meant that nationwide public medical insurance was adopted with more difficultly and ultimately less federal control than hospital insurance (LAC 1972b).

Since the adoption of medical insurance in 1968, there have been several important attempts to develop nationwide pharmaceutical insurance in Canada, but none have been successful. After the adoption of hospital insurance, and certainly after the adoption of medical insurance, adding services to Canadian health systems took on the characteristics of major or radical change. The three failed pharmacare proposals faced significant ideational and electoral barriers at the national level, in addition to the potential barriers posed by provinces' institutional veto power. Politicians' ideas about the feasibility of pharmaceutical insurance were initially limited: ideas about potentially uncontrollable pharmaceutical insurance costs appear in policy discussions in the late 1940s and early 1950s. The precise origins of these ideas are not clear, but they are remarkable for both their longevity in Canadian policy discussions and for their variable and sometimes tenuous connection with the realities of pharmaceutical policy. They first appeared well before the therapeutic revolution in pharmaceuticals increased drug prices in the 1960s, and they persisted through changing economic circumstances in Canada and developments in pharmaceutical management both in Canada and in other countries with broad insurance or benefit schemes.

An incremental pace of policy development also meant elite ideas about the scope of the health system were restricted to those services that were adopted first, and the discourse of staged health insurance placed limits on public expectations. The top priority or priorities were discussed in public as part of election campaigns, newspaper coverage, and parliamentary debate, but later priorities by definition received less attention, and this resulted in a cycle of limited discussion, little public attention, and little policy action – feeding back into low levels of salience.

The low priority of pharmaceutical insurance became self-reinforcing. Governments' public debate and deliberation on hospital and medical insurance was crucial to the development of public expectations for services and therefore electoral incentives to act. However, there were few chances for this to occur for pharmaceuticals. Pharmaceutical insurance was rarely debated outside the closed circuit of the DHW and the federal Cabinet, and until the 1970s neither private drug insurance nor provincial drug benefits were widely available. This meant there was little basis for the formation of public expectations about pharmaceutical insurance that were analogous to the development of expectations for hospital and medical insurance over time.

Drugs were not entirely absent from the public agenda, however. In the late 1950s and throughout the 1960s, Canadian publics and governments became very concerned about the high prices of prescription drugs. This resulted in an alternative track for pharmaceutical policy development that was surprisingly but consistently separate from health insurance debates. The one exception is discussed below: in the early 1970s, the DHW unsuccessfully proposed a Drug Price Program that would use broad public insurance to manage drug prices, among other concerns.

The alternative track of policy development focused on price control and patents and contributed to limited ideas about pharmaceuticals through more than three decades of policymaking at the federal level. The following sections trace these ideas and demonstrate how they contributed to the failure of three specific opportunities for the adoption of nationwide pharmaceutical insurance, in 1972, 1997, and 2002. There was also a proposal for pharmaceutical insurance in the 1964 *Report of the Royal Commission on Health Services*. The report is discussed in chapter 6 as an important contributor to major change in public medical insurance in Canada, and this chapter briefly discusses why the commission's additional proposals, including pharmaceutical insurance, were not seriously considered by the federal government of the day.

## An Alternative Path of Pharmaceutical Policy: Drug Prices and Patents

In Canada, pharmaceutical *insurance* was little discussed. However, pharmaceutical *prices* were of greater public concern. In the late 1950s and early 1960s, public expectations and the attendant electoral incentives they produced actually helped ensure the place of pharmaceutical prices and their management on the federal government's agenda. Federal investigation of drug prices began in 1958 with an internal report by the director of investigation and research, Combines Investigation Act, called the "Green Book."

Between 1958 and 1969, drug prices were the subject of at least four more government inquiries, both internal and public.[14] The problem was identified as drug patents, which produced monopolies and high prices. The solution was a series of changes to patent law and tariffs on drugs, the centrepiece of which was a new allowance for compulsory licensing of imported pharmaceutical products. Compulsory licensing creates a legal requirement for a drug patent holder to let other firms produce its drug before the patent expires, in return for a specified level of royalties from the new generic product.

The new compulsory licensing provisions passed in 1969 reduced the patent life from seventeen years to six or seven (and arguably the effective patent life to zero, given that most of that time is pre-market, while the drug is undergoing trials) and introduced competition between branded and generic medicines (Eden 1989). This had a significant impact on drug prices (Gorecki 1981, xii), but an unintended consequence was to further restrict policymakers' views of pharmaceutical policies in a way that made it very difficult for them to consider later proposals for pharmaceutical insurance.

## Public Expectations and the Demand for Price Control

Although there is little evidence to suggest that the Canadian public expected government drug insurance, they were clearly concerned about drug prices. In 1960, an Ontario parliamentary committee noted, "For some reason the public has attached great importance to the spread in drug prices" (*Globe & Mail*, 6 October 1960). Complaints about drug prices were provided as the main rationale for the first Canadian investigation, which described its work as prompted by "a large number of complaints that prices of drugs in Canada were exorbitant," and "informal complaints about the high cost of drugs" (Director of Investigations and Research 1961). That same report noted that discussion of the profits of manufacturers had been widespread, particularly since the high-profile investigation into monopolistic drug pricing by U.S. Senator Estes Kefauver, begun shortly after the first internal government study started in Canada in 1958.[15]

Public concern was also likely influenced by the increase in "wonder drugs." Although sulfonamide drugs and penicillin to treat infection had been available since the 1930s and mid-1940s, respectively, the rate of discovery was increasing. Corticosteroids were introduced in 1949, the first classes of tranquilizers in 1953, and the first synthetic, patentable antibiotics to deal with drug-resistant infections in 1958 (Director of Investigations and Research 1961; Mann 2004). Canadians were certainly experiencing increases in their out-of-pocket drug costs, which was likely a combination of increased drug use and higher prices for new products. The Department of National Health and Welfare (Research and Statistics Division) (1963) found that "each Canadian in 1961 spent nearly twice as much in retail drug stores on prescribed drugs as he spent in 1953," although at this time the percentage of personal health expenditures spent on prescription drugs (7 per cent) remained about the same as it had for many years.

Finally, public concern was exacerbated by interventions from interested individuals and groups. The Canadian Congress of Labour (CCL), a union umbrella group, had played an ongoing role with the CCF in pressuring the Liberal Party to act on hospital and medical insurance (Maioni 1998), and in 1955, the *Globe & Mail* reported that the CCL had asked the government to look into drug prices. According to the labour group, "Drug prices are too high and it appears that someone is gouging the public." Prime Minister St Laurent responded that complaints should be directed to the Restrictive Trade Practices Commission, an arm's-length body of the Department of Justice (*Globe and Mail*, 16 December 1955), and perhaps these are some of the public complaints the "Green Book" mentions in its report.

The public statements of Jules Gilbert, the owner of an eponymous generic drug manufacturing company in Toronto, about problems with drug pricing also appear to have been an important impetus to early government investigation of drug prices. Lang (1974, 28) suggests this connection, quoting an out-of-print booklet that states, "It was partly the publicity caused by Gilbert's statements to the press and to anyone else who would listen, which forced the Canadian Parliament to initiate its own investigation" (Stephenson 1967, 29). Although the Green Book and Restrictive Trade Practices Commission (RTPC) studies do not mention Gilbert, archival evidence demonstrates that he was a very active contributor to the debate and a dogged participant in later public commissions on drug prices. Gilbert's campaign to expand the market for his lower-priced generic drugs had an unpredictable effect on policy development, in that theory has difficulty predicting the potential impact of one particularly motivated individual. However, it appears that this effect was significant. In a 1961 profile of Gilbert, Pierre Berton argues, "If any single man can be said to have focused public attention on high drug prices in Canada, it is Gilbert ... For the past two years he had been regularly in the headlines, appearing before commissions and panels, issuing statements, making speeches and (until members of the pharmaceutical industry refused to appear with him) taking part in consumer panels" (LAC 1961c).

Gilbert argued, "There isn't a valid drug patent written in Canada" (LAC 1961c), and furthermore, the Food and Drug Directorate disadvantaged generic manufacturers such as him with overly strict regulation of manufacturing plants and products. In 1966, Gilbert wrote to the chairman of the Interdepartmental Advisory Board on Standards for Pharmaceutical Manufacturers about an unsatisfactory plant inspection and alleged that the Food and Drug Directorate, "under its present method of operation, is designed … to be the basic cause for maintenance of high drug prices and to be the future cause for increasing drug prices" by blocking competition (LAC 1966). The file on Gilbert held by Library and Archives Canada contains almost a decade's worth of similar correspondence and news coverage. Although Gilbert's actions were undoubtedly self-interested – as Berton reports, he was "the first to admit … that this particular crusade has also been a profitable one for him" (LAC 1961c) – it also alerted the Canadian public and policymakers to the issue of high drug prices in Canada in a way that provided strong electoral motivation for policy action *and* prompted a particular type of policy response, given Gilbert's focus on the role of patents in causing high prices.

## The Developing Consensus on Drug Prices

The internal investigation of drug prices begun in 1958, the Green Book, was submitted to the RTPC in 1961 with a request that the commission conduct public hearings and report on the manufacture, distribution, and sale of drugs in Canada. This was an important step, because the Green Book findings were not made public until the request for further investigation went to the RTPC (*Globe & Mail*, 4 February 1961).[16] The choice of venue for this investigation was also important in shaping the government's understanding of the problem and the eventual choice of policy solutions. The prime minister's statement in 1955 that the Canadian Congress of Labour should direct its complaints about drug prices to the RTPC was almost certainly an instance of buck-passing; however, any federal response to public expectations for action on drug prices was also constrained by the limits of federal jurisdiction over pharmaceuticals. Policy development occurred only where it was possible for the federal government to exercise centralized authority over the policy area.

The Food and Drugs Act (1953) and the Narcotics Control Act (1961) were the only pieces of federal legislation that directly mentioned drugs: the former focused on the safety of drugs, while the later was concerned with trade controls (Department of National Health and Welfare [Research and Statistics Division] 1964). Although drug prices were the subject of "considerable concern" for both federal and provincial levels of government throughout the 1960s (Gorecki and Henderson 1981), the federal government's constitutional jurisdiction over trade and commerce, specifically the Combines Investigation Act (1952), contributed to the fact that initial investigations were conducted in an arena that allowed unilateral federal action.

Following the Green Book, government investigations tended to be more public and to encompass a broader range of federal government departments. The RTPC investigation began holding public hearings in 1961, and in 1962 a Special Committee of the House of Commons on Drug Costs and Prices (later known as the Harley Committee) was formed. In late 1964, an Interdepartmental Committee on Drugs was established to provide advice from the Departments of Justice, Finance, and Health and Welfare, among others. Also in 1964, the Royal Commission on Health Services (the Hall Commission) released its report, which acknowledged the investigations of high drug prices and agreed with their conclusions. The commission recommended a Prescription Drug Benefit to be introduced by the provinces and included a wide variety of recommendations for drug-price control (Royal Commission on Health Services 1964, 40–1). By 1965, these reports and investigations had produced a consensus that "Canadian drug prices [were] among the highest in the world" (LAC 1965b) and that drug manufacturers "taking undue advantage of the tariff structure," along with the current rules around drug patents, were to blame (Director of Investigations and Research 1961; Lang 1974).

Lang argues that this consensus, particularly among bureaucrats, was an important policy driver: "The initial investigations into drug costs in Canada had been begun by the civil service in 1958. By 1965, the same civil servants had developed a self-induced commitment to lower the cost of drugs and to defeat what they considered to be an arrogant industry" (Lang 1974, 136). As part of the strong, centralized executive characteristic of Canada's parliamentary system, the civil service is an important policy actor. However, as will be demonstrated with the failure of the 1972 proposal for national pharmaceutical insurance, bureaucratic enthusiasm is not sufficient to introduce a major new program or pass a significant policy change. The difference between the 1972 program and these earlier amendments to the Patent Act was that, in 1969, the bureaucrats were able to get politicians onside, presumably because there were external, electoral incentives for government action on drug prices. This allowed for the passage of compulsory licensing provisions that significantly reduced the patent life and hence price of new drugs.

Another important element in the success of the drug price reforms was the fact that the Patent Act amendments were a type of policy that was fundamentally different from the subsequent proposals for pharmaceutical insurance. They required limited outlay of federal resources, could be enacted without consultation with provincial governments, and although they required confrontation with one major organized interest, the pharmaceutical industry, this actor enjoyed far less influence and prestige than the Canadian Medical Association, or industry groups in other countries like the United Kingdom.

Despite an intense lobbying effort, the Pharmaceutical Manufacturers Association of Canada could not block federal action on patents (Lang 1974). The Canadian pharmaceutical industry was not in a strong position vis-à-vis government at this time. It was not a major part of the economy and did not conduct much of the economically important research and development in Canada (27). According to a federal report, "The great majority [of Canadian-controlled firms] ... are small in size, and mostly involved in the production and distribution of proprietary medicines, household remedies and sundry drugs" (Department of National Health and Welfare [Research and Statistics Division] 1964, 30). The report concludes that "in many respects" the Canadian pharmaceutical market was "simply an extension of the United States market" (31). Therefore, although organized groups could have posed some barrier to the development of regulation in this area, the federal government did not face provincial objections or pressing financial concerns and was motivated to act by a combination of consensus on a clear causal idea (that patents produced high prices) and the public salience of the drug price problem. These developments set the stage for the failure of future pharmacare proposals at the national level.

## 1964: The Royal Commission on Health Services

The Royal Commission on Health Services, or Hall Commission, reported around the same time as many of the above-mentioned studies and appears to have been strongly influenced by their concern with drug prices and patents. Its recommendation for pharmaceutical benefits had to compete with its focus on drug price control and with the much greater emphasis placed on medical insurance. Although commentators sometimes (incorrectly) describe the commission as the first proposal for pharmaceutical insurance at the national level in Canada, this element of the commission's report does not appear to have received serious political attention.

The commission made two recommendations related to pharmaceutical insurance. First, that the federal government make grants to the provinces "for the purpose of introducing a Prescription Drug Benefit within the Health Services Programme" and that these grants cover 50 per cent of the cost of such a program. Second, that patients be required to make a one-dollar "contributory payment" for each prescription, although it might be waived for "drugs required for long-term therapy" (Royal Commission on Health Services 1964, 41). The commission was clear on the importance of including all drugs as part of a comprehensive health service, noting that covering only a selection of drugs or only drugs in hospital could result in adverse incentives for physicians and prescribers, and "could affect the quality of therapy" (346).

These two recommendations were followed by an additional twenty-three for controlling drug prices and costs. Despite the importance of pharmaceutical benefits to the goal of a comprehensive health service, the report devoted considerably more research and analysis to drug prices and patents, including the removal of federal tax on prescription drugs, the study of a voluntary price-restraint program by industry, and changes to patents and tariffs (Royal Commission on Health Services 1964, 41–3). Furthermore, the report maintained the incremental approach of earlier health insurance proposals, noting that its overall recommendations for health services would be "introduced in stages" and acknowledging "that this whole programme cannot be put into effect immediately or simultaneously in all provinces" (14). As discussed in chapter 6 of this book, nationwide medical insurance was a clear priority for both the commission and the federal government receiving the report, so pharmaceuticals and other auxiliary services were again pushed down the agenda. The recommendation for a co-payment for pharmaceuticals and the focus on drug prices also set pharmaceuticals apart from medical insurance in the type of policy problem they presented.

The DHW prepared draft comments in response to the commission's recommendations on pharmaceuticals, which noted that it would be possible to integrate "prescription drug benefits with the Hospital Insurance and Diagnostic Services programme and a medical services insurance programme" as the report called for, and also that "a more limited initial approach" to pharmaceuticals was also possible, although the details of this approach were not included (LAC n.d.[a]). The department also provided a detailed response to the commission's recommendations on drug prices. However, outside this one reference to the potential feasibility of including pharmaceuticals, which rested on the problematic assumption that the cost-sharing arrangements used for hospital insurance were still politically viable, there is no evidence that pharmaceuticals were part of the federal government's discussions or plans for health insurance at this time. In terms of political consideration, pharmaceutical benefits were completely overshadowed by the thorny problem of medical insurance, which became a major focus of federal-provincial negotiation over the next five years (Taylor 1987; Maioni 1998; Bryden 1997).

## 1972: The Drug Price Program

At the 1965 Federal-Provincial Conference, Prime Minister Lester Pearson referred to the ongoing work of the Special Committee of the House of Commons on Drug Costs and Prices, saying, "We hope that its recommendations will have the effect of reducing the prices of drugs, and thereby make it easier for a complete health service to make drugs, prescribed for major illnesses, available on a prepaid basis" (Canada 1965, 16). Interestingly, this is one of the only instances of a politician linking control of pharmaceutical prices to public pharmaceutical insurance; they were not even explicitly linked in the commission's report, although it made separate recommendations on both issues. Despite the bureaucratic and public attention given to drug prices since the late 1950s, policies to deal with drug prices were pursued quite separately from those of pharmaceutical insurance. This is consistent with the expectation that limited policy ideas about the problem of pharmaceuticals will channel policy development towards issues that appear more tractable.

Although the changes to patent law in 1969 had a significant impact on drug prices (Gorecki 1981, xii), the unintended consequences were their reinforcement of previous ideas about the prohibitive cost of drugs and direction of politicians' views of pharmaceutical policies in a way that made it very difficult for them to consider later proposals for pharmaceutical insurance. The dominant idea of pharmaceutical *insurance* was a program with the potential for uncontrollable costs. Pharmaceutical patents and price control, or pharmaceutical *management*, was seen as a much more tractable problem. It did not involve jurisdictional issues, since the national government had authority to regulate pharmaceuticals, and it was a relatively inexpensive regulatory policy, rather than a costly new benefit program. This meant when federal politicians considered pharmaceutical issues, they understood the relevant problem to be prices (which they dealt with through patents, although an insurance program might also affect prices), and they understood insurance to be an unfeasible or undesirable option.

This separation between pharmaceutical management and pharmaceutical insurance, at least in the minds of the political elite, is evident in the failure of a proposal for a Drug Price Program discussed between 1971 and 1972 that would have linked the two issues. In 1971, the minister of health proposed a Drug Price Program that would include the extension of medicare (as nationwide health insurance was known) to cover prescription drugs (LAC 1971). The bureaucratic authors of the proposals clearly saw them as a principled policy choice that would not only reduce drug prices, which were an ongoing concern, despite the mitigating effect of new patent laws (Lang 1974, 248), but also fill a gap in the provision of health care and rationalize the use of public services. A draft memo from the DHW entitled "Some Social Reasons for Pharmacare" argues that "society has come to think of health care as being part of a total system and as a result has recognized that an important segment of the health care system is not presently being covered by an insurance program," and furthermore, that "it does not make much sense to pay a physician under Medicare to examine and prescribe for his patient if the patient is unable to benefit" because the prescription is unaffordable (LAC n.d.[b]). They recommended benefits be introduced on a universal basis, since the federal government would have the most bargaining power over prices as the single purchaser of drugs (LAC 1972b).

These ideas about pharmaceutical insurance as a way to lower the *social* cost of pharmaceuticals contrast with the position of cabinet ministers. Consistent with their limited ideas concerning health and pharmaceutical policy, they did not consider the department's recommendation for a universal program, and seemed most concerned with containing the cost of pharmaceuticals *to the federal government*. In cabinet, the prime minister said he did not wish to extend Medicare to drugs "because of the considerable expenditures involved and the difficulty of getting the provinces to pay their share" (LAC 1971). Ministers thought pharmaceutical insurance should be avoided because "the government's first priority should be to restore public confidence in its economic policies" (LAC 1972b),[17] and that "pharmacare would be the beginning of a very expensive program which would undermine the confidence of the middle-income groups in the government's ability to control the budget" (LAC 1972b).

Although the primary focus of the memorandum was price control, and the Cabinet debate focused on overall cost, there was also some reference to the interests of organized groups. The memorandum's authors argued that the program would be popular with health professionals and the drug industry. This possibility did not appear to convince Cabinet ministers, who suggested that the "drug lobby [pharmaceutical industry] would learn of the interdepartmental studies [of drug insurance] and would react violently against them," and that the inclusion of prescription drugs in the still-new medicare scheme would "only exacerbate" the medical profession's dissatisfaction with it (LAC 1971).

There is reason to be sceptical about the strength of opposition from the pharmaceutical industry. At the time, pharmaceutical industry groups were engaged in an expensive and ultimately unsuccessful lobbying effort against the new compulsory licensing regime (Lexchin 1993, 150), and it is possible that internal government proposals for insurance schemes were simply of less importance to them. Crucially, the proposal for drug insurance never left the confines of Cabinet, so the validity of these concerns was not tested. Furthermore, the quotes above represent the complete interest group discussion. Ideas about costs were much more prominent.

Provincial preferences and policy development also received little attention in federal Cabinet. When Cabinet reviewed the Drug Price Program, it had not yet been presented to provincial governments (LAC 1972a). DHW predicted that the program would be popular with the Quebec government, which had previously requested federal cost-sharing for drugs for low-income seniors and social assistance recipients, and was generally optimistic about the potential for provincial cooperation (LAC 1972c). However, ministers did not discuss the proposals in light of the provinces' preferences or their existing pharmaceutical insurance programs, but instead concentrated on opportunities for the federal government to claim credit with voters. The minister of health, John Munro, commented that he did not anticipate opposition from the provinces, but he was concerned that the federal government should be able to claim credit for any program, saying it would be preferable to make a positive initiative than to wait for provincial consensus to develop. In Cabinet discussion, other ministers argued "that the federal government would only get credit for a new initiative if it was put forward as a major Pharmacare program; it would not get much credit for an offer to discuss with provincial governments the possibility of introducing a staged program" (LAC 1972a).

Despite this concern, and on the recommendation of the minister of health, Cabinet focused on a "staged program" that would provide drug coverage to the elderly and eventually expand to cover children and other groups. The result was that drug insurance proposals were not debated as a principled extension of medicare: Cabinet ministers explicitly rejected the bureaucratic authors' attempts to draw a link between existing hospital and medical insurance and the proposed pharmaceutical insurance. Instead, the proposals were considered as one of a number of unrelated options for assisting elderly Canadians (LAC 1972a). One minister expressed the opinion that "if anything were to be done for older people, it should be simple and dramatic," such as "a once-and-for-all increase to $100 for the OAS [Old Age Security program]" (ibid.).

Thus, DHW attempts to frame pharmaceutical insurance as a tool for price control failed, and this failure is a legacy of politicians' policy ideas about the nature of both the drug price and drug insurance problems. Elites had developed a consensus that patents caused high drug prices. This allowed for strong action in this policy area, but it also made it difficult for politicians to conceptualize the drug price issue in any other way. Despite the name of the proposal, in Cabinet discussions of the Drug Price Program the issue of drug prices received few mentions. Politicians interpreted the proposals solely as a benefits program that had historically been dismissed for cost reasons, and in the end decided pharmacare for seniors was only one of "various possible ways of providing further assistance to older people [that] should be considered in the more comprehensive financial content of the budget and deferred until such time as that could be done" (LAC 1972a).

There is limited evidence on electoral motivations for drug coverage at this time, but there were few opportunities for public expectations to develop. A memo arguing for the Drug Price Program noted that federal departments "have received and continue to receive many letters from the public complaining about the high cost of prescription drugs and many requests that a drug insurance program similar to Medicare be made available" (LAC 1972b). However, the same memo goes on to discuss strategies for implementing a program and says that since the federal government is not in a position to act unilaterally, it could "wait ... for provincial and public pressures to build up," or actively encourage these pressures in hopes of igniting a desire for intergovernmental cooperation on the issue (ibid.). This suggests that proponents of pharmaceutical insurance recognized the potential for public opinion to aid policy development, but that the necessary pressure did not yet exist.

Furthermore, most provinces did not begin to introduce targeted public drug benefits (for seniors and social assistance recipients) until the early 1970s, so Canadians' first experience with public insurance for drugs was both late and restricted to a relatively small portion of the population (Grootendorst 2002). Private insurance was also limited: a 1964 study of prescription drugs in Canada reported that "insurance against expenditures for prescribed drugs became available in Canada only recently, in a few prototype schemes" (Department of National Health and Welfare [Research and Statistics Division] 1964, 105). Eight years later, the situation remained much the same. A report of the Canadian Pharmaceutical Association noted that private, third-party prescription drug insurance programs "are not believed to cover a significant portion of the population" (Commission on Pharmaceutical Services 1971, 96). Certainly the campaign promises of political parties, and policy agendas of governments, never alluded to pharmaceutical insurance as anything other than a vaguely distant possibility. Although it is possible that the public was beginning to develop expectations about drug insurance based on a perceived "gap" in the now-comprehensive public hospital and medical insurance they enjoyed, there is little evidence for this kind of public pressure.

## 1997: National Forum on Health Proposes Universal Insurance

After the quiet failure of the 1972 Drug Price Program, pharmaceutical policy at the federal level continued on a track of managing prices and patents. In 1985, the Commission of Inquiry on the Pharmaceutical Industry presented recommendations to the federal government on new patent rights and price competition in the industry (Eastman 1985). The Commission's only comment on pharmaceutical insurance was a recommendation that provincial governments ensure public benefit programs require a "significant contribution to each purchase by the consumer, arranged in such a way that price competition in induced," and encourage private plans to do the same (xvii). In 1987, federal Parliament made significant changes to the compulsory licensing provisions that had helped limit Canadian drug prices since 1969, and compulsory licensing was abolished in 1993 (Douglas and Jutras 2008).

The next federal attention to pharmaceutical insurance came in 1997, with the report of the National Forum on Health. The forum was chaired by the prime minister but drew its membership from non-governmental policy experts and was convened to fulfil a commitment in the 1993 Liberal "Red Book" platform (Liberal Party of Canada 1993, 78). Interviewees said it was seen in government as an opportunity to consider general health reform "without being in crisis mode," to assess and improve cost control, and in the words of one respondent, "to buy time."[18] Its final report, published in February 1997, made a bold though high-level recommendation for nationwide, public, and universal pharmaceutical insurance: "Because pharmaceuticals are medically necessary and public financing is the only reasonable way to promote universal access and to control costs, we believe Canada should take the necessary steps to include drugs as part of its publicly funded health care system" (National Forum on Health [Canada] 1997, 22).

This proposal received more attention than any previous call for pharmacare at the national level. The June 1997 Liberal platform "endors[ed] pharmacare as a long-term national objective" and pledged to work with provinces and territories "to develop a national plan and timetable for introducing prescription drugs into our medicare system" (Liberal Party of Canada 1997). The November 1997 Speech from the Throne announced a plan to reinvest $300 million in health initiatives, including a Health Transition Fund that would, among other things, "help the provincial governments innovate in the areas of primary care and provide more integration in the delivery of health services, home care and pharmacare" (Canada, Governor General 1997). In the same speech, the government also stated its intention to "develop a national plan, timetable and a fiscal framework for providing Canadians with better access to medically necessary drugs" (ibid.).

These promising plans did not, however, result in significant policy development. According to Marie Fortier, executive director for the Secretariat of the Forum and former associate deputy minister of health, "After the Forum, the whole idea of national pharmacare sort of fell down ... in a black hole."[19] When pharmaceuticals next appeared on the federal government's public agenda in 2000, the focus had returned to pharmaceutical management policies (Canada 2000).

Given the apparent momentum of the National Forum's proposals, why did they fail? One important reason was that the proposals came at the end of a very difficult economic period in Canada. The pain of a severe recession in 1990 and 1991 was extended when high levels of public debt at both the federal and provincial levels resulted in a downgrading of the country's triple-A credit rating. As one interviewee noted, when the Liberal government came to power in 1993, "there was no money at that time. Canada had been declared nearly bankrupt, a third world country, in the *Wall Street Journal.*"[20] After four years of deep cuts, including federal health transfers to provinces in the previous year, the country was just on the cusp of recovery when the proposals were made public (Treff and Perry 1997, 1998). Provincial governments were angered by the federal changes to health transfers and only beginning to recover themselves, and were in no mood to negotiate what they called "boutique programs," according to Paul Genest, a former advisor to two federal health ministers. He explained that provinces "were not ready to talk about these new horizons or adding new things on when they felt that they were struggling mightily to deal with the core."[21]

Another possible economic barrier to the National Forum's pharmacare proposal involved a more specific issue of pharmaceutical regulatory policy. There is some evidence that the 1993 passage of Bill C-91, which abolished compulsory licensing, increased drug prices (Lexchin 1997), which would have increased the cost of an expanded public pharmaceutical insurance program. However, the federal House of Commons Standing Committee on Industry reviewed the legislation abolishing compulsory licensing in April 1997, and committee members apparently did not make this link. Their first recommendation, which they admitted was on a topic "strictly outside the Committee mandate," was "to investigate the feasibility of a national pharmacare program" following the recommendations of the National Forum on Health (Standing Committee on Industry 1997b). Their third recommendation was to retain the twenty-year patent protection granted by Bill C-91, despite hearing testimony from both the Canadian generic industry association and former National Forum experts that this would tend to affect the cost of a national pharmacare program (Standing Committee on Industry 1997a).

These immediate circumstances clearly had a role in the failure of the National Forum plan, but I argue elites' limited policy ideas and correspondingly limited public expectations were crucial barriers. These ideas regarding pharmaceuticals and the scope of the health system, which developed in the 1940s and 1950s and blocked policy expansion in 1972, were also evident in this later policy episode, preventing the extraordinary ideational and electoral circumstances that might have overcome immediate institutional and fiscal hurdles.

I expected to find statements by policy elites about the necessity of "fixing what we have" versus "adding something new" when considering whether to adopt pharmaceutical programs, and this was reflected in the comments of federal policymakers and advisors on the failure of the National Forum proposals. Interviewees consistently reported prioritizing improvement of the existing health programs over system expansion. Although elites tended to frame limited ideas about the scope of the health system as a response to the long period of government cuts, these ideas are also evident at earlier periods (such as the 1972 Drug Price Program), and later during relatively good economic times (such as the 2002 Romanow and Kirby proposals).

A policy advisor recalled that when the Liberals were planning their 1993 election platform, the main goal in health was to "reassure people that medicare did not need to be dismantled."[22] The federal and provincial governments shared responsibility for health and faced an overlapping constituency of potentially concerned voters, so reassuring the public also meant appeasing provinces, which had suffered from federal cuts to health transfers. Fortier suggests when the National Forum reported, it was "too early in the post-deficit years to think about something big like [pharmacare], also some of the cuts were still hurting ... There was a lot of anger [in the provinces] about the ... reductions overall in transfers."[23]

Roy Romanow, who was premier of Saskatchewan when the National Forum report was published, confirmed this sense of provincial attitudes. He recalls that most premiers at this time were "more preoccupied with the withdrawal of federal funding to the overall healthcare system in the 1990s ... than it was about specific programs."[24] Genest noted that he did not think the provinces took the National Forum's pharmacare proposals seriously enough, but also admitted that "when they're having trouble affording bread and butter and we're saying, 'Let's work on cheese,' you can appreciate their point of view."[25]

In short, even when health reforms were on the federal agenda, expansion through the adoption of additional services was not. A sense of crisis about the sustainability of existing services precluded the possibility of drawing positive lessons that might apply to pharmaceuticals. In 2008, Abby Hoffman, assistant deputy minister in Health Canada in charge of pharmaceutical management policies, summed up the lack of serious attention to pharmaceutical insurance by federal governments: "I think, reflecting back on the last fifteen years, I don't see any government actually seriously saying, 'The next building block in the evolution of Canadian medicare is a comprehensive, universal pharmacare regime' ... nobody has gone down that road."[26]

This limited idea of what the health system should do posed an important barrier to reform, but so did a limited idea of pharmaceutical insurance itself. I expected that if elites' ideas about pharmaceuticals become more limited over time, they should make "explicit, consistent reference" (A.M. Jacobs 2009, 262) to a dominant understanding of insurance as unfeasible or too expensive and should pursue policies on a non-insurance track aligned with this understanding, and this was the case in Canada.

A policy advisor remembers that during the deficit period, "the fear of opening the floodgates to something hugely expensive and uncontrollable [like pharmacare], which you could never take away from anybody, was there for everybody."[27] Similarly, Hoffman said that after the National Forum, "there wasn't real political appetite to really carry these ideas forward ... even if there was some sort of publicly and privately funded universal program, the costs were just regarded as so daunting." She went on, "Even if ... a universal system would provide more access and be less burdensome on the economy than this fragmented mess that we have today, this is a great example of a terrific academic idea ... that is impossible to sell, and it will continue to be impossible to sell as long as costs ... go up at the rate they are going up."[28]

Provincial pharmaceutical programs did not appear to influence federal policy ideas in this area, perhaps because political decision-makers did not have detailed knowledge of them. One policy advisor commented on the perception that the federal government did not have much experience delivering health care, and the provinces for the most part did not trust the federal government to know what to do.[29] To the extent that federal elites did know about provincial programs, their knowledge reinforced ideas about pharmaceutical insurance being financially unfeasible. In an interview, a political advisor detailed the measures the Chrétien government had undertaken to control the federal deficit in the 1990s and suggested pharmacare did not fit into these efforts, saying, "The experience in the provinces was that costs are runaway."[30]

After the National Forum made its proposals in 1997, there was a shift in focus towards management policies aimed at controlling drug prices and ensuring cost-effective prescribing – an echo of the 1970s focus on prices rather than insurance. A policy advisor noted that the next major intergovernmental discussion of health policy, the 2000 First

Ministers Meeting, concentrated on pharmaceutical management rather than insurance because it was about cost containment, and this was easier to get agreement on than insurance.[31] She recalled that the provinces' message to the federal minister was "'Don't give us another responsibility, we're drowning ... if you ask us to do anything big, we will refuse.'"[32] Instead, the conference communiqué included a statement that federal and provincial health ministers would develop "strategies for assessing the cost-effectiveness of prescription drugs," while the federal government would work to strengthen surveillance of drugs that were already on the market (Canada 2000).

A year later, the Annual Conference of Federal, Provincial, and Territorial Ministers of Health announced progress on pharmaceutical management goals, citing plans for a nationwide common drug review, a national system to provide "critical analysis of price, utilization and cost trends," and a review of reports on increasing drug costs (Canada 2001). The communiqué focused on drug prices and optimal use of drugs rather than insurance or expanded government purchasing of drugs.

As in previous periods, the absence of strong political backing for an expert proposal on pharmaceutical insurance contributed to limited public salience, which in turn reinforced elites' limited ideas about the feasibility and desirability of a nationwide pharmaceutical program. There are few direct measures of public awareness of or support for broad public pharmaceutical insurance at this time. However, the relevant polls do suggest that public attention to health issues was firmly focused on the problems of existing services, while elites tended to focus on existing services *and* the role of alternative institutions in dampening the salience of public pharmaceutical insurance.

Elites consistently and without prompting cited the prevalence of private, employer-sponsored drug insurance for the middle class, and the high levels of concern about the problems of the existing system of medical and hospital insurance, such as wait times and overcrowded hospital emergency rooms, as reasons that the public did not pay attention to proposals for universal pharmaceutical insurance. Hoffman offered that while there are significant numbers of Canadians without sufficient drug coverage, "it is not something that affects a large number of Canadians all the time." She noted that Canadians are concerned about wait times and doctor shortages, but drugs have not captured the public imagination.[33]

Jane Coutts, a former health reporter for the *Globe and Mail* who covered the National Forum on Health, suggested that Canadians didn't focus on pharmaceutical insurance because they were (and are) insulated by private, employer-sponsored drug plans or public plans for seniors in most provinces, but wait times for hospital and medical services were much more visible. However, she also cited the legacy of limited expectations about pharmaceutical insurance, saying, "They [Canadians] don't expect it. They expect fast care ... but [pharmacare] has never been part of medicare and never seems as urgent."[34] Another political advisor commented on the media attention directed towards overcrowded emergency rooms in the late 1990s, saying, "It was on the news every night ... it was like a national disaster," and this greatly increased the pressure to boost transfers to provinces for primary care. He contrasted this issue with pharmacare, which, he said, "probably wouldn't come up as a top-of-mind issue" for voters.[35]

These assessments are borne out in public opinion polls released in 1997 and 1998. Beyond concern with problems in existing health services, there was a high level of concern with economic problems. When questioned about it directly, voters were concerned about health care and supported increased health spending, but their response regarding the most important problem facing Canadians was unemployment and the economy. At the beginning of 1997 these were the most frequent responses at 43.6 per cent and 11.7 per cent, respectively, while "other health/medical" was the most important problem for only 4.4 per cent of respondents (Environics Canada 1997–1).[36]

A poll at the end of the year asked voters about their knowledge of the Speech from the Throne, where the government set out its agenda for the coming parliamentary session. This provided an unusual opportunity to observe voters' knowledge of pharmacare promises, since they were mentioned in the Throne Speech (Canada, Governor General 1997). However, only 21.5 per cent of respondents were "somewhat familiar" or "very familiar" with the speech, and only 1.7 per cent of these reported that mention of a drug plan had attracted their attention, compared to 8.6 per cent who noticed the promise of a balanced budget, and 5.4 per cent who noticed a promise to restore funding for health care (meaning hospital and medical services) (Environics Canada 1997–2).

In a comprehensive review of Canadian public opinion on health prepared for the Commission on the Future of Health Care in Canada, Mendelsohn (2002, 62) found that, when questioned about a range of policy options in 1998, Canadians preferred tax breaks for the poor, home care, and increased transfers to the provinces over pharmacare. He notes, "When told that prescription drugs are publicly insured in most other countries, only 27 percent still believe that there should be no pharmacare program in Canada" but concludes that "many proposals for new national programs are greeted favourably in polls because trade-offs or costs are not made explicit in the question" (14). The implications of these results are that the limited elite discussion of pharmacare had not drawn public attention away from the higher-profile issues of general reinvestment in health services – "fixing what we have" – and therefore the public provided no clear electoral motivations for politicians to act on pharmacare.

## 2002: Catastrophic Drug Coverage

The two most recent public proposals for nationwide pharmaceutical insurance are contained in the *Report of the Commission on the Future of Health Care in Canada* (the Romanow Report) and the *Report of the Standing Senate Committee Social Affairs, Science & Technology* (the Kirby Report). The Romanow Report was commissioned by the federal government in 2001 to "inquire into and undertake dialogue with Canadians about the future of Canada's public health care system" and to make recommendations about its sustainability (Commission on the Future of Health Care in Canada 2002, xi). A Senate committee undertook the research for the Kirby Report. Its order of reference calls for an examination of "the pressures on and constraints of Canada's health care system and the role of the federal government in Canada's health care system" (Senate Standing Committee on Social Affairs, Science and Technology 2002), although in the words of one interviewee, "Kirby started because he didn't think Romanow would get it right."[37] Both Romanow and Kirby reported in 2002, and federal and provincial governments responded to their recommendations in two Health Accords, or intergovernmental agreements for health policy development, in 2003 and 2004.

The pharmacare proposals in both reports respond to some of the major concerns with earlier options by outlining a more limited goal of "catastrophic drug coverage," where citizens would be protected against drug expenses exceeding a certain portion of their incomes. Although catastrophic drug coverage had been discussed before, these two reports certainly contributed to its dominance of subsequent discussion. Senator Wilbert Keon, a member of the Senate committee, reported that they recommended catastrophic drug coverage because the committee believed that most people had reasonable coverage through private or provincial plans and that only those with very high drug costs were vulnerable.[38] The former director of research for the Commission on the Future of Health Care in Canada has indicated that Romanow's recommendation for catastrophic drug coverage was strategic, and that the commission believed that starting with a more limited universal program would allow for later expansion (Forest 2004), a position that is confirmed by a policy expert involved in researching the proposal.[39]

The switch to catastrophic drug coverage as a policy goal also had the potential to make the proposal more attractive to both the pharmaceutical and private insurance industries, since it would mainly target patients who might have previously had to forgo drug treatment for financial reasons and would act as a complement rather than a substitute for private insurance. In fact, representatives from both individual pharmaceutical companies and the national association of research-based pharmaceutical companies have indicated their support for the concept of catastrophic drug coverage as recommended by the Kirby and Romanow reports, a position published on the organization's website in 2010 (Rx&D 2010).[40]

Romanow and Kirby reported during relatively good economic times, when the federal government presented its fifth consecutive balanced budget, and debt-reduction targets continued to be met (Treff and Perry 2002, 2003). Pharmacists' professional groups supported the catastrophic drug coverage proposals (Canadian Pharmacists Association 2001a, 31; Canadian Pharmacists Association 2001b, 9), and a medical association interviewee noted that the infusion of federal cash in the system meant physicians were more interested in "enhancing these other areas" of health care than they had been previously, although their main concern was that patients have access to drugs and that physicians face the minimum additional administrative tasks.[41] The budget immediately following the reports' releases, in February 2003, pledged "a five-year, $16-billion Health Reform Fund to provinces and territories to target improved primary health care, home care and catastrophic drug coverage" (Canada 2003a). So why did expanded pharmaceutical insurance fail to materialize?

Despite the differences in the details of the plan and the economic circumstances, the calls for catastrophic drug coverage failed for the same reasons the calls for first-dollar coverage did in 1972 and 1997. First, because of restricted policy ideas of elites that told them fixing existing services was more important than expanding services, that pharmaceutical insurance of any type was not analogous to existing services, and that initiating this type of benefit would result in an expensive program with no potential for cost control. Second, because of public expectations that mirrored and reinforced those ideas.

The 2003 First Ministers Accord on Health Care Renewal included language about catastrophic drug coverage but no clear commitments and devoted equal or greater attention to pharmaceutical management, in line with theoretical expectations. The 2003 Accord listed catastrophic drug coverage as a priority, along with primary health care, home care, access to diagnostic/medical equipment, and information technology, including an electronic health record (Canada 2003b). It listed a number of pharmaceutical management goals and promised that "First Ministers will take measures, by the end of 2005/06, to ensure that Canadians, wherever they live, have reasonable access to catastrophic drug coverage" (ibid.). However, there was no indication of what this might entail or how it would be achieved, and certainly no conditions placed on provinces to receive funding. The First Ministers Communiqué the following year pledged to "develop, assess and cost options for catastrophic pharmaceutical coverage" but devoted significantly more space to discussions of pharmaceutical management (Canada 2004). It created a ministerial task force to draft a National Pharmaceuticals Strategy. In 2006, the task force recommended additional research on catastrophic drug coverage along with four other management priorities, but has issued no further reports (Health Canada, Strategic Policy Branch 2006).

Those closely involved in the creation of the Romanow and Kirby reports tend to cite situational factors in explaining why their recommendations were not adopted. Senator Keon argued that Kirby's catastrophic drug coverage proposals failed for lack of an individual or group at the provincial or federal level to handle the issue, although he also noted criticism of the proposal as potentially extremely expensive.[42] Roy Romanow was generally positive about what the commission achieved but noted that "the report fell into the Martin-Chrétien battle," when leadership of the governing federal Liberal Party was in question, and this hampered adoption of its recommendations. According to Romanow, the new Health Reform Fund fixed the funding problem highlighted by the report, but unfortunately without conditions, so provinces were not obliged to make changes to pharmaceutical insurance programs.[43]

However, the response of federal policy advisors and observers reflects the influence of longstanding policy ideas about pharmaceuticals and the scope of the health system as well. Interviewees emphasized the degree to which pharmaceutical insurance competed with other reform priorities (a focus on "fixing what we have") as well as the barriers

posed by cost, the desirability of focusing on management as a more
feasible policy option, and jurisdictional issues.

A senior federal official involved in planning the 2003 and 2004 First
Ministers Meetings summed up these barriers, saying, "Caution was
the order of the advice." He said the 2003 Health Reform Fund was "a
classic example" of the problem of multiple priorities: "We have a number of priorities overall. Getting deeply into in this one [pharmacare]
could be very expensive and could detract from our focus on those
other areas." He went on to say pharmaceutical insurance was less attractive than other issues because "analytically and in policy terms, it
was extremely complex ... and it is costly." Finally, there was the jurisdictional issue: "Did the federal government want to get involved ... in
actually administering a program?"[44] Fortier indicates that in 2004,
questions of pharmaceutical insurance and management were separate, and management was emphasized because "everyone deliberately
wanted to make progress on pharmaceuticals without having to open
the insurance can of worms." According to her, pharmacare "is kind of
a non-story, really, because with pharmaceuticals, at least the insurance
side of it, has just been dismissed time and time again."[45]

As was the case in 1972 and 1997, there is little evidence of provincial
pharmaceutical programs affecting federal ideas about the policy area.
When asked how provincial programs influenced federal goals for
pharmacare after the 2000 Health Accord, Genest noted that federal
health policy analysts were making compendiums of different provincial programs, and there was certainly a bureaucratic interest in these
options, but "as far as models [of pharmacare programs go], I wouldn't
say that really percolated up to the top level. We weren't in that space.
The legwork was being done, but I don't think there was a view that
we'd take on a Saskatchewan approach or a Trillium [Ontario] approach."[46] Mr Romanow himself indicated that the commission had
been interested in Nova Scotia's approach to pharmaceuticals and had
also looked at Quebec and British Columbia,[47] but this was not evident
in the final report.

Assessing public expectations for expanded public drug insurance
after the Romanow and Kirby reports is problematic, because there is a
lack of publicly available polling data on how aware voters were of the
reports, and the recommendations of which they were most aware.
Certainly pharmaceutical insurance was a low priority for Canadians
prior to the reports' release. Mendelsohn (2002) reports on a qualitative
research project in 2002 that asked Canadians to rank their goals for

health system reform and found that "adequate numbers of nurses, doctors and specialists across the country" was the top priority, while pharmacare was the lowest – a finding he notes was repeated in "a large survey conducted around the same time" (15).

The release of the Romanow and Kirby reports generated slightly more media coverage of pharmaceutical insurance than the National Forum on Health. A review of coverage of pharmaceutical insurance in three national-level, English-language newspapers between 1990 and 2010 found fewer than thirty substantive articles on pharmaceutical insurance in the months around the release of the Romanow and Kirby reports in 2002, and fewer than ten articles around the release of the National Forum's report (Daw and Morgan 2013, see figure 2). However, neither level of coverage is particularly high, and while a nationwide, universal pharmacare program was one of three major recommendations by the National Forum (along with home care and improved health information systems), the smaller-scale proposals for catastrophic drug coverage were one of approximately twenty-three recommendations from the Kirby Report, and forty-seven recommendations from Romanow. In the absence of clear evidence that catastrophic drug coverage stood out in the public's mind, it seems plausible that it was even less publicly salient than the National Forum's earlier pharmacare proposal.

Interviewees were in consensus about the lack of public salience of expanded public drug insurance. This is significant because even if a variety of advisors all made the same mistake about public opinion, their assessments were being passed on to political decision-makers. Their assessment of low public salience in 2002 was similar to that of 1997 and was based on two factors: the public was more concerned about fixing or funding existing services (e.g., dealing with wait times for hospital and medical services), and the idea that a combination of private and targeted provincial insurance programs served most people fairly well.

Keon explained the Senate committee's decision to focus on catastrophic drug coverage, saying that although the patchwork of provincial plans was complex, the coverage it provided was generally acceptable: "The one outstanding issue ... was individuals who were subjected to catastrophic costs."[48] Owen Adams, the assistant secretary general in charge of policy analysis for the Canadian Medical Association, argued that in terms of public attention, pharmacare "is losing in the competition ... and governments know this. Expanding medicare doesn't roll ... because most Canadians have some kind of coverage."[49]

Two Liberal policy advisors offered more direct insights to the government's priorities for health reform in the early 2000s. Fortier noted that although pharmacare was mentioned in 2003 and 2004 Health Accords, Prime Minister Martin and his team chose to focus on wait times, and put a lot of money into it, because "they were looking for something that affected people and that people understood. Wait times were a big top-of-mind issue at the time."[50] Genest echoed this view, saying that in the 2004 Accord, "I think they went for popular pieces: wait times was way up on the radar screen of what the public wanted; pharma policy was merely good and sound policy but so many people had private insurance ... The Martin government was very much a poll-driven government, and because it wasn't way up there in the polls, they decided to put their eggs in the wait times basket."[51]

Stephen Lewis, a policy advisor and researcher who was a member of the National Forum and also involved in the Romanow Commission, reiterated that pharmacare stays off the agenda because the middle class has private insurance and most provinces provide coverage for seniors. As he eloquently put it, "I think the public's expectations have been stripped in this area. They have bought the argument that it's not affordable, even though they are paying for it in the end."[52]

## Australia

In Canada, the limited and negative ideas about the possibility of pharmaceutical insurance in the immediate post-war period were gradually reinforced as politicians and at times the public focused on the problem of pharmaceutical prices and patents. These ideas were important barriers to the adoption of broad pharmaceutical programs when they were proposed in subsequent years. In Australia, there was an abrupt, partisan shift in ideas about health policy that prevented further health policy development. In 1949, a Liberal-Country coalition government that was opposed to compulsory public health insurance was elected. As might be expected, it did not continue the Labor program of public health policy development. One author has described the Liberal-Country government's health policy choices during its next twenty-three years in power as "a pragmatic, unplanned set of benefit programmes cobbled together in the face of intense suspicion from the BMA" (Gillespie 1991, 278). However, in 1950 the new government *did* choose to implement the Pharmaceutical Benefits Scheme designed by its Labor opponents, with some modifications. The remainder of this chapter will focus on this surprising instance of policy stability. It explains how the new government was able to overcome the implementation problems that had plagued its predecessors, and why it chose to do so.

## Barriers to Policy Implementation

The Labor government first passed legislation for the Pharmaceutical Benefits Scheme in 1944, but when it lost power in 1949, the scheme was still not providing benefits to Australians. Understanding the barriers to policy implementation faced by the Labor government is key to explaining how the Liberal-Country coalition government chose to implement the PBS in 1950. The new government made changes to the original program that brought the PBS more in line with its own ideas about health policy and provided later opportunities for reform with compensation.

Gillespie argues that one of the reasons pharmaceutical benefits and hospital benefits were attractive first and second priorities for health policy development by the Labor government was because "both (it appeared) could be implemented immediately without waiting for the long and cumbersome negotiations with the medical profession" (Gillespie 1991, 210). This was a reasonable expectation: to this point, the medical profession's main concern was that there be no changes to medical service until after the war, as health minister Holloway promised in 1941, so benefit schemes that subsidized drugs or hospital beds without touching on the contentious issue of physician remuneration seemed promising. Furthermore, physicians already participated in the limited Repatriation Pharmaceutical Benefits Scheme, which provided free medicines to veterans on a basis similar to that of the proposed PBS (Sloan 1995). However, the government did not predict that the BMA would view the PBS as the wedge towards socialized medicine and would oppose it "with a furor and effectiveness which decided its fate" (Hunter 1965, 412).

The government's strong expectation of cooperation can be seen in its decision not to consult with doctors until December 1943, six months after successful consultations with the pharmacists, and to present the scheme as a fait accompli – a choice that did not endear government planners to the BMA's Federal Council (Hunter 1965, 415). After the passage of the Pharmaceutical Benefits Act in 1944, the BMA convinced the attorney-general of Victoria to launch a constitutional challenge to the Commonwealth government's ability to legislate on pharmaceutical benefits, and the High Court ruled in Victoria's (and the BMA's) favour, disallowing the Pharmaceutical Benefits Act in 1945. In the court's decision, the chief justice wrote of the PBS, "It is just the kind of Statute which might well be passed by a Parliament which had full power to make such laws as it thought proper with respect to public health-doctors, chemists, hospitals, drugs, medicines, medical and surgical appliances. The Commonwealth Parliament has no such power" (quoted in Hunter 1965, 420).

The Commonwealth government then held a national referendum, in 1946, where a question on social services was approved and gave the Commonwealth power over various benefits to individuals, including pharmaceuticals (Australia 2003, section 51[xxiiiA]). This allowed for the passage of new PBS legislation.

Once the PBS was adopted, the BMA prevented the scheme from functioning by simply refusing to use the government prescription forms necessary for patients to obtain free drugs at the pharmacy. The doctors' most overt objection was to the proposed Commonwealth Formulary or list of subsidized drugs. A Cabinet submission in 1947 concluded, "The whole controversy in relation to pharmaceutical benefits revolves around the matter of the use or non-use of the Formulary" (NAA 1947b). Doctors preferred either no list (so every prescription would be subsidized) or a very limited list (so government would subsidize and therefore control only a small number of expensive drugs) (NAA 1947a). Both options would preserve doctors' autonomy: if the PBS subsidized a reasonably comprehensive but still finite list, as the Labor government proposed, doctors would be under pressure to prescribe mainly from the list and accept government guidelines on amounts and frequency of prescriptions.[53] Doctors argued that being constrained to even a broad formulary would compromise their patients' care and that they would cooperate with the government's Formulary Committee only when it agreed to the principle that "where a drug is ordered which is not within the formulary the patient shall nevertheless be supplied with such drug without cost" (NAA 1944b), which would render a formulary meaningless.

Labor policymakers did aim to cover a broad range of drugs, promising that "the formulary will be as comprehensive as the medical professional desires, [and] no restriction will be placed on the number or variety of drugs and compounds used except where it is necessary to avoid redundancy or to preserve efficiency," (NAA 1944e). However, this goal was tempered by the experience of New Zealand, which introduced a program of pharmaceutical benefits without a formulary in

1938, and by the mid-1940s was struggling with much higher costs than anticipated (NAA 1945e). In 1944, the government reminded the BMA that it was "paying for the entire scheme and therefore must maintain a certain amount of control over what it will pay for … Experience in other countries suggests that, without the use of a formulary, the cost per script tends to rise year by year" (NAA 1944f). The government believed that a formulary was necessary to maintain "the greatest economy in [drugs'] usage" during the war, as well as to lower administrative costs and provide a quick and easy method of prescribing, since it would standardize prescriptions that were often still compounded for each individual patient (NAA 1943c). The government also noted, in a 1943 memo, "The public, under war time conditions, will more readily accept limitations – such as a restriction of dispensing to a formulary" (NAA 1943a).

The BMA was not satisfied by these claims, and their concerns with the PBS formulary overlaid a more basic fear of major changes to the medical profession and the introduction of "socialized" or "nationalized" medical services. At the first reading of the bill in 1944, physician, long-time BMA advocate, and later coalition health minister Earle Page commented that "this provision may be the thin end of the wedge of nationalization of the medical profession … My own strong view is that the nationalization of the medical profession would cause a deterioration of the caliber of its future personnel" (quoted in Crowley 1973, 101). In a 1945 article in the conservative *Argus*, a doctor argued, "In addition to the formulary, the individual practitioner was indignant because he saw in the Pharmaceutical Benefits Act a threat to nationalize the medical profession" (NAA 1945f).

The BMA fought the PBS in private meetings with the minister (NAA 1947c, 1948b) and in public. It issued newspaper statements to argue that the formulary would constitute a cap on total pharmaceutical expenditure (NAA 1944a) and published pamphlets to explain to patients that doctors "are not, in their patient's interest, prepared to drift into a groove bounded by the narrow limits of a formulary," particularly since, "in the minds of the Minister and the Government, a method of pricing is more important than the patient's welfare" (NAA 1945a). The Labor government was not successful in countering this campaign; in fact Gillespie (1991, 231) argues that "the Chifley government … proved singularly inept in mobilizing public support" for the PBS, and this meant the BMA was able to prevent the implementation of this first priority for five years.

*Barriers to Further Policy Development*

The Labor government did not abandon attempts at other health policy initiatives during the conflict over the PBS, but it was not able to implement further elements of a universal public health insurance or benefits program. In 1945, Labor passed the Hospital Benefits Act, which authorized negotiations with states on hospital benefits. The resulting Commonwealth-state agreements provided states with a subsidy of six shillings per day for each occupied bed in public and private hospitals, on the condition that public ward treatment in public hospitals be offered free without a means test, and non-public wards reduce their fees by six shillings (Sax 1984, 56). Gillespie (1991, 197) calls this policy "striking" in "the extent to which it ignored the advice of the NHMRC and the JPCSS," which had called for direct Commonwealth involvement in hospitals.

States and doctors were initially suspicious, the former because they (rightly, as it turned out) did not think the subsidy would cover their operating costs, and the latter because they saw the means test as a crucial tool for maintaining a scope for private practice (Sax 1984, 57; Gillespie 1991, 203). However, while the subsidies eliminated the charitable element of hospital care, they did not change the basis of the system (Gillespie 1991). Sax (1984, 57) notes that after a year in operation, "doctors were reporting that the abolition of the means tests had not affected practice in public hospitals to any significant extent," and most patients who had formerly paid at least in part for hospital services continued to do so.

Labor's 1948 National Health Service Act, meant to provide for medical services, was similarly limited. Work on this element of health policy was postponed earlier in the 1940s, as the BMA refused to discuss the government's proposals for a universal service, and government became occupied with the protest over the PBS and serious balance of payment problems (Sax 1984, 57; Gillespie 1991, 247). The legislation passed in 1948 after it was amended by compromises with the BMA, including a provision making doctors' participation in the scheme voluntary (Sax 1984, 58; Gillespie 1991, 248).

Labor lost power in 1949 without having implemented the PBS or the more limited National Health Service Act, and the change in government was a decisive factor in blocking further health policy development. The Liberal-Country government led by Robert Menzies was opposed to the extension of compulsory, public health insurance and instead took health policy development in Australia down a path very different from the one envisioned by previous Labor governments.

In Australia health policy remained an issue of partisan contention for decades longer than in the United Kingdom or Canada. Instead of tax-funded public coverage, the Liberal and Country Parties emphasized contributory insurance measures: the 1946 Liberal platform called for "the encouragement of supplementary voluntary schemes in addition to government schemes" for social security (D.M. White 1978, 146). This platform focused on public health initiatives such as vaccination programs and stated the party's opposition to "the nationalization of the medical profession and service" (146). Menzies's speech for the 1949 election that returned a Liberal-Country coalition to power called for a focus on preventative health, more doctors and hospitals, the inclusion of diagnostic clinics in hospitals, and argued that, "side by side with these matters, we need to encourage those voluntary schemes of medical benefit which now exist," meaning private health insurance (Menzies 1949, 21–2). Menzies concluded the health portion of the speech by saying, "We are utterly opposed to the Socialist idea that medical service should become salaried government service, with all its implications, penalising skill and experience and destroying the vital personal relationship between doctor and patient" (22).

Although Labor lacked consensus on an overarching idea for health services that might have put a broad, universal program at the top of the policy agenda, the party was at least sympathetic to the concept of compulsory insurance. In contrast, the Liberal Party's ideas for health emphasized physician autonomy (which precluded a nationalized program similar to the British NHS) and private, voluntary insurance. In his memoirs, Earle Page recalls that when the Liberals took office, "the essence of my suggested attack [on the health policy problem] was to help those who helped themselves – to encourage the formation of new, and strengthen the working of existing, voluntary insurance organizations to handle the problems of administration involved, and to provide a real nursery for democracy" (Page 1963, 375).

The first step for the new government, somewhat surprisingly, was to complete the implementation of the PBS. Although the Liberal-Country government did make changes to the scheme, its version of the PBS still provided universal, and at the time, free public coverage of drugs. However, its other health policy choices aligned with the parties' general preference for limited government involvement in health and social services. Gillespie (1991, 256) notes that when the Liberal-Country coalition took power, it "accepted that the Commonwealth could not withdraw from the finance of health care," but it did wish "to depart radically" from Labor's preference for administration by the Commonwealth Department of Health and instead shift administration to private, not-for-profit organizations. Its subsequent health policy decisions laid the foundations for the system of private insurance with public subsidies that existed in Australia for almost twenty-five years.

The alternative private institutional arrangements for health insurance were initially quite popular. The subsidy for voluntary hospital insurance was announced in November 1951, and the following month, a Gallup poll found that 70 per cent of respondents knew of the program, and 86 per cent of these were in favour of it (Gallup Poll [Australia] December 1951–January 1952). The Liberal-Country government's plan for a subsidy for voluntary medical insurance, announced shortly thereafter, was similarly popular (Gallup Poll [Australia] July–August 1952, August–September 1953). The fact that subsidies made private insurance more affordable for the average Australian likely dampened demand for public services for some time, although as discussed in chapter 6, by the mid-1960s gaps in coverage provided by the voluntary system had become increasingly problematic and salient to voters.

The Liberal-Country government's ideas about health were clearly quite different from the Labor Party's, as reflected in its decisions supporting and expanding private hospital and medical insurance in the 1950s and 1960s. Those ideas did not coincide with the universal provision of free pharmaceuticals under the PBS, and yet the new government chose to implement the program. The PBS was also opposed by a powerful interest group: the BMA had expended considerable time and resources fighting the PBS, although they were prepared to be mollified by a Liberal government that was much more in tune with their interests. Given these factors, the lack of expansion to public health insurance after 1950 is expected, and the real puzzle is to explain the Liberal decision to implement a modified PBS. I argue that this decision is an example of how quickly public expectations of service can take hold, a conclusion supported by the evidence contradicting any alternative explanations for the PBS's implementation, such as support for the scheme from within government or from a major interest group.

## Implementing the PBS

When the Liberal-Country coalition took power in 1949, the PBS had been on the books for five years, but lack of cooperation from doctors meant very few people were receiving benefits. Although the Liberals criticized the Pharmaceutical Benefits Act when it was introduced in 1944 (Crowley 1973), once the scheme was nominally in place, there seems to have been a different attitude, reflecting the difficulty of removing outright an existing benefit (Pierson 1994).

In the 1946 election speech where he called for contributory health insurance, Menzies also promised that "no person who enjoys any social service payment today will have it taken away or reduced by a Liberal Government" (McAllister and Moore 1991, 165). The turning point came in 1948, when the Liberals added pharmaceutical benefits to their party platform: the health section called for "the free provision of certain specific drugs vital to the preservation of life (such as insulin)" (D.M. White 1978, 155). This hinted at the Liberals' eventual restriction of the PBS formulary but nonetheless demonstrates that some level of pharmaceutical benefits was understood to be desirable, or at least inevitable. Roskam (2001, 278) notes that, when Menzies became prime minister in 1949, he "endorsed the central elements of welfare policies adopted by Labor in the 1940s, and he recognised that first the Great Depression, and then war, had changed community expectations about economic and welfare policies."

By 1950, the PBS had become a reasonably salient issue: it had been the subject of two High Court cases, one only a year previous, and a successful constitutional referendum. Furthermore, opinion polls demonstrated that the public was also reasonably attached to the idea of a public pharmaceutical program. In March 1950, when the Liberal-Country government's scheme for a less comprehensive PBS was first introduced, Gallup reported that "at this stage, the public is not keen on the idea" (Gallup Poll [Australia] March–April 1950). The poll asked whether people favoured a scheme where all medicines were free (like the original PBS), a scheme where only expensive medicines were free (as was proposed by the new government), or if they preferred no free medicines. Overall, 43 per cent of respondents favoured "all medicines free," and 37 per cent preferred that only expensive medicines be free. As expected, there was some difference along party lines, with 57 per cent of Labor voters supporting the "all free" scheme, versus 33 per cent of Liberal-Country voters. Crucially, however, only 15 per cent of respondents overall favoured "no free medicines" (ibid.), suggesting a new set of expectations based on government's policy promises. A few months later, this dropped to only 11 per cent of respondents preferring no free medicines (Gallup Poll [Australia] June–July 1950), so taking some sort of action on a pharmaceutical program was clearly an electoral winner across party lines.

Interestingly, the Liberal minister of health, Earle Page, was well aware of the power of public expectations, and this informed his strategy to avoid having his new version of the PBS blocked by the Labor-controlled Senate. Page introduced the scheme through regulations while Parliament was in recess and reports, "It was my assumption that during that period the public would become accustomed to the use of free medicines and other items included in my programme" (Page 1963, 376). The Senate could veto the new PBS when it returned, but Page correctly reasoned that "with public approval of the scheme – which should be assured when it had been working satisfactorily for three months – it would be difficult for the Labour Opposition to use its majority in the Senate to disallow the regulations and thereby take from the people the benefits they were receiving" (ibid.).

The Liberals recognized the significance of having the PBS already in place, if not operating, even when they criticized Labor's approach to health policy. In 1948, a Liberal opposition member asked whether the government was "sincere in introducing a 'free medicine' scheme for the benefit of the public, or does it believe that the inauguration of such a scheme will pave the way for the nationalization of all medical services?" and in the same speech deplored the fact that citizens were paying taxes for free medicines that they were not receiving (NAA 1948a). This type of rhetoric set the stage for the early Liberal implementation of the PBS when they took power, although the scheme began operation in September 1950 with a significantly more restricted formulary than the original Labor design. In the next chapter, I describe these differences and explain how they shaped opportunities for minor changes to the PBS. I argue the Liberal-Country government's initial design was shaped by its ideological position opposing comprehensive health services and the need to secure doctors' cooperation, and that its later choice of cost-control measures was influenced by the need to manage public expectations of service.

## Conclusion

This chapter has explained policy stability in the Canadian and Australian health systems over time. Specifically, the chapter has asked why incremental health policy development stalled in each country, despite early suggestions that each would adopt one health service initially and add the others over time.

In Canada, pharmaceutical insurance was described as a "later stage" of health insurance in early policy documents, but by the time nationwide hospital and medical insurance programs had been adopted, pharmaceutical insurance had fallen off the agenda and was consistently blocked when expert groups proposed programs over the next forty years. In Australia, a pharmaceutical benefits scheme was adopted with the acknowledgment that it was only one part of a comprehensive plan for health and social security. However, it was implemented only after a lengthy controversy with the medical association and a change in government. The new government held quite different goals for health policy and effectively prevented the consideration of additional public insurance or benefits for thirty years.

Australia presents perhaps the most obvious case for a stalled or blocked process of policy development. Although the Labor government made more attempts than the Canadian Liberals to expand public health policy in the 1940s, their choice of an incremental approach combined with significant opposition to their first priority for service adoption meant they were actually less successful than their Canadian counterparts. Given that the Liberal-Country government elected in 1949 was opposed to public insurance for health, we would not expect additions to the health system that its Labor predecessors initiated with the Pharmaceutical Benefits Scheme. The only unexpected element of the story is the implementation of the PBS by the Liberal-Country government, which this chapter argues was a result of the public expectations for pharmaceutical benefits that developed over the five years during which the program was being debated.

The situation in Australia provides an interesting parallel to the more puzzling Canadian case, where additional policy development – the introduction of some form of nationwide pharmaceutical insurance – was rejected by the same political party that developed public health insurance at the national level and initially suggested that pharmaceuticals and other services such as dental and optical care would be part of a comprehensive health system. In both cases, the conditions associated with an incremental pace of policy development were major contributors to the lack of further policy development.

In the immediate post-war period, political elites in Canada and Australia lacked a consensus on an overarching policy idea about the appropriate scope and goals of a health system. The lack of elite prompting resulted in limited public expectations and demand for services. Over time, these two dynamics reinforced one another and blocked major policy change in both countries. Elites' restricted ideas about what government should or could do in health policy meant there were few prominent proposals for additional services and little public discussion of these issues. This in turn limited opportunities for public expectations of service to develop, which fed back into elites' lack of attention. Thus, the type of policy ideas and public expectations that contribute to incremental policy development initially *also* contribute to barriers to major policy change as they are reinforced over time. The next chapter will take up the question of how limited ideas and public expectations affect opportunities for minor change – adjustments to policies that do not significantly or immediately expand or contract the scope of coverage – and finds that, when comparing similar pharmaceutical policy reforms in Australia and the United Kindgom, limited ideas and expectations actually make retrenchment easier to accomplish.

# Chapter 5

# Opportunities for Minor Change

Studying the role of entrenched ideas in blocking major policy change also provides an opportunity to investigate the role of ideas in minor policy change – adjustments to policies that do not significantly and immediately change the range of services covered or the portion of the population receiving benefits. This chapter investigates the role of ideas in minor changes to services in Australia and the United Kingdom. It will not provide an exhaustive review of policy reforms but will instead focus on the first changes to pharmaceutical services in both countries, as they adopted very similar reforms in response to higher-than-expected pharmaceutical expenditures. However, the politics and outcomes of these policies were conditioned by their history of incremental versus radical paces of health policy development.

In Australia, the first adjustments to the Liberal-Country government's version of the Pharmaceutical Benefits Scheme – introducing a patient charge or co-payment – was accomplished with significantly less controversy than in the United Kingdom, which attempted a similar set of early policy reforms to try to rein in pharmaceutical expenditures. An incremental approach to health policy development produced barriers to major change in Australia. However, the lack of broad policy ideas about health also allowed for a flexibility in services that did not exist to the same extent in the United Kingdom with its radical pace of change and radical, popular ideas about the nature of public health services.

## Minor Changes to the Australian Pharmaceutical Benefits Scheme

In Australia before 1972, major changes to the health system, such as the addition of medical or hospital services to the national, public, and universal scheme that covered pharmaceuticals, were blocked by the election of a government with a very different set of ideas and priorities for health policy. However, examining early reforms to the PBS – instances of minor change – provide an opportunity to see how a lack of overarching ideas in a policy area initially shapes public expectations and affects the flexibility of a program over time.

In Australia, there was much greater consideration of the costs of pharmaceutical benefits than there were for prescription services or other elements of the NHS in the United Kingdom. The PBS was designed with one main tool for cost control: formulary control, or management of the list of drugs available for subsidy. Conflict between the government and the medical profession over the formulary was a key determinant of when and how the PBS was eventually implemented, and over time, the power to select which drugs would be subsidized, and under what conditions they would be subsidized, became a key strategy in Australian policymakers' struggles to control overall costs of the PBS. This contrasts with the situation in the United Kingdom, where aside from a fairly insignificant Selected List (introduced in 1984), any drug approved for sale in the United Kingdom is potentially available for subsidy.

In the 1940s, the Labor government stressed the importance of a broad formulary in its initial design for the PBS. However, the scheme implemented by the Liberal-Country government in 1950 had a much more restrictive formulary. Once the unintended consequences of this scheme for the way doctors prescribed and for the cost of the program became clear, the formulary was expanded and patient contributions were added. This choice was driven by cost concerns, given the predictable explosion of expenditures under the original scheme, but here public expectations played a role. Patient charges were less politically risky in Australia than in the United Kingdom because of the legacy of limited commitment to comprehensive health services, and because the government was able to mollify the public by combining new charges with a wider formulary, an opportunity for compensation that was not available in the United Kingdom.

## Revised Formulary and Doctors' Preferences

Although the literature emphasizes the similarities between the original Labor PBS and the PBS eventually implemented by the Liberal-Country government (Hunter 1965, 413), archival records show that at the time policymakers and stakeholders regarded the two schemes as "fundamentally different" (NAA 1952b, 1952c). The restricted formulary proposed by the Liberal-Country coalition differed from the Labor plan and allowed it to secure the BMA's support and finally get the PBS underway. Although polls in 1950 indicated a slight public preference for the original scheme where all medicines were to be provided free (Gallup Poll [Australia] March–April 1950, June–July 1950), the public had never actually experienced a functioning pharmaceutical program, and this may have lowered expectations. In February 1951, Gallup interviewers reminded respondents that under the new PBS "pensioners now get all medicines free, and that the general public gets the expensive life-saving drugs free," and then asked, "Do you think that's enough, or should all medicines be free?" Overall, 51 per cent of Australians thought the Liberal plan was "enough," which breaks down to 59 per cent of Liberal-Country voters and 40 per cent of Labor voters (Gallup Poll [Australia], February–March 1951).

The original Labor formulary was to "constitute all reliable combinations of medicines covering a whole range of the practice of medicine" (NAA 1944d). In notes prepared prior to the second reading of the Pharmaceutical Benefits Act in 1944, the government reiterated its "very definite intention ... that when the Commonwealth Formulary is published it will be one of the most comprehensive and up-to-date formularies in the world" (NAA 1943b) and again in 1945, that "the Commonwealth Pharmaceutical Formulary is far more comprehensive than any formulary previously published in Australia or, as far as we know, the world" (NAA 1945b).

The PBS formulary implemented by the Liberal-Country government was quite different: it was limited to "life-saving and disease-preventing drugs" (Sloan 1995, 3) and was aimed at "prescribing for serious disease and not minor aliments" (NAA 1959e). Liberal politicians emphasized the differences between the two schemes when they were discussed in Cabinet: for example, the treasurer compared the old formulary, which covered a "wide range" of drugs, to the new list, which could cover "life-saving and costly drugs – about 50 in all – which do not require compounding by the chemists" (NAA 1950c). Minister of health Earle Page argued that the broad Labor formulary "makes it very difficult to limit the volume of medicine prescribed and breeds the expectation of a free bottle of medicine on every visit to the doctor," while the new scheme with its limited formulary was "comparatively simple and safeguards against extravagant waste of drugs" (NAA 1950a).

In 1950, a committee of the Commonwealth Department of Health predicted that the new limited formulary would cover about 20 per cent of prescriptions (NAA 1950b). This satisfied the Liberal-Country coalition's ideological desire to avoid any hint of "nationalization" in its provision of social benefits, and the government's concern about controlling costs. It also ensured doctors' cooperation, since it matched their desire to have freedom to prescribe outside the formulary: many types of drugs were not listed and therefore available only on private prescriptions. However, the limited formulary had some unintended (if not entirely unpredictable) consequences for costs. The same departmental committee predicted that limiting the formulary would "attract constant pressure for change and expansion" (NAA 1950b). It went on to note that the proposed formulary would encourage the overuse of expensive drugs, since patients would pressure doctors (and perhaps doctors would prefer) to prescribe a more expensive, listed drug when a cheaper unlisted drug would be equally effective or appropriate. The treasurer made many similar warnings (Gillespie 1991), and this was in fact what occurred. In 1960 rising costs forced the Liberal-Country government to reconsider their program of formulary control and to introduce a new tool for cost control: patient contributions.

## Patient Contributions and Public Expectations

Cabinet documents show that concerns about the rising costs of the PBS were present as early as 1952 (NAA 1952b). Government's initial response was to further control the formulary, by "limiting the use of several of the more costly drugs to certain specified diseases [and] further revision of the list of drugs available for prescription" (ibid.). However, this additional formulary control was not sufficient to control costs, and in 1959, the Liberal-Country government recognized the need for more drastic options.

In early July, Cabinet met "to review developments in connection with Pharmaceutical Benefits, particularly the rapid increase in costs, and to suggest measures which might be considered" (NAA 1959b). Cabinet debated closing the formulary to expensive new drugs, but this was deemed too difficult. Other suggestions were to broaden the list of free drugs in hopes of encouraging doctors to be more economical in their prescribing, to (further) restrict use of expensive drugs to certain diseases, and to impose a patient contribution. On this last option, the health minister's submission noted, "It has the obvious political disadvantage, but is the one sure way to control over-prescribing" (ibid.). On 13 July, the prime minister considered a proposal to introduce a fee for prescriptions and at the same time broaden the formulary, which was the option selected for implementation in 1960 (NAA 1959c).

The different focus of private government deliberations versus public policy announcements demonstrates that the government made a conscious attempt to frame these changes to the PBS so as not to thwart public expectations of service. The prime minister's memo (written by his staff in preparation for an upcoming Cabinet meeting) focuses on the introduction of the fee, while the later public materials announcing the two policy changes focus almost exclusively on the broader formulary. The prime minister's memo discusses the problems with relying on doctors to adopt more economical prescribing habits and concludes, "It seems clear that the only way to provide any effective brake is by the charging of a fee. *This would be more acceptable to the public if it associated with a wider range of drugs being available under the scheme,* and the evidence in the submission suggests that the latter would be no burden on the Commonwealth" (NAA 1959c; emphasis added).

The Liberal government's strategy is a clear example of what Pierson calls "strategies of compensation," which recognize that "offering something positive to the victims of retrenchment policies will diminish prospects for heated opposition" (Pierson 1994, 23). Offering a broader range of subsidized drugs as compensation for the introduction of a prescription charge was a particularly effective strategy because the characteristics of pharmaceutical benefits allowed it to avoid the two main drawbacks of strategies of compensation: additional cost and policy irrationalities, or the potential of creating new problems through attempts to compensate for retrenchment (24). As the quote above suggests, expanding the formulary to cover inexpensive and previously excluded drugs was unlikely to increase the cost of the program so much that it would outweigh the revenue generated by a charge for every prescription. Furthermore, an expanded formulary was potentially simpler to administer, since the same procedures would now apply for most drugs. The change would avoid certain perverse incentives built into the original program, such as prescribing costly drugs in place of equally effective and cheaper options, when the government paid for only the costly drugs.

The government's internal consideration of the merits of adding a prescription charge and expanding the formulary can be contrasted with the public announcement of the change, in February 1960, which focused on the new formulary. It stated, "The Government regarded the new scheme confidently as an economical method of extending to the community as a whole the hitherto limited application of the pharmaceutical benefits legislation" (NAA 1960). The minister said the five-shilling (about fifty-cent) fee was necessary to "stabilize the ever-increasing cost of the previously free scheme – a consideration which the more thoughtful taxpayer would readily appreciate. More important, however, *it made possible the expansion of the former list of free medicines to a greatly widened area of prescribing* ... Drugs would be available in some form or other under the new scheme for the treatment of virtually every illness or disability encountered by doctors" (NAA 1960; emphasis added).

Therefore, the deliberations that led to the policy change focused on a patient contribution as the only "effective brake" on expenditure, with a wider formulary as a measure to make the change more politically palatable. The government's public announcements of the new scheme framed it mainly as a formulary expansion, "made possible" by the fee, in recognition that they would be dealing with the public's decade-long experience with having at least some prescriptions for free.

The policy change was not entirely unopposed: some Cabinet ministers were concerned that the fee might "impose great hardship on persons suffering from diseases or conditions requiring long-term drug therapy" (NAA 1959a), and pharmacists initially said they would collect the fee only if compelled by legislation, since as the Guild president complained, "Dispensing at Government rates is a dead loss ... Take away our private prescriptions and we fold up, unless, of course, the Government is prepared to pay for drugs at private rates" (NAA 1959d).

The framing effort appears to have been successful as far as the public was concerned. The archival records of the policy change record only the complaints of pharmacists and some doctors who were concerned that they might face government pressure to prescribe inexpensive drugs more often (NAA 1959d), and there are no records of public outcry in newspapers or letters to ministers, as there are in the United Kingdom after the introduction of prescription charges. A review of Australian Gallup Poll news releases from this period does not indicate any opinion polling on the new policies.

When cost-control measures were first introduced, the Liberal government was able to forestall potential electoral backlash using a strategy of compensation, but this option was available only once: the program was already universal, so after coverage was extended to all drugs, there were limited options for further expansion. The fact that subsequent cost-control policies also encountered limited opposition suggests that the lack of founding ideas about public health insurance in Australia made this easier. As PBS expenditures continued to rise in later years, government returned to patient contributions as an effective policy option with limited concerns about political risk.

In 1965, the fee was described to a policymaker in another country as both a "brake" on pharmaceutical expenditure and as a policy "in line with the principle of 'self-help' upon which the Australian National Health Scheme is based" (NAA 1965). In 1970, the fee was doubled (to one dollar), and in a Cabinet meeting discussing the change, the Department of Health justified the fee because patient contributions had not increased since they were introduced in 1960, while the annual costs of the PBS continued to rise, and because the fee should be considered in reference to the increase in incomes since 1960 (NAA 1971). Neither this Cabinet decision nor a similar move to double the patient contribution again in 1975 (NAA 1975) records concern about the political or electoral implications of increasing the fee.

This situation contrasts with the one in the United Kingdom, where for many years every increase in the patient contribution was the subject of much political angst (TNA 1949a, 1956a, 1956b, 1956c, 1956d, 1964d, 1968a). In Australia, the Liberal-Country government was sensitive to the possibility of thwarting public expectations of a free service in 1960 and countered it by linking the new fee to a wider formulary. They were aided by both the opportunity to use a strategy of compensation and the fact that patient contributions were never as politically charged as they were in United Kingdom.

No Australian government, and particularly no non-Labor government, had ever promised free health services the way British Labour did. The bald statements by Chifley in 1946 and 1949 saying which legislation had been passed on health (McAllister and Moore 1991) can be contrasted with British Labour's more expansive promises to "vigorously develop the health services" (in 1935), and to provide a "new National Health Service [where] there should be health centres where the people may get the best that modern science can offer, more and better hospitals, and proper conditions for our doctors and nurses" (1945) (Craig 1975, 109, 129). The 1950 British Labour election manifesto reminded voters that "Labour has honoured the pledge it made in 1945 to make social security a birthright of every citizen. Today destitution has been banished. The best medical care is available to everybody in the land" (Craig 1975, 158). Furthermore, Australians always had to pay for many prescriptions, since before 1960 some common drugs were not included on the formulary. This made patient contributions an easier policy tool and made it possible for Australian fees to increase at a faster rate and to a much higher level than the nominal charges in British prescription services.

## Minor Changes to U.K. Prescription Services

Like Australia, the United Kingdom faced early challenges from increasing pharmaceutical expenditures and adopted an almost identical policy response. A Conservative government introduced the first patient charges in 1952, and subsequent governments of both political stripes presided over the increase, abolition, and reinstatement of charges during the 1950s and 1960s. Because of the different circumstances around the adoption of U.K. prescription services, there was no opportunity to cushion the introduction of charges by expanding the range of subsidized drugs at the same time, as there was in Australia. This, combined with the different rhetoric that accompanied the NHS's adoption, made U.K. prescription charges much more politically contentious than those in the Australian PBS and placed different limits on the types of policy changes that politicians could introduce. The politics of minor change in a country that had initially adopted a radical pace of health policy development were very different as the result of the radical consensus on policy ideas and corresponding public expectations for health services.

Pharmaceuticals were not a main focus in some of the earlier and more prominent statements of British health policy ideas. They were not mentioned specifically in the Beveridge Report, despite its emphasis on the need for a complete range of health services and its receipt of submissions from both the Pharmaceutical Society of Great Britain and the National Pharmaceutical Union. Pharmaceuticals appear briefly in the 1944 White Paper, which states that arrangements for dispensing will be discussed "with appropriate pharmaceutical bodies" (Great Britain 1944, 37).

However, policymakers were clearly planning to include pharmaceuticals. Archival records show extensive discussions of which health professionals would be allowed to dispense prescriptions in which types of settings (TNA 1943, 1946), consideration of pharmacists' remuneration (TNA 1947b), and a somewhat surprising amount of debate over the issue of medicine bottles: as the result of a shortage of glass bottles (and their expense), pharmacists wanted patients to buy or supply their own bottles for prescriptions, while the Ministry of Health was concerned that this would make the service look "rather squalid to the middle-class patient" (TNA 1947a).

By 1943, policymakers took the comprehensiveness of the NHS for granted, so the inclusion of pharmaceuticals was also taken for granted. However, there was still some effort prior to the implementation of the NHS to consider the specific problems of administering a prescription service. As the remainder of the chapter will argue, the distinctiveness of these problems became clear to policymakers almost as soon as the service was implemented, leading to conflict over the need to control costs while maintaining the principles of the original program.

### Concerns about the Cost of Prescription Services

Although prescription services were introduced as part of a broad health scheme, they raised distinct political problems. Initially, any prescription drugs and many appliances and bandages were provided free of charge. There were no policies for pharmaceutical management, but escalating costs quickly demonstrated that this was a mistake. However, the problem was not entirely, or even primarily, related to policy design. During the later 1940s until the late 1960s, pharmaceuticals were undergoing a "therapeutic revolution," as the mass screening of chemical entities for therapeutic properties resulted in a large number of new, effective drugs, and drug companies began patenting synthetic versions of these naturally occurring substances (Morgan, McMahon, and Greyson 2008). Costs would have escalated even in the absence of a universal program (as was the case in Canada), but the original design of NHS prescription services had no capacity to deal with these problems.

In the first nine years the NHS was in operation, the total cost of prescriptions doubled (Hinchliffe 1959, 24). Concerns about the overall cost of the NHS led to the early introduction of prescription charges as a strategy for recouping revenue and limiting demand. The low fees, and later the introduction of widespread exemptions, meant that prescription charges were never particularly lucrative (Klein 2010, 35). In addition, in 1959 the government's Hinchliffe Committee on the Cost of Prescribing expressly recommended against their continued use, concluding that "the present prescription charge is a tax which, beside stimulating the wrong incentives, has proved disappointing financially"

(Hinchliffe 1959, 11). However, patient charges for prescriptions have persisted and increased, always accompanied by some degree of political controversy.

Klein (2010) notes that there was strikingly little analysis of the financial implications of the NHS before its adoption, but there was at least some consideration of the cost of drugs. In 1944, a Ministry of Health memo estimated that the drug bill would be "somewhere about £10,000,000 and it will, therefore, be worth while to set up some considerable machinery to ensure that we get what we are paying for" (in terms of the quality of drugs) (TNA 1944). The following year, health minister Anuerin Bevan told Cabinet that although "only very approximate estimates are possible of the cost to public funds of the comprehensive health service ... in the early years of the service the annual expenditure might be £145 million" (TNA 1945). Thus, drugs accounted for only about 7 per cent of early estimates of NHS costs.

In December 1948, after less than a year in operation, Bevan reported to Cabinet on cost overruns in the NHS, where the total gross cost was £225 million, saying, "That, then is the cost of social innovation. The justification of the cost will depend upon how far we get full value for our money" (TNA 1948b). Regardless of the value for money, the cost of prescriptions was also significantly higher than originally anticipated and made up almost twice as much of NHS expenditures as was expected in 1944. The gross cost of prescriptions dispensed in 1949/50 was £31,674,000 (more than three times the budget predicted in 1944, and about 14 per cent of the total cost of the NHS the previous year) (Hinchliffe 1959, 24). It appears that the Ministry of Health was not successful at estimating NHS costs at this time, even when it attempted to do so, and the actual cost of prescription services was unexpected.

Since the limited National Health Insurance program of 1911 covered prescription drugs for workers, we might expect that policymakers would have learned from this previous experience. The Hinchliffe Committee report did refer to the influence of the NHI drug coverage when it considered current problems with the cost of prescribing, saying that under the NHI, "it was found necessary at an early stage to take administrative action to control costs" (Hinchliffe 1959, 15). These actions included prohibitions on doctors prescribing "non-drug preparations," educational materials in which prescribers were "urged to prescribe with economy," and financial penalties for individual doctors who were found to be prescribing excessively (ibid.). Prior to the Second World War, the prescribing environment was quite different, as there were very few effective drugs (Rivett 1998, 55). However, it is curious that the lessons of the earlier restricted plan for prescription services were not applied more systematically to the design of NHS prescription services.

The apparently limited learning from previous restricted pharmaceutical benefit policies provides additional evidence for the importance of policy ideas, since the desire to adopt free, universal, and comprehensive health services, including pharmaceutical coverage, may have trumped previous experience with the problems of pharmaceutical expenditure increases. Moreover, even those lessons noted by the Hinchliffe Committee all emphasized physicians' prescribing behaviour as the key to cost control. Politicians were reluctant to impose regulatory limits on physicians' clinical autonomy in this regard,[54] and when the need for cost control became unavoidable, politicians chose patient charges. However, after the initial shock of higher-than-expected drug usage and rising prices, physicians' behaviour became a second major policy challenge, as doctors proved adept at avoiding or minimizing prescription charges on behalf of their patients. The Hinchliffe Committee reported, "The charge is regarded by patients as a tax and … it stimulates all the instincts which taxes usually arouse in ordinary people, viz. to avoid paying more than they can help and to obtain as much as possible for what they have to pay. At the same time the doctors' representatives have told the Committee that they regard the charge as a tax on illness and old age" (Hinchliffe 1959, 89).

## Prescription Charges, 1952–1956

A radical pace of health policy development makes programs less flexible once adopted, since they were introduced under conditions of consensus on broad policy ideas from politicians, and high levels of attention and support from the electorate. This means that any change to a program that threatens its key characteristics (in the NHS, a comprehensive range of free and universal services) should prompt backlash from those politicians who had strong preferences for the policy and, perhaps more importantly, from the public who had developed strong expectations about the type of services to which they were entitled.

The introduction of prescription charges in the United Kingdom provides evidence to support this expectation, especially when considered alongside Australia's different experience with the same type of policy change. Patient charges for prescriptions clearly clashed with the principle of a "free" service, and this was the main source of public backlash and governmental concern. Implementing this change aroused much greater opposition than the same policy did in Australia, and prescription charges continued to be a politically controversial issue in the United Kingdom for much longer than in Australia, while remaining significantly lower and more narrowly applied.

Prescription charges had been on the policy agenda in at least some parts of government since the NHS was implemented. A Treasury report on the history of prescription charges, completed in 1968, notes that in 1948, "the size of the estimate [for prescription services] alarmed Treasury officials so much that they began almost at once to propose a prescription charge" (TNA 1968b). Although it is clear that prescription charges were adopted in response to financial pressures, the exact reasoning for the policy design is a matter of some debate. The 1968 Treasury report notes a range of possible reasons for charges, from "general disinflationary measures" to "concern over increase in drug bill" to "prevention of 'abuse.'" However, it finds that charges were not a particularly effective response to any of these problems and goes on to say, "It never seems to have been clear precisely what officials believed to be the situation at any time. The drug bill was large and was rising, but whether this change was caused by 'abuse' was never properly investigated" (TNA 1968b). The authors of the Treasury report conclude, "It seems as if the Treasury, having assumed the charges were good without further analysis, concentrated merely on tactics, i.e. waiting, on each occasion, till it was thought that ministerial opinion was ripe for a further attempt [to get charges]. Thus miscalculations took place on each occasion" (ibid.).

At the time, politicians saw the introduction of charges as financially necessary and a less painful option than alternatives such as cutting back services (TNA 1950a), a position that was repeated in subsequent debates. For example, in 1956 the Conservative minister of health explained, "When it was decided that money should be raised from the Health Service, it was felt that the least harmful way would be from the Drug bill" (TNA 1956c). However, elite discussion of the policy change demonstrates that government was still quite concerned with the public's reaction. This concern was justified, given the continued popularity of the free, universal NHS: in 1950, the Gallup Poll of Britain reported that 71 per cent of respondents thought that the nationalization of medical services had been good (BIPO/Gallup Poll, 13 November 1950).

When prescription charges were first proposed in the House of Commons in 1949, it was as part of the Labour government's proposals to deal with the difficult post-war economic situation. Prime Minister Clement Attlee proposed prescription charges as the last of a list of expenditure reduction items but still linked the measure to "good policy" motives of preventing abuse of the system rather than economic necessity. On 24 October 1949 he told the House of Commons, "The purpose [of the charges] is to reduce excessive and, in some cases, unnecessary resort to doctors and chemists ... resultant saving will contribute about £10 million, although this is not the primary purpose of the charge."[55] However, the Treasury report notes that although Attlee justified the charge in light of evidence of excessive prescribing, "this 'evidence' is not available in Treasury papers" (TNA 1968b).

When prescription charges were debated in Cabinet in 1950, policymakers were also attentive to the potential for backlash. The chancellor of the Exchequer argued that if charges were to be implemented, government must immediately try to get the medical professions (and particularly doctors) onside, since "they would be quick to see the fruitful possibilities of working up an agitation, among the public no less than among themselves" (TNA 1950b).

The chancellor's concerns proved to be well founded, as doctors began to find ways to subvert the charges almost as soon as they were implemented by a Conservative government in 1952. The charges were originally levied at one shilling per prescription form, which at that time was about equal to the cost of a loaf of bread.[56] If a patient required multiple prescriptions at one doctor's visit, these were typically written on one form. A Ministry of Health circular explaining charges to doctors said, "Doctors are asked not to increase either the number of prescriptions on one form or the quantities ordered in one prescription" (TNA 1952b), but it appears that this direction was not taken to heart by physicians.

A letter from the pharmacy chain Boots Drugs to the ministry in June of 1952 complained that in order to minimize charges, doctors were prescribing potentially dangerous quantities of drugs in a single prescription and putting all prescriptions for a family on a single form, so it was not clear who should get which medicine (TNA 1952a). Perhaps in part because of doctors' avoidance, and perhaps because excessive prescribing was not as severe a problem as policymakers assumed, Treasury found that after the introduction of the charge in 1952, the reductions in the number of prescriptions were "nowhere near the 10% reduction apparently expected" (TNA 1968b).

This led to a change in how prescription charges were administered. In 1956, a Conservative government moved from a shilling charge per prescription form to a shilling charge per item, effectively increasing the charge for people taking more than one drug. The Conservative government used the same language of financial necessity as previous Labour governments when justifying this change. In 1956, the minister of health wrote to chemists to say, "This alteration ... was made with great reluctance, and only because it is regarded as unavoidable in the present financial and economic situation" (TNA 1956a). In a Cabinet meeting to discuss the change, the minister of health raised concerns that the charge per item would cause hardship and suggested that the BMA could mitigate this with "generous prescribing in particular cases," such as a larger prescription of insulin for diabetics. Others noted that "the Local Medical Committees could confidentially be instructed to disregard heavy prescribing in cases of chronic sufferers. It could then be stated that doctors would not be penalized for generous prescribing in suitable cases" (TNA 1956a). It seems that ministers were looking for a way around their own policy in certain cases, and again, this became a source of concern later when doctors acted on it.

Ministers were also concerned with more public methods of blame avoidance, saying, "It might ... be easier to meet criticism of the increased charge if some concession in the health field could be announced at the same time, for instance, the provision of local authority chiropody services for old people" (TNA 1956a). Despite these plans, and a policy allowing low-income patients to apply to the National Assistance Board for a refund of their prescription charges, increased charges still caused public consternation. In November 1956, a constituent wrote to her member of Parliament to say that once the new charges were in place, her prescriptions would cost five shillings each time, "Yet how can I possibly afford to pay 5/- every two weeks. I have three young children and our income is considerably small. Do you think you have given this scheme fair consideration?" (TNA 1956d). This file, which was maintained by the Ministry of Health concerning the amendment regulations for the new charge, contained similar complaints from other constituents, so the public appears to have been concerned even before the change was implemented.

A Conservative government doubled prescription charges in 1961, and this again was the subject of much policy discussion, despite the fact that the cost of the average prescription had increased to the point that doubling the charge still resulted in patients paying a slightly lower proportion of the cost of each prescription than they did when charges were first introduced in 1952.[57] The government's justification for the increase focused on the rising cost of prescription services and the need to maintain sufficient budget room for other priorities, such as hospital construction. A draft statement prepared for the minister of health stated, "The Government are determined to continue their policy of developing the Health Services and to carry through a long-term programme of modernizing our hospitals. These objectives would be endangered if the cost of the Service to the Exchequer were allowed to go on increasing at so high a rate" (TNA 1961a). An internal memo argued, "It is the duty of the Government to do everything it can to limit the cost of the Pharmaceutical Service to that reasonably required for effective treatment" (TNA 1961b).

The Conservative government's somewhat weaker commitment to NHS principles is demonstrated in a question-and-answer memo on prescription charges that argued, "The Government adheres to the principle that a patient under the National Health Service shall be supplied with all necessary drugs, but they must be paid for and it is reasonable that patients should pay a reasonable share" (TNA 1961d), contrary to the original principle of a "free" service. The government's rationale was rejected by a pharmacists' group who wrote to the Ministry of Health, "We have always held the view that the levy [patient charges] system is socially unjustifiable" (TNA 1961c).

## Prescription Charges, 1964–1968

The ongoing political relevance of prescription charges is demonstrated by the Labour Party's push to abolish them, which was part of the party platform starting in 1955.[58] It was not an election-winning issue, but the fact that this fairly specific aspect of the NHS received individual attention in the manifesto statements is significant. In their 1955 election manifesto, Labour promised, "In order to restore a free Health Service, we shall abolish all charges, including those on teeth, spectacles and prescriptions." The Conservatives countered by emphasizing hospital building and preventative medicine, and saying, "We rank [these priorities] higher than free wigs or free aspirins" and won the 1955 election (Craig 1975, 198), but the Labour promise persisted in manifestos in 1959 and 1964.

Labour won the 1964 election with a bare majority and moved quickly to fulfil its promise about prescription charges. In a letter to Prime Minister Harold Wilson just a month after the election, first secretary of state George Brown said, "I am worried by the omission from the

Budget Speech of any reference to the date for the abolition of Health Service prescription charges. *I think it matters that we should take the greatest credit for this* and proclaim it at an early date, and it ought to operate from the earliest date practicable" (TNA 1964a; emphasis added). In his reply, Wilson agreed with this assessment.

This exchange shows Labour was aware of credit-claiming opportunity and potential electoral payoffs for abolishing prescription charges, but there is also evidence that some politicians, in particular health minister Kenneth Robinson, may have wished to get rid of charges because of his own commitment to the idea of free health services. A Treasury memo notes that, "The Minister (Mr. Kenneth Robinson) has personally pledged abolition of prescription charges, and has attacked the charges on many occasions" (TNA n.d.). Robinson wrote to the chancellor of the Exchequer, James Callaghan, in November 1964 to argue against postponing the abolition of charges until spring 1965, as this "would have forced the chronic sick and the elderly to endure another full winter of the charges and exposed us to the accusation of dragging our feet" (TNA 1964b). As will be seen below, Robinson's ideas about the need to abolish charges were also in evidence during his vigorous but ultimately unsuccessful attempt to prevent his own government from reinstating the charges four years later.

Both policy ideas and strategic considerations were evident in internal government debates about the feasibility of abolishing charges. A Treasury memo written immediately after the 1964 election cautions that "the total cost of the Health Service is growing fairly rapidly, and the abolition of prescription charges will add significantly to the total cost." In order to deal with this, the memo's authors suggest, "Unpalatable measures to control or pay for this expenditure might be easier to present at the same time as the abolition of prescription charges rather than at a later date" (TNA 1964c). This acknowledgment of both the financial implications of abolishing prescription charges and a potential need to compensate for them suggests that, by 1964, prescription charges had taken on a special political meaning that made it more electorally expedient (or ideologically acceptable, for some politicians) to address these charges, even if it meant other, perhaps less visible, cost-control measures in other parts of the health service.

During the controversial reintroduction of charges, Cabinet minister Richard Crossman recalls that he was against abolishing prescription charges in 1964 (as was the chancellor of the Exchequer) and that "the decision was taken by Harold Wilson, who argued that we'd made the pledge in the election manifesto and we couldn't let the electors down" (Crossman 1975, 646), pointing again to the electoral significance of prescription charges.

Prescription charges were reinstated in 1968 by the same Labour government that had abolished them four years earlier. The internal party debate and public dismay over this change demonstrates the conflict and electoral trade-offs between the need to control health spending and demonstrate economic responsibility to the voters, and the policy ideas and public expectations about NHS services that were pushing politicians the other way. This can be compared to the evolution of patient co-payments for drugs in Australia, where increases to co-payments were made with little debate and public attention, and there was never a move to abolish charges by either major party.

A ministers' briefing note prepared by the U.K. Ministry of Health in 1968 calls the reintroduction of prescription charges "a regrettable necessity forced upon the government by the economic situation," and goes on to compare the reintroduction of charges to other cost-cutting measures such as "(a) cutting out some element of the health service altogether; (b) cutting the hospital building programme ... Of these, (a) would be repugnant, [and] (b) would involve cutting back a long-term programme of planning and construction which has taken years to build up and would take correspondingly longer to restore" (TNA 1968a).

Here, politicians made two justifications for prescription charges, given the financial imperative to reduce health spending. First, they implied a hierarchy of NHS principles, arguing it was better to impinge on the principle of free services than to limit the range of services provided. Second, they argued in this case that prescription services were a lower priority than other elements of the NHS. This view is supported in archival materials from the Treasury concerning prescription charges. In December 1967, health minister Robinson wrote to Roy Jenkins, the new chancellor of the Exchequer, to describe the difficulty he was in, given his personal association with the abolition of charges, *and* his conclusion that hospital building should also not be cut, as the necessary savings "could only be achieved, if at all, by wrecking the entire hospital building programme" (TNA 1967a). Robinson further elaborated his opposition to prescription charges in a memo written at the same time, raising concerns about the hardship they would cause, despite proposals for a system of exemptions, and about the political repercussions of such a move, saying, "I can see no advantage whatever in reducing Health Estimates (assuming they must be reduced) by a method which would cause the maximum political dissension, and probably disaffection, which would yield an uncertain revenue and certainly far less than the alternative I have suggested [an increase in the general NHS contribution]; which would pose considerable administrative problems and require extra staff; and which would *breach a public pledge by the Prime Minister and others* at the time of devaluation, by specifically taxing the sick" (TNA 1967b, emphasis added).

Interestingly, proponents of the prescription charge within Treasury also seemed aware of the potential electoral consequences and toll on Labour Party unity posed by this policy but were more sanguine about the benefits outweighing the costs. In December 1967, a Treasury official wrote that the "reintroduction of prescription charges would be the quickest, simplest and most economically effective course. Here again it is politically the most difficult, but the most rewarding in terms of public confidence," perhaps in reference to the improvement in the economic situation (TNA 1967c).

The issue of prescription charges and a new system for exempting the chronically ill from these charges continued to be a major source of discussion within government and in the House of Commons throughout the summer and fall of 1968.[59] Excerpts from Hansard from this period reveal that the Labour government was attacked by its own backbenchers using language that reflected both a commitment to the founding ideas of the NHS and concerns about public expectations.

During debate in the House of Commons on 16 and 17 January 1968, Labour members chastised the government for "seeking to tax the sick" and emphasized that "the reintroduction of prescription charges will cause bitter disappointment among many people in the Labour movement" and "hits at the very basis and principle on which the [National Health] Service was established."[60]

Prime Minister Wilson assured the House that the charges were being reintroduced only "after the most serious consideration and with the utmost reluctance" and argued that "it would not have been possible to do what was necessary to get the economy right without making some cuts in the social services, which account for a very high proportion ... of total Government expenditure" and that maintaining funds for the hospital building program was a priority.[61]

Although Wilson referred repeatedly to the proposed scheme of exemptions from charges, whereby "something like one-half of the prescriptions dispensed in this country will be the subject of the exemption categories I listed ... the charges on the stamp will be on those who, in the main, are in work and who can afford it,"[62] members did not appear to put much stock in this scheme. Similar doubts were expressed in private by Wilson's own health minister. Early in January 1968, Prime Minister Wilson announced the plan for exemptions to Cabinet, and Crossman notes that "a reply had come from Kenneth Robinson that no formal exemption was administratively possible. Of course I recognized at once this was a political tactic ... to prevent any increase of prescription charges" (Crossman 1975, 637). When recounting the next week's Cabinet meetings, Crossman refers to the resistance to prescription charges in the Labour backbenches and says that when the meeting discussed charges "despite all my efforts Kenneth Robinson had produced a lamentably inadequate paper. It was clear that he was trying to make as many difficulties as he possibly could" (644).

The events of 1964 demonstrate that there were both ideational reasons for the government in power to abolish charges, and electoral incentives to do so. In 1968, these two factors were still at work. They were trumped by the financial imperatives of an increasing expensive health service during a difficult economic time, which created countervailing electoral incentives,[63] and charges were reinstated. However, in comparison with Australia, U.K. prescription services still appear more strongly conditioned by the policy preferences and public expectations generated by the radical circumstances of their adoption. Although both countries reformed their pharmaceutical policies to control costs, the British reforms imposed lesser burdens on patients in terms of the extent of charges and their impact on the program's comprehensiveness. If we take the counterfactual situation of U.K. prescription charges to be a system of charges like Australia's, rather than no charges at all, the British policy is a much more moderate system of pharmaceutical management. Charges were relatively low: only 20 pence per item in 1971. In contrast, in March 1971 the Australia co-payment was fifty cents per prescription, and the rate increased to one dollar in December of that year. Charges were also applied much less broadly than in Australia. The system of exemptions from NHS charges in the United Kingdom began when charges were reinstated in 1968 and has expanded to cover new groups since that time. In contrast, in Australia a system of lowered co-payments for concessional categories of beneficiaries (based on income and health status) was put in place only in 1983.

## Conclusion

In 1950, the Australian and British health systems looked quite different from one another. Australia had chosen an incremental pace of health policy development and adopted only one public health service, pharmaceutical benefits, before an abrupt shift in the governing party's goals and ideals for health halted the development of public insurance or benefits. The United Kingdom chose a radical pace of policy development and had a comprehensive range of health services included in its free, universal program. However, both countries faced the challenge of pharmaceutical expenditures that were increasing beyond all predictions and placing significant pressures on government budgets. The choice of policy tools to deal with these pressures was almost identical: both aimed to shift some of the burden of pharmaceutical expenditures onto the patient by introducing a flat charge on prescriptions. However, the way these tools played out in the political arena was influenced by the legacy of each country's earlier choices about the pace of policy development and especially by the types of ideas about health policy held by political elites and the public.

This chapter focused on opportunities for minor change to existing programs, and found that an incremental pace of policy development, with its more limited policy ideas and public expectations regarding health services, makes programs more flexible and can ease certain types of retrenchment. In the next chapter, we return to major changes to the health system – changes that significantly increase or decrease the range of services covered or the population eligible for coverage. While chapter 4 makes a case for major change being difficult and rare, it is not impossible. The next chapter addresses the problem of major change through program expansion using the two examples provided by the study countries: the adoption of public medical insurance in Canada, nine years after nationwide public hospital insurance, and the adoption of public hospital and medical insurance in Australia, more than twenty years after the adoption of the Pharmaceutical Benefits Scheme.

# Chapter 6

# Explaining Major Change: Rare Conditions for Program Expansion

Thus far, this book has argued that certain conditions make a country more likely to take a slow, incremental approach to health policy development versus a radical approach, and that the pace of policy development matters because incremental processes tend to create significant barriers to the later expansion of public health services. This chapter sets out the rare conditions when these barriers can be overcome, asking when and how countries that adopt an incremental pace of health policy development can accomplish major change later in the process.

One barrier to change occurs because, in the absence of public policy development, alternative institutional arrangements such as non-governmental or commercial insurance arise to fill health service needs. However, chapter 4 demonstrated that incremental proposals for program expansion may face barriers even before alternative arrangements develop, as with pharmaceutical insurance in Canada. A second barrier to change arises through the adaptive expectations of elites and the public. The lack of elite consensus on an overarching policy idea leads to restricted public expectations about the sorts of health services voters want or deserve, which in turn reinforces a narrow elite focus on the problems of existing health services rather than program expansion.

As barriers to change increase over time, accomplishing the "next steps" in an incremental program of health policy development becomes a radical change rather than an automatic or unproblematic progression. However, just as radical change is possible at an initial critical moment for policy development, it may also be possible later if certain conditions are met. As was the case with an initial radical pace of change, later program expansion in countries that have taken an incremental approach to health policy should require centralized institutional authority (or a temporary weakening of institutional vetoes over change), new elite consensus on a high-level idea for policy reform, and electoral motivations to act.

This chapter argues that the three conditions were present in Canada in the 1960s and in Australia in the 1970s, both examples of countries that had taken an incremental approach to health policy and had stalled after the adoption of an initial service. These conditions allowed for the adoption of nationwide public medical insurance in Canada and nationwide public hospital and medical insurance in Australia, both of which faced significant barriers. The chapter therefore steps away from the focus on the adoption and reform of pharmaceutical insurance in order to test the plausibility of the proposed mechanisms for major change in an incremental policy process, in hopes of setting directions for future research into this type of change.

**Canada**

Chapter 3 described what was to be an incremental process of health policy development in Canada, starting in the 1940s. Policymakers and politicians decided fairly quickly that the only feasible option for health policy was a "staged approach" of insuring one service at a time. There was some debate about the correct order of services to be adopted, but hospital services were eventually chosen as the first priority, and in these discussions, medical services were always the expected next step. However, the struggle to implement nationwide medical insurance in the 1960s was in many ways more difficult than hospital insurance, demonstrating the way barriers to policy development increased over time. The history of this struggle has been well documented (Taylor 1987; Naylor 1986; Maioni 1998; Bryden 1997); this chapter does not aim to add new details, but rather to interpret the degree to which the conditions for the adoption of nationwide medical insurance in Canada match the theorized conditions for radical policy change.

*Barriers to Program Expansion*

The Liberal government that designed and negotiated the majority of the nationwide hospital insurance program in Canada lost power in the June 1957 election, leaving it to be implemented shortly thereafter by the new Conservative government led by Prime Minister John Diefenbaker. Medical insurance had been discussed as a closely related second priority during the development of hospital insurance, but progress towards this goal essentially stalled for a number of years.

Despite the change in government, the main barrier to the development of nationwide public medical insurance was the growth of alternative institutional arrangements for medical insurance in the absence of federal government action, rather than objective economic problems or clearly defined partisan opposition. Although a national program would require new revenues (Taylor 1987, 356), in the early 1960s, financial conditions did not seriously constrain further policy development. The economic situation between 1962 and 1966 was particularly good: one economic historian calls these years "almost a golden age for the economy" (Perry 1989, 15), although after 1966 the financial situation worsened and federal budgets went into deficit (Taylor 1987, 373). The Conservative government had challenged certain aspects of the nationwide hospital insurance program while in opposition, but once elected it implemented the plan with very few changes (231–4). Furthermore, the Conservative government sought to delay consideration of medical insurance, or medicare as it came to be known, rather than reject it outright, calling a Royal Commission on Health Services at the request of the Canadian Medical Association in 1960 (Maioni 1998, 123). The Liberal Party was returned to power in 1963, shortly before the commission made its report.

In the early 1960s, there were a number of alternative sources of medical insurance available. Commercial insurance companies offered private (or to use the term more common at the time, voluntary) medical insurance. There were also not-for-profit, physician-sponsored voluntary plans, which developed an umbrella organization, Trans-Canada Medical Plans (TCMP), in 1951 (Shillington 1972, 109). In 1961, about 4.5 million Canadians had some coverage through physician-sponsored plans, and an additional 4.2 million had coverage through for-profit agencies (for a combined total of about 48 per cent of the population with coverage),[64] although some estimates indicate that these plans covered only 20 to 45 per cent of medical costs (Naylor 1986). The Canadian Conference on Health Care, an organization that combined the TCMP and the Canadian Health Insurance Association (CHIA), estimated that about 62 per cent of Canadians had voluntary surgical and/or medical insurance in 1965, and this figure went up to almost 67 per cent in 1966 (Shillington 1972, 200).[65]

This growth in voluntary, non-governmental insurance meant that private insurers, the TCMP, and the medical profession all had a growing interest in retaining a system of multiple insurers, which they saw as the only protection against doctors becoming "prisoners of such bureaucratic operations" as represented by broad government insurance (Shillington 1972, 140). Each group, jointly and separately, lobbied accordingly. Each submitted numerous briefs to the Royal Commission on Health Services and pressured the federal government to drop its plan for a nationwide public medical insurance plan in 1965 (Taylor 1987, 338). Later, when it appeared that passage of the necessary federal legislation was faltering, the Canadian Medical Association (CMA) met with the government to urge a fallback to a program that would provide services to the medically indigent, rather than the entire population (Taylor 1987).

Provincial governments also began to develop their own medical insurance programs in the absence of federal policy action. Saskatchewan was the first to announce a provincial medical insurance program in 1959; it began operating after a bitter doctor's strike in 1962 (Maioni 1998). Saskatchewan's program was compulsory and similar in structure to existing public, universal hospital insurance. However, Alberta, Ontario, and British Columbia took a different approach. They were much more receptive to lobbying from the CMA, CHIA, and TCMP and moved to subsidize private, voluntary insurance starting in 1963 (Taylor 1987, 341). This may have made federally led health reform less pressing or attractive, and in Alberta, it reinforced the provincial government's ideological opposition to compulsory public insurance.

In addition, provinces were becoming generally more assertive in their dealings with the federal government and less accepting of "shared-cost" or "conditional grant-in-aid" programs, where federal money came at the cost of provincial autonomy in a policy area (Taylor 1987, 355). Provinces did not respond strongly to the broad federal proposals for medical insurance at the June 1965 Federal-Provincial Conference, but after the more detailed legislation was introduced in Parliament, opposition increased. By 1966, no province had announced plans to take up the federal conditions and offer of medicare funds, and some federal Cabinet ministers began to speculate about including a role for the private plans as a way to break the stalemate (Bryden 1997, 151). As described below, the federal government was able to use financial inducements and threats to get the provinces on board, but it still took three years after the inauguration of the federal medicare program for all provinces to meet the requirements for federal funding (Taylor 1987, 391).

A few years after the adoption of nationwide hospital insurance, supporters of expanded health policy in Canada faced a strengthened private insurance industry, a wary medical profession, and provinces that, with the exception of Saskatchewan, were uninterested if not outright opposed to national health projects. The types of barriers to new public services predicted by standard path-dependent accounts of policy development had begun to appear even in the short time since the first service was implemented. How, then, did the federal Liberal Party decide to take up this issue once again, and how did they eventually succeed in introducing nationwide, public, universal medical insurance in 1968?

### New Leadership and New Policy Ideas

Chapter 2 argued that if politicians are motivated by a new idea about health policy or pressured by a new wave of public expectations for service, they are more likely to find ways to overcome institutional barriers to major change. It suggested that ideational change might be endogenous, but it was still expected to be extraordinary, requiring a high volume of new information and potentially a policy entrepreneur who worked to increase the issue's salience. In Canada, the adoption of medical insurance did not require an entirely new policy idea. It *did* require that existing ideas about the extension of health insurance become more prominent with elites, after having been mostly dormant since the adoption of nationwide hospital insurance in 1957. This was accomplished through a combination of new leadership within the federal Liberal Party and an electoral context that made the fulfilment of old policy promises newly attractive.[66]

The Liberal Party's electoral losses in 1957 and 1958 prompted a "period of partisan introspection," including a reconsideration of health insurance, which had been in the party platform since 1919 (Bryden 2009, 319). As Maioni (1998, 127) describes it, the 1958 landslide election loss convinced the Liberals that they needed to take up a new position "as the party of social reform." The new Liberal leader, Lester Pearson, was more sympathetic to the idea of broad health insurance than previous leaders, and with him came a new group of more progressive party members, including Tom Kent (later a key advisor in the Prime Minister's Office), Walter Gordon (later finance minister) and Judy LaMarsh (later health minister) (Taylor 1987, 352; Bryden 2009, 319). As Taylor (1987, 361) notes, when the Liberals were re-elected in 1963, "for the first time, there was genuine enthusiasm [for public health insurance] in the Prime Minister's Office," and in Canada's executive-dominated policy process this was a key change.

In 1960, the Liberals sponsored a "Study Conference on National Problems" in Kingston, Ontario, which became an important source of policy ideas for the party (Bryden 2009, 319). It included a sixty-six-page paper by Tom Kent titled "Towards a Philosophy of Social Security" where Kent laid out an agenda for social programs including medicare. A summary of the conference reports that this paper "was very well-received by the majority" (QUA 1960). The Liberal Party's 1962 and 1963 election platforms promised to "establish, in cooperation with the provinces, a medical care plan for all Canadians" (Taylor 1987, 333), and Peter Newman (quoted in Taylor 1987, 353) traces the origins of these policies to Kent's paper, saying it supplied "many of the more radical ideas" in the Liberal policy renewal. This focus on the extension of health insurance did pick up on an available idea, in the sense that medical insurance had been discussed as a closely related priority during the hospital insurance debates of the 1950s, but it also represented a significant increase in the number and prominence of strong supporters within the Liberal Party and eventually government.

Ideas about broader health insurance were also made more prominent by the 1964 *Report of the Royal Commission on Health Services*, which had a galvanizing effect on elites and the public. Like the Beveridge Report in the United Kingdom twenty years earlier, this report was both high profile and specific. Maioni (1998, 123) says it "ended up fanning the flames of the health insurance debate," while Taylor (1987, 353) calls it "a rallying cry of support" for those within the Liberal Cabinet and caucus who hoped for broader health insurance. Bryden (2009, 324) argues that the report was the "one thing [that] could push the Liberals into action" on health insurance after a difficult negotiation of a national pension program and a disastrous first budget.

The commission's report was wide-ranging, recommending medical services, dental and optical services for certain populations, prescription drugs services, prosthetics, and home care. It called for "a comprehensive, universal Health Services Programme for the Canadian people," although it acknowledged that each province might exercise "the right to determine the order of priority of each service and the timing of its introduction" (Royal Commission on Health Services 1964). Despite its broad scope, medical insurance was clearly a priority in the commission's recommendations: they called it the "next essential service" after hospital care (28). It was the first service recommended for adoption (Naylor 1986, 223), and although the commission's press release reiterated its objective of a comprehensive set of personal health services, it acknowledged that medicare was the first expectation (LAC 1964b).

The Royal Commission on Health Services did not necessarily provide all new ideas about health insurance – as we have seen, the Liberal
Party had been developing its policy ideas on this issue since 1960.
What the commission did provide was a clear, cohesive statement of
goals and means for achieving them, ruling out some options (such as
subsidizing voluntary insurance) and privileging others (such as the
early adoption of universal medical insurance).[67] The report was high
profile and called for immediate action, urging a Federal-Provincial
Health Conference within six months of its release (Royal Commission
on Health Services 1964, 14–15). It thus provided a strong basis for developing consensus about medical insurance within federal political
elites, although the consensus was by no means perfect.

The federal Liberal government proposed four principles for a
nationwide, universal system of health insurance and called for "comprehensive physicians' services as an initial minimum" at the Federal-
Provincial Conference of July 1965 (Canada 1965, 16). The party was re-
elected with a second minority government in November 1965, which
led to a major Cabinet shuffle. The result was a shift in power within
government away from the progressive supporters of broad medical
insurance like Walter Gordon and Judy LaMarsh, and towards more
fiscally cautious ministers like Mitchell Sharp, who was quite sceptical
of broad government health insurance, and who replaced Gordon in
Finance (Bryden 1997, 150). This ideological dissensus within the governing party made it more difficult to extend health insurance. However,
the legislation did pass in December 1966, with the support of 177 out
of the 179 members of Parliament (Taylor 1987, 374). Kent recalls that
Sharp would have preferred to postpone the implementation of medicare "indefinitely," but in 1968 "Mr Pearson thankfully put his foot
down and went ahead,"[68] demonstrating again the importance of centralized institutional authority in pushing radical change.

*Electoral Motivations*

The convictions of new progressive members of the Liberal Party were
one important factor in the decision to expand health services, but this
was also a strategic choice. Electoral factors contributed to the Liberal
decision to push for the extension of health insurance in a number of
ways. First, the electoral losses of 1957 and 1958 prompted the Liberal
Party to reconsider previous policy ideas. However, these losses did
not dictate the choice of ideas: it was conditioned by the ideals of the

progressive leadership that was coming into power in the party. Once the Liberal Party won minority governments in 1963 and again in 1965, there was a second source of pressure from the New Democratic Party (NDP), who strongly supported health insurance and whose support the Liberal government needed to stay in power. This pushed the Liberals to take bolder action on health than they might otherwise have chosen, both to retain the NDP's support in Parliament and to avoid losing their most left-leaning supporters to the NDP (Maioni 1998, 128; Hacker 1998, 105; Taylor 1987, 353).

Finally, there was the role of public expectations, but this type of pressure was less important in making the decision to pursue medical insurance, and more important in supporting that course of action once it was underway. Taylor (1987, 352) argues that public expectations had been conditioned by previous insurance policies at the federal and provincial levels to the point that medical insurance was a "natural, normal expectation." However, as was the case with hospital insurance, the strongest evidence of public expectations comes in response to polling questions directly about medical insurance, *after* its appearance in Liberal platforms and especially after the report of the Royal Commission on Health Services, which sparked public interest in the issue (Bryden 1997, 130).

Public opinion summaries do not show a major change in the salience of health insurance that might motivate government action. Unemployment remained the most important problem in Canadian's minds when they were asked for an unprompted list of their concerns for most of the years between 1960 and 1967 (Canadian Gallup Polls July 1960, May 1961, May 1962, June 1962, September 1962, March 1963, August 1964, June 1966, December 1966, June 1967).[69] The fact that health failed to move up on this important measure of salience may be related to the peculiarities of Canadian public opinion at this time: in 1966, Gallup reported, "Canadians seem to have something of a fixation about unemployment. They still name it as our chief problem, despite the fact that the ratio of those out of work is lower than it has been for years" (CIPO/Gallup Poll of Canada, 5 January 1966). However, when questioned directly about medical insurance, voters were aware of the issue and were basically positive about it. In January 1963, after medicare had featured prominently in both Liberal and NDP electoral platforms but before the Liberals had been re-elected, 50 per cent of Canadians had heard of medicare, and of those, 87 per cent thought "a satisfactory plan between government, patients, and doctors could be worked out" (Canadian Gallup Poll, January 1963). In September 1965, after the summer Federal-Provincial Conference where the federal government made its medicare proposals, 74 per cent had heard of the plan, although slightly more than half of these thought the program should be voluntary rather than compulsory (Canadian Gallup Poll, September 1965). By November 1967, 59 per cent of Canadians were willing to see a tax increase in order to have medicare implemented without further delay (Canadian Gallup Poll, November 1967).

Although there was not an obvious jump in the salience of health insurance at this time, its generally positive reception with the voters and the pressures from the NDP were sufficient to make it much more important in Liberal electoral strategy in the 1960s, and to overcome the objections of private insurers and the medical profession.[70] Liberal pamphlets from the 1962 election promised "Health Care as Needed" and proposed coverage for medical services, with "other services" such as pharmaceuticals to follow later (LAC 1961a). Other election materials informed voters that they "shouldn't have to worry about heavy medical costs" (LAC 1961b). After the Liberals were elected in 1963, the extension of health insurance remained an important promise. In a campaign memo in July 1965, Tom Kent advised Prime Minister Pearson, "The theme of the campaign should be what we have done and what we want to do if we have a chance to govern. What we have done means more employment, pensions, flag, etc. – a short list of the best. What we will do means medicare and a few other things in a shorter list" (QUA 1965b).

Kent's comments to Pearson illustrate the degree to which the government anticipated that medical insurance would be an important electoral tool: he said, "We are prepared in effect to appeal to the public over the heads of the Provinces" on this matter (QUA 1965a), thus limiting provincial governments' effective veto power over the extension of health insurance. The extent to which the Liberal government needed to and was able to do this was the final piece of the medicare puzzle.

*Overcoming Institutional Barriers*

Once the federal government decided to act on medical insurance, there was still an issue of jurisdiction. Major changes to the health system required provincial approval and cooperation, and provincial governments would not accept federal conditions unquestioningly, as demonstrated by the difficult negotiations over nationwide pensions at around this time (Bryden 2009, 325). However, despite these challenges, we should not overstate provincial opposition to medicare. Alberta's government, under Premier Ernest Manning, was clearly opposed to medicare on ideological grounds, but no other provincial government held this philosophical opposition to the idea of broad government insurance. Some, like Quebec, were newly progressive and interested in extending social provision. Overcoming institutional barriers therefore required some strategy from the federal government – the fairly detailed structure of hospital insurance was no longer suited to the climate of federal-provincial relations. It also required financial inducements to get laggard provinces in line. In the end, however, the institutional barriers needed only to be temporarily circumvented, not erased entirely.

The Royal Commission on Health Services had suggested structuring medicare similarly to hospital insurance, and an initial consultation with provincial health departments in the spring of 1965 found a favourable response to this plan (LAC 1965). However, Tom Kent said the royal commission and this professional, rather than political, survey was out of date on federal-provincial relations, and that Kent himself and other political advisors knew that the hospital insurance version of medicare was not acceptable to provincial governments or premiers.[71] Pearson and his advisors thus rejected the traditional conditional grant-in-aid program, as well as the requirement that a majority of provinces sign on in order for plan to be adopted, as was the case with hospital insurance (Taylor 1987, 361). A different type of plan was proposed by Al Johnson, the newly appointed deputy minister of finance, before the 1965 Federal-Provincial Conference. A traditional shared-cost program meant the federal government enacted legislation setting out the details of the service, and provinces signed a formal agreement with the federal government. Johnson's plan allowed the provinces to simply pass their own legislation in conformity with certain broad principles "enunciated by the Federal Government after, and as a consequence of, consultation with the provinces" (Bryden 2009, 326). These principles or criteria to receive federal funding were that provincial medical insurance programs would be universal, comprehensive (in the sense of covering all physicians' services), portable, and publicly administered.

The provinces' response to the federal proposals at the 1965 Federal-Provincial Conference was muted. Provincial governments were not necessarily enthusiastic, but they did not object to the proposal outright, with the notable exception of Alberta. Tom Kent recalls Premier Manning's first response to the proposal: "He reacted absolutely in horror … he said, 'You'll be proposing grocery care next!'"[72] As delays mounted at the federal level, however, provinces had time to develop their concerns. By 1966, all provinces were worried about the cost of establishing such a significant new program, and only Newfoundland, New Brunswick, and Saskatchewan were committed to a universal program, as the other provinces complained about the conditions for federal funding and called for an additional federal-provincial conference (Bryden 2009, 328; 1997, 153).

Despite these concerns, Kent argued that the promise of federal funds to cover half the new program was impossible for provincial governments to turn down. As he said in an interview, "They all wanted the money, of course! They grumbled about it in detail, and they have grumbled about it since. But they sure wanted it."[73] Bryden (1997, 162) argues that the federal plan went ahead despite provincial objections because of the convictions of certain federal ministers – especially Walter Gordon – who were able to convince Prime Minister Pearson to finally make a decision and require Cabinet solidarity. Taylor (1987, 374–5) concurs, saying that the "price which the federal government was to pay" for this decision was high in both political and economic terms.

The new federal plan therefore went ahead, although it put significantly fewer conditions on the funding of medical insurance than it had tied to hospital insurance funding nine years earlier (LAC 1972b). When provincial governments were slow to implement their programs after the inauguration of medicare in 1968, the federal government used a final financial threat to get them on board. In what Boychuk (2008, 130) calls a "dubious constitutional move," the federal government created a 2 per cent "social development tax" clearly intended to finance health care contributions. This was an addition to federal income tax, but since it was coming from their residents, provinces needed to start their own medicare programs in order to get this money "back" (Taylor 1987, 392).

In Canada, the gap between the introduction of the first element of a public health scheme (hospital insurance) and the second (medical insurance) was nine years, and the two services were closely linked in policy discussions about the order of priorities during the 1950s. This would seem to provide the best-case scenario for adoption of additional services under an incremental process of policy development: there was only a short period in which barriers such as alternative institutional arrangements for health insurance could develop, and initial ideas about medical insurance saw it as positive and as a high priority for service adoption. However, the adoption of nationwide medical insurance still required a fortuitous combination of newly prominent policy ideas and favourable electoral conditions in order for the federal government to overcome the barriers to its implementation and strike a deal with provincial governments. The context for major health policy change in Australia involved different policy histories, players, and institutional rules. However, there are some striking similarities in the conditions that were necessary to overcome barriers to change and introduce expanded public health services in that country.

**Australia**

In Australia, the barriers to the introduction of additional health services were arguably much higher than in Canada – they were certainly more longstanding. When Medibank, Labor's public hospital and medical insurance program, was first introduced in 1972, it had been more than two decades since the adoption of the Pharmaceutical Benefits Scheme. In that time, states had developed alternative institutional arrangements for hospital care, and private health insurance had flourished. A continuous period of Liberal government, with its preference for private, voluntary health insurance, had limited opportunities for competing ideas about universal public insurance to gain prominence.

However, the longer period of alternative insurance also meant that there was time for serious problems with the system to arise, and by the 1960s, Australians were struggling with rising premiums and reduced coverage from private insurers. Similar to Canada, public hospital and medical insurance was championed by a political party that was actively seeking new policy ideas in an effort to regain power, and when a Labor government under new leader Gough Whitlam was elected in 1972, after twenty-three years in opposition, it was able to increase the public salience of the issue and temporarily overcome institutional barriers to this major change in the health system.

*Barriers to Program Expansion*

Chapter 4 described how, when the Liberal-Country coalition government came to power in Australia in 1949, it implemented a modified Pharmaceutical Benefits Scheme but made no further attempts to develop public health insurance – unsurprisingly, given the parties' ideological opposition to compulsory government insurance. Instead, the Commonwealth government introduced subsidies for the individual purchase of private, voluntary insurance, in a program that came to be called "the Page scheme," after the Liberal health minister who oversaw its adoption.

The Page scheme initially continued a Labor policy of making payments to the states based on the number of beds occupied in public hospitals, but added a transfer to individuals who chose to purchase private hospital insurance, and allowed states to reinstitute patient charges for public hospital beds (Kewley 1973, 355). By 1962, the Commonwealth had eliminated direct assistance to states for operating public hospitals and focused entirely on individual subsidies for private insurance (358). The Page arrangements for medical insurance were similar, but here there was no role for the state governments. The Commonwealth paid a benefit to members of registered private insurance funds, although the combination of Commonwealth subsidies and fund benefits still retained significant out of pocket payments for contributors (360–1; Sax 1984, 64).

The operation of the Page scheme throughout the 1950s and 1960s allowed ample time for state governments to establish their own programs for public hospital services. Like Canadian provinces, Australian states had constitutional jurisdiction over hospital care and expertise in running hospital systems. This gave them a veto over changes and made them "reluctant to see federal involvement in this area on bureaucratic and electoral grounds as well as partisan ones" (Holmes and Sharman 1977, 196–7). The schemes they had developed were quite varied, which made them less inclined to accept a single set of Commonwealth conditions. For example, Queensland had maintained a system of free hospital care since 1944, despite Commonwealth incentives to require private insurance, while Victoria provided very few public hospital beds (197; Butler 1991, 173).

It is also significant that when Labor was in power federally from 1972 to 1975, four out of six states had non-Labor governments. The national Liberal-Country Party coalition was able to press its co-partisan state governments to reject the Whitlam government's proposals for compulsory insurance (Holmes and Sharman 1977, 197). However, even states with Labor governments had reasons to object to the Commonwealth plan, which Crichton (1990, 81) notes "put financial stress on the states, as well as annoying them by the attempts to strengthen lower-level regional and local initiatives."

The long operation of the Page scheme also reinforced the medical profession's opposition to any broader government program for medical insurance. Under the Page scheme, there was no attempt to impose standardized fees for physician's services. Physicians might raise their fees as they chose, and Commonwealth benefits could increase or not in response. Indeed, a fear of prompting increased medical fees was one reason given for *not* increasing Commonwealth benefits (Scotton and Deeble 1969, 237; Sax 1984, 76). The result was that doctors had significant autonomy over their incomes, and the medical association was vehemently opposed to any reforms that threatened that autonomy, as a universal public program must (Scotton and Deeble 1969, 237; Palmer 1979, 104).

In Canada, the medical association expressed its opposition to universal public medical insurance mainly by lobbying federal and sometimes provincial governments, but in Australia, physicians had a different institutional avenue open to them. After the election of the Whitlam Labor government, the Liberal-Country Party retained control of the elected Senate. The Australian Medical Association, along with insurance companies, was able to lobby this group of sympathetic politicians quite successfully to hold up the Labor government's health insurance legislation (Crichton 1990). Duckett (1984, 962) in fact argues that it was the Australian Medical Association's "well-funded attack" that led the Senate to block the enabling legislation for Medibank on two occasions, although certainly the Liberal and Country Parties had ideological reasons to oppose the scheme as well.

Despite the barriers to program expansion that developed over its relatively long tenure, the Australian system of voluntary insurance also faced significant criticism in the years before changes were proposed and adopted. The Page scheme was never expected to be universal, but over time it was providing less coverage at more expensive premiums, leading to "growing dissatisfaction" from subscribers (Scotton and Macdonald 1993, 19). By the late 1960s, research by academics such as Richard Scotton, John Deeble, and Ruth Inall describing these problems was gaining public attention (Kewley 1973, 391). Kewley (385) argues that this research stimulated "widespread demand for change" and in 1968 prompted the Liberal-Country government to appoint an independent enquiry into hospital and medical insurance schemes. The enquiry, known by the name of its chair, John A. Nimmo, had a limited mandate. It was to make recommendations "in the context of both a voluntary health insurance scheme, and the obligations at present accepted by the State Governments," which was interpreted as no significant institutional changes to state-Commonwealth agreements or to the voluntary insurance industry (Scotton and Deeble 1969). However, the committee's final report was quite critical of the existing scheme, saying it was too complex, too expensive to administer, provided insufficient coverage to contributors, and was too costly for many Australians to access (Kewley 1973, 504; Scotton and Deeble 1969, 259–60). This criticism, and the growing public discontent it reflected and amplified, was an important motivator for change.

## New Leadership and New Policy Ideas

Dissatisfaction with the system of voluntary insurance combined with ideational and electoral factors to prompt an attempt at major policy change. As was the case in Canada, new leadership came to power in the party traditionally associated with public health insurance – in this case, Gough Whitlam became leader of the Australian Labor Party. Also like the new cadre of Canadian Liberals, Whitlam was looking for new or revitalized policy ideas that were progressive and would assist the party in returning to power, although Labor had a much longer period in opposition than the Canadian Liberals.

Holmes and Sharman (1977, 195) note that the new Labor government elected in December 1972 was strongly committed to the promise of universal health insurance for electoral reasons but also "because they were compatible with broader party aims ... their new health policies fell within the mainstream of the party." Retrospectively, Whitlam himself wrote about the obligation of the party to provide "all Australians with adequate health treatment as a social right, rather than as a function of their income" (Whitlam 1985, 337). However, the Australian Labor Party at this time was in a position similar to that of the Canadian Liberals, in that a broader public health system had long been part of the party platform. So why did Whitlam choose to make it the centrepiece of the party's 1969 and 1972 election campaigns, and a key goal for policy development during his short time in office?

As will be detailed below, much of the impetus for the new prominence of health policy in the Labor Party was electoral. Whitlam was looking for a way to lead his party out of the political wilderness and believed that clear and specific policy promises were key to this effort. However, the choice of policy promises was "partly fortuitous" because the party found a specific idea about health policy reform in the work of two Melbourne University economists, Scotton and Deeble (Kewley 1973, 385). Whitlam records in his memoirs, "Although well aware of the inadequacies of the existing health insurance system, I was yet to develop a viable policy alternative on behalf of the ALP. The solution came in 1967 when Cass asked me to his home to meet John Deeble and Dick Scotton of the Institute of Applied Economic and Social Research at Melbourne University ... Deeble and Scotton were preparing an alternative health insurance program which built upon the criticisms, identical to my own, that they had developed of the existing system. Medibank was conceived that night" (Whitlam 1985, 335).

In Scotton's own account of that meeting, he recalls that although he and Deeble had been doing research on the "provision, cost and use of health services," which "prompted skepticism about the social outcomes of the voluntary [health insurance] system," in 1967 their "ideas were still quite tentative" (Scotton and Macdonald 1993, 24). However, they put them into writing at Whitlam's urging, and by February 1968, presented a plan for compulsory health insurance to Liberal government health officials, who rejected it as impractical (ibid.). Scotton and Deeble's plan was adopted by the Labor Party as a prominent part of its election speeches in 1969 and 1971 (Kewley 1973, 507), and it formed the basis of the Medibank proposals once Labor came to power (Palmer 1979).

As was the case in Canada, Labor leaders were looking for a new policy idea and found a clear, cohesive concept for expanding health insurance in the work of policy experts or academics. There was also the high-profile public enquiry by the Nimmo Committee that increased the prominence of this policy idea. Scotton and Macdonald (1993, 25) note that in 1968, "the Pandora's box which had contained public debate on health insurance was now well and truly open," and the greater salience of this policy idea about how health insurance should work helped fuel electoral incentives for reform.

*Electoral Motivations*

The electoral motivation for Labor to attempt major health policy reforms developed in a number of ways. First, there was simply the worsening objective condition of the voluntary scheme. Whitlam also saw a practical social policy as an important electoral tool. He felt that Labor needed to become a more programmatic party, and upon taking leadership, "set out to formulate activist, reformist and thoroughly documented policies on all areas of significance," including health (Scotton and Macdonald 1993, 19). Whitlam writes that Labor's electoral defeat in 1963 "convinced me that the Party was providing inadequate alternatives to the policies of the Menzies [Liberal] Government. New and attractive policy programs, meeting the aspirations of both the Party and the electorate, had to be developed if the Party was to regain government" (Whitlam 1985, 4).

Health reform was an attractive policy program because it clearly distinguished Labor from Liberal policies, fit with party ideology, and involved a clear distribution of benefits to voters. The research published by Scotton, Deeble, and others, as well as the "unusual energy and vigour" of Labor Party members like W.G. Hayden, shadow minister for health, helped make health reform a topic of public discussion (Kewley 1973). Scotton and Macdonald note that after universal health insurance was adopted as Labor policy, it "rapidly assumed increasing prominence as an issue" in the 1969 election (Scotton and Macdonald 1993, 32–3).

Although Labor lost this election, they increased the pressure on the Liberal-Country government to reform the health system. The coalition government of John Gorton moved to introduce changes immediately after the election, including free or subsidized insurance for low-income Australians, offered through existing voluntary funds (Sax 1984, 89; Duckett 1984, 960). Furthermore, the public seemed to warm to the promise of universal insurance: a Gallup Poll from September 1969 found that 58 per cent of respondents "favoured Whitlam's scheme" for health (Kewley 1973, 509). Compulsory health insurance remained an important part of the 1972 Labor election campaign (Palmer 1979, 105), and "'free medical services' were identified by 46.3 per cent of respondents – more than any other item – as the most important single issue in a public opinion poll conducted in September 1972" (Scotton and Macdonald 1993, 51).

As the salience of health insurance reforms was increasing, so was the popularity of compulsory insurance. A March 1969 poll found that most voters preferred to keep the voluntary insurance system rather than to increase income tax by 8 per cent to fund a free medical and hospital program (Gallup Poll [Australia] March–May 1969).[74] However, in August 1969, Gallup reported, "The ALP [Australian Labor Party] promises most likely to swing voters from the Liberal-CP to ALP are free medical services and pensions without a means test," and 58 per cent of all voters favoured a revised proposal for a free medical service with a 1.25 per cent levy on taxable income (Gallup Poll [Australia] August–September 1969).[75] Whitlam saw public health insurance as a potential policy "winner," in terms of electoral support, and its increasing importance to and popularity with voters seemed to confirm this assessment.

## Overcoming Institutional Barriers

Once the Whitlam Labor government was elected in 1972, its policy ideas on health and the apparent salience and popularity of health reforms with the voters led to the proposals for Medibank. However, they faced two main institutional barriers: states' veto over health reform, where they held constitutional jurisdiction, and obstruction from the elected Commonwealth Senate, which was controlled by opposition parties. Although both barriers were "state" issues in the sense that the Australian Senate is made up of representatives of the states, a key difference is that the Commonwealth government was able to negotiate with state governments, but was able to overcome Senate opposition only through a long process of extraordinary parliamentary procedure.

The opposition Senate was the first and perhaps most serious institutional barrier facing Medibank. The Labor Party had a majority in the House of Commons: sixty-seven seats to the Liberal-Country coalition's fifty-eight. However, the Liberal-Country coalition still controlled the Senate, and they rejected several key pieces of Labor legislation through 1973 and 1974, including the two health insurance acts. The conflict came to a head in April 1974, when the Senate refused to pass the House's appropriation bills, necessary to fund the civil service and government activities (Harris 2005, 461).

The Australian constitution has provisions for resolving such conflicts between the houses of Parliament. If the Senate fails to pass legislation that has passed in the House of Commons three times, and a waiting period has elapsed, the prime minister may ask the governor-general to call a "double-dissolution" election. Normally, elections for the Senate and House of Commons are staggered, but as the name suggests, in this circumstance both houses are dismissed and face the electorate at the same time. This is what happened in May 1974. Whitlam's policy speech in the 1974 election accused the opposition parties of having "falsified democracy," and, with regards to health, said, "In defence of the wealthy friends and vested interests, [the opposition] preserved the inequity, inefficiency and injustice of an antiquated health scheme" (Whitlam 1974). Of his own party's plans for health, he promised to "give all Australians access to high quality health care at reasonable cost," but there were further obstacles once Labor was returned to government. Although Whitlam's government was re-elected with a loss of two seats, Labor still lacked a majority in the Senate.

Immediately upon opening the new Parliament, the Whitlam government reintroduced the bills the Senate had failed to pass in the previous session, including the health insurance bills. They were again rejected by the Senate. This triggered Australia's first and only joint sitting of the Parliament, a further constitutional provision to resolve deadlock between the houses. Both the House of Commons and the Senate met together to debate the bills, which were passed with an absolute majority of the combined legislators (Harris 2005, 473–5). Health insurance legislation was in place at the Commonwealth level: now it remained to secure the states' cooperation.

Holmes and Sharman (1977, 196) argue that while the new Labor government was expecting opposition to Medibank from the Liberal and Country Parties as well as the medical profession and private insurers, it did not anticipate the states' objections. However, even the two states with Labor governments were reluctant to enter into an untried new arrangement for hospital funding that put an important revenue source, direct patient contributions, out of reach. The four states with non-Labor governments were even more problematic, and the delays in adopting Medibank at the federal level favoured the states, as worsening economic conditions and waning popularity of the administration overall weakened Whitlam's position (198).

As was the case in Canada, the Commonwealth government was able to overcome these barriers to the expansion of health insurance with a combination of strategic policy design and financial clout. In early 1975, the Commonwealth government realized it would be "forced to buy off the states" (Holmes and Sharman 1977, 198) by offering special payments to states who did sign on, making a more open-ended financial commitment to cover public hospital expenditures than was originally planned, and providing fewer incentives for states to economize on the use of hospital beds (Palmer 1979, 108). The Commonwealth government was able to negotiate with each state individually, starting with the Labor governments in South Australia and Tasmania. Gray (1991) argues that once these states had joined Medibank and started receiving funds, there were greater electoral and financial incentives for the remaining states to fall in line, as the flow of financial benefits to South Australia and Tasmania was now apparent.

This assessment is supported by Victorian newspaper editorials from this time. In March 1975, the left-leaning Melbourne *Age* published an editorial titled "States Must Not Miss Out on Medibank," where it called the Victorian government's opposition to the federal proposals "strongly ideological and stubbornly political in flavor," and accused the state government of being too much influenced by the medical profession, private insurers, and private hospitals (Editorial 1975a). It argued that by not reaching agreement with the Commonwealth government, state politicians were denying Victorians access to free hospital care, and denying both public and private hospitals new sources of funds. A second editorial, published in June 1975, chastised the state government for not being prepared to meet the 1 July deadline for joining Medibank, and argued that Victorian voters "should not readily forgive the political misjudgment and administrative ineptitude of those responsible" (Editorial 1975b).

The states did eventually sign on to Medibank, as they "could not afford to lose the large sums of money that would be involved" if they refused (Sax 1984, 118). Victoria's premier overruled his health minister and accepted the Commonwealth's conditions in June 1975, and Queensland, Western Australia, and finally New South Wales followed suit in time for cost-sharing to start on 1 October 1975 (ibid.). The Whitlam government had little time to enjoy its success. In late 1975, it faced a growing crisis with conflict over vacant Senate seats, a scandal in the sourcing of an overseas loan for energy projects, and ministerial resignations (Clarke 1989, 258–62). The Senate again blocked appropriation bills, and after nearly a month of deadlock, the governor-general dismissed the Whitlam government on 11 November and called on John Malcolm Fraser, leader of the opposition, to form a caretaker government. The appropriation bills were passed and Parliament was dissolved later that day (Harris 2005, 462–6). An election was held on 13 December 1975, and the Liberal-Country coalition was returned with a majority in both houses.

## Australian Epilogue

This return to Liberal government could have put the new health insurance program at risk – certainly, the Liberal-Country coalition had been hostile to the legislation while it was moving through Parliament and Commonwealth-state negotiations. However, it appears that the same rapid adaptation of public expectations and resulting electoral dynamic that caused the Menzies Liberal government to implement the PBS in 1950 was at work in this instance. Since the early 1970s, public and universal health insurance had been gaining public salience and popularity, and this made it very difficult to reverse entirely.

In his 1975 election speech, Fraser promised to "maintain Medibank," despite the fact that many in his party "were strongly opposed ideologically to Medibank, and [the party's] broad election policy involved a commitment to massive reduction of government expenditure" (Scotton and Macdonald 1993, 235). According to Scotton and Macdonald (36), "Fraser's position [on Medibank] was a logical response to evidence of the growing popularity of Medibank shown in public opinion polls," and Palmer (1979, 124) also notes that there was "probably an awareness in government circles that any attempt to return to the pre-1972 system ... would be politically disastrous."

In October 1976, the Fraser government introduced "Medibank II." It included a levy on taxable income that would help fund public insurance, with an opt-out provision for those who chose to purchase private hospital and medical insurance. The Commonwealth government also made new arrangements with the states regarding hospital funding, which limited Commonwealth liability for hospital budgets (Palmer 1979, 113–14). In 1981, the Commonwealth announced that it would not renew hospital cost-sharing agreements with the states. Although the Commonwealth still provided funding to the states through what were known as "identified health grants" in the general revenue grants program, this move reduced Commonwealth support for states' public hospitals and resulted in the reinstatement of patient charges for public ward treatment (Butler 1991, 170).

Writing shortly after the first changes were introduced, Palmer (1979, 116) argued that the reforms retained "most of the equity gains of Medibank I," although they increased the administrative cost of the system. Somewhat later, Duckett (1984, 965) offered a different assessment, saying the changes under the Fraser government had "succeeded in dismantling most of the reforms of the Labour years and produced a financing system almost identical to that existing in 1972," before Whitlam was elected. However, the popularity of the original scheme is evidenced by how easily it was reinstated when a Labor government took power again in 1983. As Whitlam sums up the electoral significance of Medibank, "Medibank ... had been one of the decisive issues in the great campaign of 1969. It was crucial to our victory in 1972. Its rejection by the Senate Opposition contributed significantly to victory in May 1974 ... Fraser acknowledged its popularity by his specific promise to retain Medibank in 1975. Hawke won in March 1983 with a simple one-line undertaking: 'We will restore Medibank'" (Whitlam 1985, 349).

## Conclusion

Both Canada and Australia took an incremental approach to health policy development. The national government in both countries adopted one element of a universal public health service initially, with the expectation that other services would be added in stages. However, health policy development stalled after the adoption of the first service. In Canada, cautious, somewhat sceptical political leadership under Prime Ministers King and St Laurent, and then a change in government in 1957, led to a loss of momentum after the adoption of nationwide public hospital insurance. In Australia, a new government implemented the Pharmaceutical Benefits Scheme but then pursued a policy of supporting private, voluntary health insurance in accordance with its ideological position.

Over time, barriers to the expansion of public health insurance increased in both countries. Provinces and states developed alternative institutional arrangements to deliver health insurance, and private commercial and physician-sponsored insurance filled the policy gaps. The development of these alternative institutions, with the attendant costs, increased opposition to national, universal insurance from these key stakeholders. The lack of elite consensus on ideas for a comprehensive health system that contributed to an incremental approach initially meant there were limited opportunities for a countervailing public demand for services to develop.

These barriers made major change – the expansion of public health services – unlikely. However, both Canada and Australia were eventually able to expand their public health systems to an extent. Canada added nationwide public medical insurance before policy development stalled again, preventing the adoption of pharmaceutical insurance. Australia added nationwide public hospital and medical insurance simultaneously, although this system retained a greater role for private insurance than either Australia's Pharmaceutical Benefits Scheme or Canada's system of hospital and medical insurance.

Although policy change happened on different timelines in the two countries, the conditions that prompted and permitted change were quite similar. In both cases, the political party that had traditionally supported broader public health services was trying to regain power. Both the Canadian Liberals and Australian Labor had new, progressive leadership that saw a renewed focus on public health insurance as an ideologically compelling policy that would help them win an election.

When the Liberals and Labor did return to government, their prominent policy promises and high-profile reports on health services had increased public interest in expanded services and gave the new governments the electoral motivation they needed to overcome institutional barriers. Their success was accomplished mainly by making concessions in policy design to give subnational governments more flexibility and by sweetening the financial deal provinces and states were to receive. Major change was achieved and the health system expanded, but doing so required an extraordinary combination of ideational, electoral, and institutional conditions.

What lessons do these instances of major change hold for current policy reformers? First, they demonstrate that ideas need a champion. Broader health insurance had been a minor part of both Liberal and Labor platforms for many years before new leaders decided to bring these ideas to prominence and develop concrete policy promises around them. Second, they suggest that public demand and expectations for major change is unlikely to be spontaneous. Despite the growing problems in the voluntary system of health insurance in Australia, public demand for change came *after* the publication of the Nimmo Report, high-profile research by Scotton and Deeble, and policy promises from the Whitlam Labor Party. Finally, the cases of Canada and Australia suggest that institutional barriers to change can be overcome at a cost. Provinces and states may object to federal conditions on health policies, and these objections may gain strength from the objections of important interests like the medical profession or private insurance industry. The question for reformers is how high a price in both policy concessions and financial resources they are able to pay in order to overcome these barriers.

# Chapter 7

# Conclusion

This book has sought to provide a new answer to an understudied empirical puzzle: why Canada lacks a nationwide, public, and universal pharmaceutical insurance program. In doing so, it has made a number of theoretical claims. First, that the pace of policy development and change is predictable, based on the institutional, ideational, and electoral conditions present at an initial critical moment. Of course there are still elements of contingency here, as in almost any social process, but the pace of policy development is neither random nor atheoretical. If we observe certain institutional, ideational, and electoral conditions, we should expect to also observe a corresponding pace of change. Second, that the pace of change is consequential, that it helps explain policy outcomes over the long term. The book examines how the pace of change prompts particular adaptive expectations by political elites and the public. In incremental processes of policy development, politicians and voters adapt to a restricted understanding of the scope of health services over time, and this increases barriers to major expansions of benefits. In radical processes, politicians and voters initially share an idea of health services as necessarily comprehensive. This makes minor changes to existing programs more difficult than similar changes to programs adopted as part of an incremental process.

The third theoretical claim is that major change is rare but not impossible and that the conditions for major change may be significantly more endogenous than other accounts focused on the role of external crisis have acknowledged. In this case, major change means temporarily restarting a stalled incremental policy development and expanding the scope of health services. This requires an extraordinary combination of institutional, ideational, and electoral conditions, similar to those present at the start of a radical policy development. These extraordinary conditions are necessary to overcome barriers to change posed by the development of alternative institutional arrangements for service provision and barriers posed by well-established expectations of political elites and the public about how health services should work and what types of policies are feasible and desirable.

The barriers posed by alternative institutional arrangements have been described by previous work on path dependence in health policy, particularly Hacker's (1998, 82) account of how delays in the development of government health services allow private insurance to expand and consolidate opposition to public programs. However, the barriers posed by adaptive expectations are a new mechanism proposed by this book to help account for instances where public policy development stalled even in the absence of alternative institutional arrangements. If additional health services have consistently been relegated to the bottom of governments' action agendas, if there has consistently been a focus on "fixing what we have" in existing services, and if certain services like pharmaceutical insurance have consistently been understood as unfeasible or undesirable, it may not be necessary for private alternatives for service delivery to block policy development; when they arise, they are simply building on more longstanding ideational barriers to policy change.

These theoretical claims are developed through a comparison of Canadian, British, and Australian health policy over the course of more than thirty years (and more than sixty years in the Canadian case). This chapter reviews the findings in accordance with the three main themes emerging from the theoretical claims: what they tell us about health system variation, the pace of change, and the role of ideas in politics and policy. It proposes directions for future research both within the health policy field and other complex policy areas, in order to test the mechanisms proposed here and better understand their limitations. Finally, it offers some suggestions to those with a practical interest in policy reform, arguing that while major change requires extraordinary circumstances, at least some of these circumstances are within the control of political actors.

**Findings about Health System Variation**

Canada does not have a nationwide, universal program of pharmaceutical insurance, despite early plans for a comprehensive health system and periodic expert proposals for pharmacare since the 1940s. As detailed in chapter 1, this is not a purely academic point of interest: the lack of broad public coverage for pharmaceuticals has significant practical implications for the equality of access to pharmaceuticals in Canada and for the social cost of pharmaceuticals overall. This policy gap exists because the initial decision to adopt health services incrementally led to increasing barriers to additional services over time. Contrary to the accepted wisdom, these barriers are not solely or even primarily financial or institutional. Instead, the relationship between elite ideas about health and pharmaceutical policy and public expectations for services is much more important. Early in the policy process, political elites developed restricted, pragmatic ideas about health policy as limited to hospital and medical services, and about pharmaceuticals as a potentially "uncontrollable" expense where broad public insurance was not feasible.

These ideas persisted in the face of changing economic situations and new policy analysis. For example, in 1972 federal Cabinet ministers seemed to ignore or perhaps did not understand arguments from their own Department of Health and Welfare that a broad pharmaceutical insurance program could lower drug prices (which was a concern for politicians at the time) and lower the social cost of pharmaceuticals. The fact that pharmaceuticals were low on politicians' agendas, and that elites took a restricted and negative view of the issue when it did appear, dampened public expectations for services. Little public demand for pharmaceutical insurance fed back into limited electoral motivations for politicians to act. As one commentator colourfully puts it, this makes pharmaceutical insurance in Canada a "zombie" issue, that "pops up every five to ten years" but does not proceed to actual policy development (Rosenfield 2011, E465, quoting Neil MacKinnon). Even when proposals for pharmacare were changed significantly in 2002, when two major national reports recommended some form of catastrophic drug coverage versus the earlier proposals for universal, first-dollar coverage, they were met by the same longstanding arguments about high costs and a need to focus on existing health services.

This new explanation for Canada's lack of nationwide pharmaceutical insurance challenges some theories of health system variation. Pharmaceuticals are a financially and therapeutically significant aspect of health policy that is simply not captured by standard accounts of the institutional and historical causes of differences among national health systems, but it is necessary to disaggregate health policy and look beyond national systems as a whole in order to see this. There is some political science literature that takes a disaggregated perspective and addresses health policies at a more specific level. Examples include literature on mental health (Tomes 2006; Wolff 2002) and the regulation of assisted reproductive technology (Montpetit, Rothmayr, and Varone 2005; Snow 2013). However, it would be helpful to have more of this type of literature, especially if it focuses on mid-level policy areas (more specific than national health systems, but more general than particular therapeutic interventions or targeted policy tools). The literature would also benefit from additional comparative work that clearly explains the implications of findings about the dynamics of mid-level policy areas like pharmaceutical insurance or benefits for the broader literature on health policy development and change. This strategy suggests that researchers should investigate whether the politics of one policy component, like pharmaceuticals, is necessarily and always synonymous with the politics of the broader policy area. If the lack of pharmacare in Canada is not just an artefact of poor timing but a theoretically consistent and predictable outcome, we may need to adjust the ways we study these complex policy areas. We need new ways to account for policy stability and change over time, and to that end I argue for a greater focus on the pace of policy change.

**Findings about the Pace of Change**

This book has argued that the pace of policy development or change is both predictable and consequential. Countries may develop policy in complex domains like health in a radical "big bang" effort that introduces a range of programs simultaneously, or they may start with similar goals but choose to introduce programs slowly and incrementally. This "choice" is in fact not an unconstrained decision by some group of policymakers but is shaped by the institutional, ideational, and electoral conditions present in an initial critical moment. A radical pace of policy development, where a comprehensive set of health services are adopted simultaneously, requires centralized institutional authority, elite consensus on a policy idea that links theory to practice and provides guidelines for what a health system can and should do, and a public that is both attentive and supportive. In the absence of these conditions, policy development defaults to a less risky and slower approach of adopting services incrementally. The choice between a radical or incremental pace of policy development has a long-term effect on policy outcomes, because it shapes the prospects for both minor adjustments and major change, and this can be seen in the process of health policy development in all three countries.

In Canada, experts initially proposed a universal public health system that would cover a full range of services. Federal politicians rejected this plan in anticipation of the jurisdictional problems it would create, and the lack of consensus on a clear idea of what the health system should do prevented bold action to overcome these institutional barriers. The lack of elite consensus on health policy ideas meant there was little opportunity for public expectations for services to develop, and this lack of electoral motivations reinforced politicians' preference for a cautious, incremental approach to health policy development.

The Canadian federal government was able to facilitate the adoption of one component of a universal public health system when it negotiated hospital insurance agreements with the provinces in the late 1950s; indeed, pressure on the minority government from a third social-democratic party in Parliament made some type of action imperative (Maioni 1998). However, previous literature has disregarded what this book argues is a key outcome of this incremental process of policy development: the delay in adopting additional services made expansion much more difficult. When nationwide hospital insurance was being negotiated, medical insurance was discussed as an obvious second priority for service adoption. However, when medical insurance made it back on the agenda some years later, there were already significant new barriers to program adoption from alternative institutional arrangements for private medical insurance.

Proposals for pharmaceutical insurance faced even greater barriers. Although alternative sources of insurance took longer to develop, elite discussions of pharmaceuticals as far back as 1949 considered them subject to uncontrollable costs, and later, as an issue where price and patent control, not insurance, was the appropriate policy tool. These limited ideas about the nature of pharmaceutical policy combined with a limited idea about the appropriate scope of public health systems based on existing services, and meant that proposals for nationwide pharmaceutical insurance in Canada have failed time and again.

In Australia, the conditions for health policy development towards the end of the Second World War were similar to those in Canada. The federal government lacked constitutional jurisdiction over health, and although in this case government was less concerned about this obstacle, there was still a lack of consensus on how a health system should take shape. Planning committees favoured a system based on public health and hygiene, but Labor politicians were concerned with more tangible cash benefits to individuals and households. Liberal and Country Party politicians were opposed to government health benefits, and this partisan split in the electorate's preferences for health policy prevented the development of clear electoral motivations for action. The result was a pragmatic, incremental approach that focused on what appeared to be a fairly inexpensive and manageable service – pharmaceutical benefits – and faltered when adopting this service was much more difficult than politicians anticipated.

The incremental pace of health policy development also had consequences for policy outcomes in Australia. It meant the Labor government was fighting health policy battles on a number of fronts in the late 1940s, as it attempted to implement its first priority, universal pharmaceutical benefits, while later also negotiating limited hospital subsidies with the states and trying to coax recalcitrant doctors towards salaried medical services. All these efforts stopped when a Liberal-Country government was elected in 1949, with a policy of encouraging private insurance rather than developing public insurance.

The fact that the new government allowed states to reinstitute fees and means tests for public hospitals and abandoned attempts to arrange free medical services is not surprising; it was consistent with the coalition parties' ideology of limited government intervention in health services. However, the Liberal-Country government's decision to implement the Pharmaceutical Benefits Scheme, which remained for many years Australia's only public, universal health program, is a puzzling example of policy stability. I argue that the Liberal-Country government implemented the PBS contrary to its ideological tendencies because of the public expectations that had developed even in the few years between the passage of the legislation, in 1944, and Labor's electoral loss. This demonstration of the speed at which public expectations for service can develop suggests that if the Labor government had been more successful at adopting or implementing other aspects of its incremental plan for health before it lost power, it likely would have been difficult for a new government to dismantle them completely.

The institutional, ideational, and electoral conditions in the United Kingdom, which took a radical approach to health policy development, were quite different from those of Canada and Australia. The centralized institutional authority created by the United Kingdom's unitary, parliamentary system was reinforced by a large majority government for the Labour Party in 1945. A series of interwar reports on health and social security led to the development of a strong elite consensus, even across party lines, on the idea of a health service that was universal, comprehensive, and "free at the point of use." The inclusion of this idea in electoral platforms and speeches, and especially in the prominent Beveridge Report on Social Security in 1942, helped create public expectations for a broad public health system, and corresponding electoral motivations for radical policy development.

While these conditions made a radical pace of policy development possible in the United Kingdom, they also affected opportunities for minor change – that is, adjustments to programs that do not significantly or immediately expand or contract the scope of benefits. Somewhat counterintuitively, I find that there is greater flexibility within the programs adopted incrementally, at least in the early days of policy implementation, than there is in simultaneously adopted health programs. The high levels of principled and strategic commitment to the idea of broad public health services that allow for a radical pace of change also constrain attempts to control costs in ways that might limit the universality or comprehensiveness of coverage, in a sense betraying the policies' founding ideas. This meant that in the United Kingdom, early attempts to limit and recoup costs by imposing a patient charge for prescriptions were very controversial and took on a political symbolism that was out of proportion with the actual cost to patients, as prescription charges remained nominal and subject to widespread exemptions.

Australia provides an interesting comparison to this dynamic, because it adopted an almost identical policy of patient charges for prescriptions around the same time. The design of the Liberal-Country PBS offered an opportunity to compensate for charges with an expanded formulary, or list of covered drugs. However, this was a one-time opportunity for compensation, and subsequent increases to patient charges also avoided the type of controversy that characterized the United Kingdom's policies. The lack of consensus on policy ideas about health, and the correspondingly more limited public expectations that contributed to an incremental pace of policy development in Australia also made the PBS easier to adjust once it was in place, as it was the subject of somewhat less high-profile rhetoric than prescription services in the United Kingdom.

Thus, an incremental pace affects policy development in at least two ways. In broad health policy outcomes, it restricts the range of services that are introduced, so policy development is constrained to the path of the service or services that were early priorities. In changes to existing programs, the ideational and electoral conditions of policy adoption affect the parameters of change that are feasible later on, so an incremental approach generates more flexibility to reform an existing program in ways that limit its comprehensiveness and universality.

Peter Hall (2010, 219) acknowledges the need for research on when and why processes of change vary: where is it frequent or abrupt, versus slow and incremental? This book has responded to this need and argued for an alternate view of the consequences of slow versus fast change, especially in policy development and expansion. Additional research is needed to refine our understanding of the conditions for minor change in both incremental and radical processes. Does the initial pace of policy development have a longstanding effect on the possibilities for minor changes later in the policy process? It would be helpful to test its impact on subsequent minor adjustments to both pharmaceuticals and other services in all three countries. Does elite consensus on a set of policy ideas, coupled with support from an attentive public, "protect" programs from minor changes, and under what conditions are such minor changes possible?

This book also suggests a need for further research on major change in incremental and radical processes. The present research has focused on major changes that expand the scope of benefits provided by the public health system, adding universal pharmaceutical insurance, medical insurance, and/or hospital insurance. The welfare state literature has long claimed, with good reason, that the politics of retrenchment is fundamentally different from the politics of expansion (Pierson 1994). Future research should investigate whether a focus on the pace of change and the conditions that determine it – institutional, ideational, and electoral – can provide points of commonality between major changes that expand health systems, and major changes that contract them. It may be that the broad conditions for major expansionary change in incremental processes have important parallels to the conditions for major retrenchment in radical processes, where the starting point is a comprehensive system.

### Findings about the Role of Ideas in Policymaking

There is a rich and growing literature on the role of ideas in politics and policymaking (Berman 1998; Blyth 2002; A.M. Jacobs 2011; Béland and Cox 2011). The book builds on this literature by distinguishing policy ideas as a cohesive, measurable concept and by providing evidence of the process by which limited ideas restrict policy development across time and space. It does this by defining the level of generality of the ideas under study, as suggested by Mehta (2011, 25). While researchers may be able to identify many types of ideas that have a role in politics, from world views, public philosophies, and zeitgeist to precise formulations of policy solutions (27), different types of ideas may have different causal effects. This book has examined the role of programmatic policy ideas that link theory and practice within a given field. It has argued that these mid-level ideas define the scope of acceptable, feasible, and desirable policy actions within health policy, and when there is no consensus on such overarching health policy ideas early in the process, more pragmatic ideas about the scope of health policy develop piecemeal, in a way that tends to restrict the agenda significantly.

The book also highlights the collective nature of ideas in politics, a point that is perhaps obvious but is both crucial and under-theorized. Policy ideas often need a policy entrepreneur or champion to bring them into political currency – this may be a particular politician or an outside expert – but in order to shape policy outcomes, a consensus among political elite must develop. The conditions under which such ideational consensus develops is an important topic for future research, but this book's findings suggest that ideational consensus among political elites may be linked to the prominence and popularity of specific statements of policy ideas, such as the Beveridge Report in the United Kingdom in the 1940s, or the Royal Commission on Health Services in Canada in the 1960s. This type of high-profile report makes ideas available not only to political elites, but also to the public, and this may push consensus for strategic electoral reasons, as well as ideological reasons.

Many authors have examined the tension between politicians' ideological or "good policy" motives and their electoral incentives – a key material interest for politicians. Authors such as Hay (2011) and Blyth (2003) argue that we cannot understand material interests without reference to ideas, since "objective" interests are necessarily interpreted and constructed by actors who do not have perfect information about the world. However, this book's contribution to the study of ideas and material interests is to argue that previous literature has underestimated the potential impact of elites' policy ideas on voters' expectations, which then feed back into electoral prompts for elites.

This relationship between elite ideas and public expectations is key because in many complex policy areas including health, public expectations are unlikely to develop in the absence of some prompting from elites. However, even a clear elite idea about how a policy should work can rarely be sustained on the agenda in the absence of some attention and support from voters. Furthermore, in an incremental process, particularly one where the steps are not attempted in quick succession, there are more opportunities for elites to develop "blind spots" about a policy area and reject attempts to address lower priorities because they do not conform to previous expectations about the nature of the problem and plausible or necessary solutions. As A.M. Jacobs (2009, 273) argues, over time policymakers develop mental models that "channel their reasoning toward certain causal probabilities and obscure others from view." Thus, the interaction between the elite ideas and public expectations becomes more important over time and is a key element in the self-reinforcing nature of low priorities in an incremental process of policy development. I expect the relationship between elite ideas and public expectations to be present in a variety of policy areas, and this suggests directions for future research on the bounded rationality of both policymakers and voters, and further investigation of the ways elites and publics construct policy problems.

**Prospects for Reform**

For those interested in the prospects for broad pharmaceutical programs in Canada, the results of this research are sobering. In previous analyses of past proposals for nationwide pharmaceutical insurance there has been a tendency to focus on institutional and financial barriers to expanded public pharmaceutical coverage, but this book has shown that ideational barriers might be even more daunting. Designing an efficient and cost-effective system in abstract is unlikely to be enough if political elites are conditioned by their policy ideas to discount the potential benefits of pharmacare, and the public has no context to demand it.

The practical implications of this research are therefore not necessarily a set of recommendations about the types of policies that should be adopted, but an acknowledgment of the barriers that face any attempts at reform, and one hopes some suggestions about how they may be overcome. As I noted at the beginning of this chapter, although the research finds that major change occurs only in extraordinary circumstances, it may be possible for dedicated reformers to engineer some of these circumstances over time.

Perhaps the first goal for setting reforms in motion is to convince a broad range of Canadians that the problem of public pharmaceutical insurance is worthy of attention and action, even amid other pressing concerns about health policy reform. Daw and Morgan (2013) have noted the lack of sustained public attention to pharmaceutical policy in Canada and linked the issue's low salience with a lack of political action, but finding ways to engage the public beyond fleeting attention to human interest stories about lack of access to a particular high-profile drug is difficult. At the time of writing, advocacy groups in Canada such as Pharmacare 2020 are using new strategies to frame research findings about the benefits of universal pharmaceutical insurance for public consumption, and additional work in this vein is crucial. Public outreach may be particularly effective if it is strategic about the way it presents the problems created by a lack of broad public pharmaceutical insurance: for example, Lynch and Gollust (2010) find that American voters are more supportive of government health insurance when it is framed it terms of social values around fairness, rather than material benefits.

A second or perhaps concurrent step is to address the entrenched policy ideas about pharmaceuticals present in provincial governments, which presently administer most of Canada's varied collection of public pharmaceutical programs and which will be crucial factors in any nation-wide reforms. Altering longstanding ideas is difficult, but many authors have pointed to the role of crisis and policy failure in promoting ideational change (Hall 1993; A.M. Jacobs 2009; Skogstad 2011b; L.A. White 2011), and this makes provinces a promising venue for new ideas. It is provincial drug plan administrators and health ministers who grapple most directly with challenges that arise in drug pricing and coverage decisions and are therefore most likely to see efficiency gains from universal coverage. However, the acceptance of new ideas among bureaucrats and experts will not be enough to prompt policy change: politicians must change their ideas, and there must some degree of consensus, if not across party lines than at least within a governing party. In practical terms, this likely means the acceptance of new ideas by both health and finance ministers, and recognition among advocates that the lower social costs of universal drug insurance still represent an increase in government expenditure.

The institutional barriers to nationwide, radical change are certainly formidable, especially at a time when the federal government has expressed a desire to become less involved in areas of provincial jurisdiction like health. However, there has been some, admittedly slow, progress towards interprovincial cooperation and collaboration on pharmaceutical policy, especially on purchasing drugs jointly in order to leverage more bargaining power, which has been recommended by experts as way to lower prices (Law and Morgan 2011). The Council of the Federation, a forum for collaboration between provincial and territorial premiers, coordinates certain interprovincial drug purchasing programs for both branded and generic drugs. Since 2010, the Pan-Canadian Purchasing Alliance has completed negotiations for thirty brand-name pharmaceuticals (Council of the Federation 2013). In 2013, the Council of the Federation announced a number of new bulk purchasing agreements between the provinces and the drug manufacturers: in January, the provinces came to an agreement on bulk purchasing of six generic drugs, and in July they announced progress towards deals on seventeen brand-name drugs and ten additional generics (Lunn 2013; Bell 2013). On a less promising note, however, a recent study has found that provincial bureaucrats have significant reservations about the viability of the broader joint negotiation of product listing agreements (another method of securing better prices from manufacturers, often in return for some guaranteed volume) without financial incentives from the federal government (Morgan, Daw, and Law 2013).

There is also some interprovincial cooperation on drug assessment through the Common Drug Review (CDR), a health technology assessment body that was created in 2002 and is housed in the Canadian Agency for Drugs and Technologies in Health. The CDR has no connection to reimbursement or pricing: participating provincial plans are not bound by the CDR's recommendations but have agreed that new drugs must go through the CDR before they are considered by the provincial agencies (McMahon, Morgan, and Mitton 2006, 340).

The relatively small number of successful initiatives for interprovincial cooperation on pharmaceutical policy may not be a sufficient basis for a universal, nationwide program, but as noted above, if there is consensus on ideas about the problems posed by pharmaceutical insurance and the range of appropriate solutions, institutional barriers to radical change may be significantly lowered. Furthermore, ongoing initiatives that involve new institutional arrangements for sharing information or collaborating on tasks related to pharmaceutical policy may also ease barriers posed by provincial jurisdiction.

Finally, the types of barriers identified here suggest that small steps to increase public coverage for pharmaceuticals – incrementalism writ small – may not ultimately lead to a universal program. If it is difficult to achieve a truly comprehensive public health system one service at a time, we might expect it to be similarly difficult to achieve a universal pharmaceutical insurance program by starting with catastrophic insurance and gradually lowering the deductible, or by starting with one population group and gradually expanding eligibility. Bold action is called for, which is challenging but consistent with the kinds of bold claims needed to disrupt entrenched public and elite ideas about pharmaceutical insurance.

Overcoming these barriers is not a small task, and certainly the history of pharmaceutical policy proposals at the national level in Canada is not an encouraging one. However, the research has demonstrated the power of a cohesive policy idea in the right context and suggests that even if policy development appears to have stalled, there is always hope for a spark.

# Notes

1 Federal spending on prescription drugs is considerably higher in the territories, which have higher Aboriginal populations (Canadian Institute for Health Information 2013, Series B).

2 Esping-Andersen's (1990) classification of these three countries as "liberal welfare regimes" has always sat somewhat uneasily with their universalistic health systems – see, for example, Castles and Mitchell (1992) on the problem of classifying Australia in this way. However, this categorization accounts for similar underlying assumptions about the nature of the welfare state in all three countries, and as argued below, their health systems also share important initial similarities, despite subsequent divergence.

3 While the constitutional amendment eased the introduction of nationwide pharmaceutical benefits somewhat, it remains to be explained why the Commonwealth government attempted pharmaceuticals, and only pharmaceuticals, as its first policy for the provision of universal health benefits. This will be discussed in chapter 3.

4 The 1944 Referendum on Post-War Reconstruction and Democratic Rights was known as the "14 Powers" referendum. If passed, it would have given the Commonwealth government jurisdiction over topics including prices, monopolies, the rehabilitation of ex-servicemen, and national health and pensions for five years after the end of the war, and it would have provided constitutional guarantees of freedom of speech and religion.

5 There is also a lively debate in the public administration literature about the balance of influence between politicians and bureaucracies (see, for example, Peters 2010; Savoie 2003). Much of this work focuses on country- and time-specific factors that affect this balance and will not be addressed here.

6 A.M. Jacobs (2011, 32) has argued that in fact policy goals can be assumed to be politicians' primary motivation: politicians seek office "for the

unparalleled opportunity ... to shape society via state action," although there is often more than one policy option that is consistent with election or re-election.

7   Tom Kent, interview, Kingston, 11 February 2008. The Canadian research draws on interviews conducted with individuals with expertise in federal health and pharmaceutical policy. They included three political advisors, three federal bureaucrats, four representatives of professional organizations or the pharmaceutical industry, two former politicians, one journalist, and two non-governmental policy experts. All interviews were conducted by the author. Interviewees are cited by name or by their chosen designation.

8   Federal-provincial coalition-building around hospital and then medical insurance was considerably more complex than can be captured in this chapter. For more on the role of territorial dynamics, see Boychuk (2008).

9   Kent, interview.

10  The following section draws extensively on James Gillespie's 1991 book, *The Price of Health*, which provides an excellent and comprehensive account of early health politics in Australia based on primary sources. Although the book addresses the adoption and implementation of the Pharmaceutical Benefits Scheme, its main focus is tensions between public health and private medical practice in Australia between 1910 and 1960.

11  The association became the Australian Medical Association in 1962.

12  The JPCSS was created by the Liberal government in July 1941 but relied heavily on NHMRC ideas and analysis (Gillespie 1991, 143; Hunter 1966, 318).

13  The first part of the decade was marked by a strong preference for contributory benefits: see Gallup Polls (Australia), December 1944–January 1945, November 1945, and September 1946.

14  The studies were by the Restrictive Trade Practices Commission (*Report concerning the Manufacture, Distribution and Sale of Drugs*, 1963), the Interdepartmental Committee on Drugs in 1964, the Royal Commission on Health Services (Hall Commission 1964), and the Special Committee of the House of Commons on Drug Costs and Prices (Harley Committee 1966/7).

15  Formal hearings before the Senate Anti-Trust and Monopoly Committee began in 1959 and resulted in the Kefauver-Harris Drug Control Act of 1962.

16  The "Green Book" report was eventually published as Appendix Q to the RTPC's final report in 1963.

17  The recession of the mid-1970s had not yet hit and the economy was still reasonably strong at this point (Perry 1989, 14–16).

18  Policy advisor, interview, Toronto, 23 October 2008; Paul Genest, former advisor to health ministers David Dingwall and Allan Rock, interview, Ottawa, 24 October 2008.
19  Marie Fortier, interview, Ottawa, 15 October 2008.
20  Genest, interview.
21  Genest, interview.
22  Policy advisor, interview.
23  Fortier, interview.
24  Roy Romanow, interview, Saskatoon, 31 October 2008.
25  Genest, interview.
26  Abby Hoffman, interview Ottawa, 16 October 2008.
27  Policy advisor, interview.
28  Hoffman, interview.
29  Policy advisor, interview
30  Political advisor, interview.
31  Policy advisor, interview.
32  Policy advisor, interview.
33  Hoffman, interview.
34  Jane Coutts, interview, Ottawa, 15 October 2008.
35  Political advisor, interview.
36  These numbers were fairly consistent for the remainder of 1997.
37  Senior federal official, interview, Ottawa, 16 October 2008.
38  Senator Wilbert Keon, interview, by phone, 6 November 2008.
39  Steve Morgan, personal communication, 29 June 2012.
40  Aimee Sullivan, manager, Life Sciences Sector Strategy, Pfizer Canada, interview, Ottawa, 17 October 2008; Mark Ferdinand and Stuart Reynolds, Rx&D, interview, Ottawa, 28 October 2008.
41  Owen Adams, assistant secretary general, Research, Policy and Ethics Directorate, Canadian Medical Association, interview, Ottawa, 21 October 2008.
42  Keon, interview.
43  Romanow, interview.
44  Senior federal official, interview.
45  Fortier, interview.
46  Genest, interview.
47  Romanow, interview.
48  Keon, interview.
49  Adams, interview.
50  Fortier, interview.
51  Genest, interview.

52 Stephen Lewis, interview, Saskatoon, 31 October 2008.

53 Doctors' preference for a limited list was framed in terms of retaining autonomy over medicines compounded by pharmacists according to individual doctors' instructions, but interestingly, pharmacists do not appear to have shared this concern. The pharmacy profession cooperated in the design and implementation of the PBS, and their main concern was limiting dispensing from Friendly Societies versus independent chemist shops, as these mutual aid groups undercut their prices (NAA 1945c).

54 The Hinchliffe Committee's insistence that "no restriction should be imposed on the doctor's right to prescribe whatever drugs he considers to be proper and necessary for his patients" (Hinchliffe 1959, 12) is typical, despite longstanding efforts to educate physicians about economical prescribing.

55 House of Commons Debates 1948–9, volume 468, c. 1016–19.

56· In 1950, a loaf of bread cost about one shilling and was no longer rationed. Joyce Williams, personal communication, 3 December 2009.

57 The average cost of a prescription in 1949/50 was three shillings, one pence, and by 1960/1 had increased to seven shillings, three pence. If the cost of prescriptions in 1949/50 was similar to 1952, patients initially paid about 32 per cent of the cost of a prescription, whereas the two-shilling charge in 1961 represented only about 27 per cent of the average prescription cost. See TNA (1961b).

58 This is despite the fact charges were first proposed by the Labour government of Clement Attlee in 1949: the Attlee government passed legislation that gave government the power to impose charges, but prescription charges were not introduced until a Conservative government under Winston Churchill came to power in 1952.

59 Internal government discussions are contained in three additional files maintained by Treasury, as well as others from the Ministry of Health. See, for example, "Reintroduction of Medical Prescription Charges. 1968. 1 March 1968–11 April 1968 (Part B)," T 227/2655; "Reintroduction ... 17 April 1968–10 June 1968 (Part C)"; T 227/2273 "Reintroduction ... 17 June 1968–20 September 1968) Part D," T 227/2656; and "National Health: Date from Which Abolition of Charges Should Become Effective; Loss to Exchequer; Reintroduction of Charges, 1964–1968," PREM 13/2805; and "NHS Prescriptions Numbers and Costs: Reports to Minister 1967–1971," MH 149/1085.

60 House of Commons Debates 1967–8, volume 756, columns 1578–1814.

61 Ibid.

62 Ibid.

63  Persistent balance-of-payment problems forced the government to devalue the sterling in 1967 (Booth 1995), which decreases the domestic standard of living and increases the burden of a country's foreign currency debts.

64  Author's calculation based on population numbers available from Statistics Canada (2012).

65  It is not clear whether this estimate used methods similar to those of Naylor (1986) above.

66  Although the Co-operative Commonwealth Federation (CCF) and its successor, the New Democratic Party (NDP), had long been champions of comprehensive public health insurance in Canada, during this time they were firmly in a third-party position, with government alternating between the Liberal and Conservative parties. The Liberal Party was thus the main, at times hesitant, actor in national health policy.

67  Kent, interview. See also Taylor (1987, 345) and LAC (1964b), where the commission found that means-tested benefits were administratively un- feasible and "not in harmony with public dignity."

68  Kent, interview.

69  Comprehensive list of Canadian Gallup Poll surveys with a "most impor- tant problem" question accessed through ODESI database; 1966 surveys identified high cost of living / high prices as the most important problem in *Public Opinion News Service Release.*

70  Bryden (1997, 130) argues that the federal government learned from Saskatchewan's handling of the doctors' strike over provincial medical insurance, saying that this difficult episode still taught them "that physi- cians did not have the power to mount a successful blockade of public health insurance."

71  Kent, interview.

72  Kent, interview.

73  Kent, interview.

74  Only 35 per cent of voters overall preferred increased tax and a free system; 63 per cent of Liberal-CP voters favoured the voluntary system, compared to 47 per cent of Labor voters.

75  There was an increase in the popularity of the compulsory option with both Liberal-Country Party voters (51 per cent in favour) and Labor voters (68 per cent in favour).

# Works Cited

**Public Opinion Polls**

Canadian Gallup Poll. July 1960.
- May 1961.
- May 1962.
- June 1962.
- September 1962.
- January 1963.
- March 1963.
- August 1964.
- September 1965.
- June 1966.
- December 1966.
- June 1967.
- November 1967.
CIPO/Gallup Poll of Canada. 8 April 1942. *Public Opinion News Service Release.*
- 6 February 1943. *Public Opinion News Service Release.*
- 22 May 1943. *Public Opinion News Service Release.*
- 8 April 1944. *Public Opinion News Service Release.*
- 24 July 1948. *Public Opinion News Service Release.*
- 6 July 1949. *Public Opinion News Service Release.*
- 13 July 1949. *Public Opinion News Service Release.*
- 1 August 1953. *Public Opinion News Service Release.*
- 14 November 1953. *Public Opinion News Service Release.*
- 18 April 1956. *Public Opinion News Service Release.*
- 21 April 1956. *Public Opinion News Service Release.*
- 5 January 1966. *Public Opinion News Service Release.*

Environics Focus Canada Polls. 1997–1, 1997–2, accessed from Canadian Opin-
    ion Research Archives, queensu.ca/cora.
Gallup Poll (Australia). May–June 1943. Polls 124–31, "National Insurance by
    Contribution Popular."
–  August–September 1943. Polls 141–52, "National Insurance by Contribu-
    tions Favored."
–  October 1943. Polls 153–61, "Support for National Medical Service."
–  July 1944. Polls 205–12, "Public Wants Medical Service Contributory."
–  December 1944–January 1945. Polls 241–8. "Social Benefits Should Be on
    Contributory Basis."
–  May 1945. Polls 264–71, "Present Taxes Too Heavy for Social Services."
–  November 1945. Polls 304–13, "Australians in Poll Insist on Contributory
    Social Services Scheme."
–  December 1945–January 1946. Polls 314–26, "Federal Social Services
    Approved."
–  September 1946. Polls 382–97, "Contributory Social Services Wanted."
–  March 1947. Poll 416–25, "Big Change in Opinion of Financing Social
    Services."
–  February–March 1948. Polls 487–91, "Lower Taxes Preferred to More Social
    Services."
–  May 1948. Polls 511–28, "Public Uncertainty about Free Medicines."
–  February–March 1949. Polls 569–78, "Medical & Dental Plan."
–  May–June 1949. Polls 590–9, "Public Still Wants Free Medicine, but Oppos-
    ition Grows."
–  March–April 1950. Polls 662–76, "Public Not Keen on Page Medical Plan."
–  June–July 1950. Polls 690–9, "Page Medicine Plan Hasn't 'Caught On.'"
–  February–March 1951. Polls 744–55, "Page Medicine Plan Goes Far Enough,
    Most Say."
–  December 1951–January 1952. Polls 822–34, "Page's Hospital Plan Popular."
–  July–August 1952. Polls 865–74, "Page Plan Strongly Supported."
–  August–September 1953. Polls 941–9, "Medical Insurance Popular."
–  March–May 1969. Polls 2105–2118, "Keep Medical Funds Voluntary."
–  August–September 1969. Polls 2132–42, "Some ALP Planks Could Be Net
    Losers."

**Archival Sources**

Library and Archives Canada (LAC). n.d.(a) (circa 1966). Draft comments on
    Hall Commission, prescription drug services – benefits. RG 29, vol. 1129,
    file 504-4-15, pt 2.

Library and Archives Canada (LAC). n.d.(b) (circa 1972). DRAFT: Some Social Reasons for Pharmacare" and "Arguments for Pharmacare." RG 29, vol. 1572, file 1016-1-2.

Library and Archives Canada (LAC). 1946. Meeting of the Cabinet Committee on Dominion-Provincial Relations: Report of the Working Committee on Health Insurance, 4 January. Brooke Claxton fonds, MG 32-B5, vol. 138.

Library and Archives Canada (LAC). 1949a. Department of National Health and Welfare / CMA studies of NHS and New Zealand health scheme. RG 29, vol. 1111, file 504-2-4, pt 2.

Library and Archives Canada (LAC). 1949b. Department of National Health and Welfare memo, 22 December. RG 29, vol. 1061, file 500-3-4, pt 1.

Library and Archives Canada (LAC). 1949c. Draft minutes of the first meeting of the Interdepartmental Working Committee on Health Insurance, 30 November. RG 29, vol. 1061, file 500-3-4, pt 1.

Library and Archives Canada (LAC). 1949d. Health insurance brief, 7 December. RG 29, vol. 1061, file 500-3-4, pt 1.

Library and Archives Canada (LAC). 1949e. Minutes of the second meeting of the Interdepartmental Working Committee on Health Insurance, 9 December. RG 29, vol. 1061, file 500-3-4, pt 1.

Library and Archives Canada (LAC). 1950. G.D.W. Cameron to Paul Martin, 27 November. RG 29, vol. 1061, file 500-3-4, pt 2.

Library and Archives Canada (LAC). 1955a. Draft report to the chairman of the Preparatory Committee for the Federal-Provincial Conference 1955 on a Personal Health Care Program. RG 29, vol. 1132, file 504-5-6, pt 1.

Library and Archives Canada (LAC). 1955b. Memo to minister on health insurance and Ontario, 5 August. RG 29, vol. 1132, file 504-5-6, pt 1.

Library and Archives Canada (LAC). 1961a. Liberal campaign pamphlet, "Health Care as Needed: The Answer." RG 33-78, vol. 51.

Library and Archives Canada (LAC). 1961b. Liberal campaign pamphlet, "Take a Stand for Tomorrow: Vote Liberal." RG 33-78, vol. 51.

Library and Archives Canada (LAC). 1961c. Pierre Berton, "Jules Gilbert's Profitable Crusade for Cutting Drug Prices." *Toronto Daily Star*, 1 November. RG 27, file 13-27.

Library and Archives Canada (LAC). 1963. Meeting of the Departmental Group to Study Health Insurance, 27 March. RG 29, vol. 1129, file 504-4-15, pt 1.

Library and Archives Canada (LAC). 1964a. Royal Commission on Health Services in Canada, news release, 19 June. RG 33-78, vol. 27, file 2-8-2, pt 3.

Library and Archives Canada (LAC). 1964b. Statement of Principle Advocated by British Columbia Respecting ... the Report of the Royal Commission on Health Services, 20–1 July. RG 29, vol. 1133, file 504-5-11, pt 1.

Library and Archives Canada (LAC). 1965a. Consolidated report of views expressed by the provinces on health services. RG 29, vol. 1133, file 504-5-12.

Library and Archives Canada (LAC). 1965b. R.B. Bryce to Health Minister Judy LaMarsh, 16 March 1965, "Possible Action on Drug Prices." RG 33-78, vol. 51.

Library and Archives Canada (LAC). 1965c. Report of the Interdepartmental Committee on Drugs, 9 April. RG 27, vol. 11, file 11-24.

Library and Archives Canada (LAC). 1966. Jules Gilbert to Dr H.S. Showalter re: plant inspection report, 8 July. RG 27, file 13-27.

Library and Archives Canada (LAC). 1971. Memo: "The Drug Price Program," 23 September, Privy Council Office. RG 2, vol. 6381, series A-5-a.

Library and Archives Canada (LAC). 1972a. Memorandum to Cabinet: "Measures to lower the unit price of drugs including a drug benefit program," 23 March, 30 March, Privy Council Office. RG 2, series A-5-a, vol. 6395.

Library and Archives Canada (LAC). 1972b. Memorandum to Cabinet, "Measures to lower the unit cost of prescription drugs including a drug benefit program [Pharmacare – handwritten]," 2 and 8 February. RG 2, vol. 6397, file 120-72.

Library and Archives Canada (LAC). 1972c. Memorandum to Cabinet, 24 November, Office of the Deputy Minister of Health and Welfare. RG 29, vol. 1572, file 1016-1-2.

National Archives of Australia (NAA). 1943a. Memorandum: The advantages of establishing a pharmaceutical benefits scheme during war time. A571, 1943/1812, pt 2.

National Archives of Australia (NAA). 1943b. Pharmaceutical Benefits Bill: Notes on general policy. A571, 1943/4513.

National Archives of Australia (NAA). 1943c. Pharmaceutical Benefits Bill: Valuations, 24 May–8 June. A571, 1943/4513.

National Archives of Australia (NAA). 1943–4a. Pharmacy manpower surveys. A571, 1943/4513.

National Archives of Australia (NAA). 1943–4b. Second reading speech, Pharmaceutical Benefits Bill (House, draft). A571, 1943/4513.

National Archives of Australia (NAA). 1943–4c. Social Security in Australia memorandum. A571, 1943/4513.

National Archives of Australia (NAA). 1943–4d. Treasury memorandum. A571, 1943/4513.

National Archives of Australia (NAA). 1944a. BMA statement, 10 August. A1928, 781/4, section 2.

National Archives of Australia (NAA). 1944b. BMA to health minister, 19 February. A571, 1943/4513.

National Archives of Australia (NAA). 1944c. Caucus meeting notes. A571, 1943/4513.

National Archives of Australia (NAA). 1944d. Memorandum, January. A571, 1943/4513.

National Archives of Australia (NAA). 1944e. Minister of health to physicians, 9 August. A1928, 781/4, section 2.

National Archives of Australia (NAA). 1944f. Notes for BMA Conference, 28 January, and Social Security in Australia memorandum. A571, 1943/4513.

National Archives of Australia (NAA). 1945a. BMA pamphlet to hospital patients. A571, 1943/1812, pt 1.

National Archives of Australia (NAA). 1945b. Chifley to Senator Lamp, Tasmania, 3 May. A571, 1943/1812, pt 1.

National Archives of Australia (NAA). 1945c. Federated Pharmaceutical Service Guild of Australia to Prime Minister Chifley, 14 October. A432.

National Archives of Australia (NAA). 1945d. Government Q&A's on the PBS, 1945. A571/1943/1812, pt 1.

National Archives of Australia (NAA). 1945e. Notes on a visit to New Zealand, January. A571, 1943/1812, pt 1.

National Archives of Australia (NAA). 1945f. "Objections to Free Medicine: Bad for Patients," *Argus*, 8 June. A571, 1943/1812, pt 1.

National Archives of Australia (NAA). 1947a. Cabinet memorandum, 24 September. A27000.

National Archives of Australia (NAA). 1947b. Cabinet submission, 19 September. A1658, 813/1/1, pt 1.

National Archives of Australia (NAA). 1947c. Transcript of meeting, minister and BMA, 21 April. A571 1943/1812, pt 2.

National Archives of Australia (NAA). 1948a. Mr Harrison, Hansard, 17 June 1. A571, 1943/1812, pt 3.

National Archives of Australia (NAA). 1948b. Transcript of meeting, minister and BMA, 2 July. A571, 1943/1812, pt 3.

National Archives of Australia (NAA). 1950a. Earle Page, "Department of Health: Pharmaceutical Benefits," Cabinet submission 22 June. A1658, 813/1/1, pt 1.

National Archives of Australia (NAA). 1950b. Major principles of the proposed National Health Scheme. A4933.

National Archives of Australia (NAA). 1950c. Treasury submission, 19 June. A571, 1950/596.

National Archives of Australia (NAA). 1952a. Cabinet submission (Sir Earle Page), 27 August. A571, 1950/596.

National Archives of Australia (NAA). 1952b. Cabinet minutes 31 March (Decision 360). A1658, 813/1/1, pt 1.

National Archives of Australia (NAA). 1952c. Keith Attiwill, "Report from Public Relations." *Gilseal News* (Pharmacuetical Guild newsletter), 16 October. A1658, 811/1/1, pt 1.

National Archives of Australia (NAA). 1959a. Cabinet minute (Ad Hoc Committee), decision no. 388 HOC, 17 August. A1658, 813/1/2, pt 1.

National Archives of Australia (NAA). 1959b. Cabinet submission, 2 July. A1658, 813/1/2, pt 1.

National Archives of Australia (NAA). 1959c. July. Notes on Cabinet submission no. 252. A5619, C523.

National Archives of Australia (NAA). 1959d. *Melbourne Herald*, 21 September. A1658, 813/1/2, pt 1.

National Archives of Australia (NAA). 1959e. National Health – Pharmaceutical Benefits – background press package, 11 August. M2568/25.

National Archives of Australia (NAA). 1960. Press statement by Dr [Donald] Cameron [Minister of Health] re: new pharmaceutical benefits, 16 February. A463, 1956/1905.

National Archives of Australia (NAA). 1965. Reply to information request from Senator, Jersey, Channel Islands. A1658, 813/1/1/1, pt 3.

National Archives of Australia (NAA). 1971. Cabinet minutes, 21 July. Pharmaceutical Benefits – Patient contribution – Decision 259 (M). A5908/192.

National Archives of Australia (NAA). 1975. Minister of health to prime minister, 13 June. A5931, CL640.

Queen's University Archives (QUA). 1960. "The Kingston Conference, September 1960." Writing series, box 6, folder "Study Conference on National Problems, Kingston Sept 1960" (1), Thomas Worral Kent Papers.

Queen's University Archives (QUA). 1965a. Kent to Pearson, 18 July 1965 (secret: Federal-Provincial Conference: strategy). Thomas Worral Kent Papers.

Queen's University Archives (QUA). 1965b. Kent to Pearson, 29 July 1965 (personal and secret). Thomas Worral Kent Papers.

The National Archives of the United Kingdom (TNA). n.d. (circa 1964). Treasury memo, "Free Prescriptions." T 227/2285.

The National Archives of the United Kingdom (TNA). 1943. Memoranda, March–April, Ministry of Health. MH 77/120.

The National Archives of the United Kingdom (TNA). 1944. Memorandum, 31 March, Ministry of Health. MH 77/120.

The National Archives of the United Kingdom (TNA). 1945. Memorandum: Proposals for a National Health Service, 13 December, Cabinet documents. CAB 129/5.

The National Archives of the United Kingdom (TNA). 1946. General Medical and Pharmaceutical Services Regulations, National Health Service Bill 1946. MH 137/75.

The National Archives of the United Kingdom (TNA). 1947a. Agenda of meeting of the Joint Committee on a National Pharmaceutical Service, 17 June. MH 135/576.

The National Archives of the United Kingdom (TNA). 1947b. Memorandum 16 April (preparation to discuss new Health Service with pharmacists). MH 135/576.

The National Archives of the United Kingdom (TNA). 1948. Memorandum (minister of health): "Payment of Eyes, Teeth, and Drugs: Cost Overruns," 13 December, Cabinet documents. CAB 129/31.

The National Archives of the United Kingdom (TNA). 1949a. Cabinet item: Consideration of proposed cuts in public expenditure including the introduction of prescription charges, 14 October. CAB 134/220/34.

The National Archives of the United Kingdom (TNA). 1949b. Chancellor of the Exchequer, memorandum EPC(49)111: "Consideration of Proposed Cuts in Public Expenditure including the Introduction of Prescription Charges," 14 October, Cabinet documents. CAB 134/220/34.

The National Archives of the United Kingdom (TNA). 1950a. Chancellor of the Exchequer, memorandum: "Ceiling on Expenditure," 29 March, CAB 129/39.

The National Archives of the United Kingdom (TNA). 1950b. Chancellor of the Exchequer, memorandum: "NHS: Charge for Prescription," 26 January. CAB 129/38.

The National Archives of the United Kingdom (TNA). 1952a. Boots Drugs Co. to minister of health, 18 June. MH 135/77.

The National Archives of the United Kingdom (TNA). 1952b. Executive Council circular. MH 135/76.

The National Archives of the United Kingdom (TNA). 1956a. "Meeting of Ministers on Prescription Charges: meeting 1." 15 November. CAB 130/121.

The National Archives of the United Kingdom (TNA). 1956b. Minister of health to National Pharmaceutical Union, October. MH 135/79.

The National Archives of the United Kingdom (TNA). 1956c. Minutes of meeting with BMA, 31 October. MH 135.79.

The National Archives of the United Kingdom (TNA). 1956d. Mrs Richards to member of Parliament, 22 November. MH 123/290.

The National Archives of the United Kingdom (TNA). 1961a. Draft statement (by minister of health on increase in charges). MH 135/73.

The National Archives of the United Kingdom (TNA). 1961b. Memorandum: "Increased Charges for Drugs and Appliances." MH 135/73.

The National Archives of the United Kingdom (TNA). 1961c. National Pharmaceutical Union to R.F. Tyras (minister of health), 2 February. MH 135/73.

The National Archives of the United Kingdom (TNA). 1961d. Q&A memo: "Prescription Charges." MH 135/73.

The National Archives of the United Kingdom (TNA). 1964a. George Brown to Harold Wilson, 12 November. T 227/2285.

The National Archives of the United Kingdom (TNA). 1964b. Kenneth Robinson to James Callaghan, 12 November. T 227/2285.

The National Archives of the United Kingdom (TNA). 1964c. Treasury memorandum re: "Abolition of Prescription Charges: Minister of Health's Letter of 19th October 1964," 21 October. T 227/2285.

The National Archives of the United Kingdom (TNA). 1964d. William Ross to James Callaghan re: need to abolish prescription charges, 22 October. BN 72/175.

The National Archives of the United Kingdom (TNA). 1967a. Kenneth Robinson to Roy Jenkins, 18 December. T 227/2652.

The National Archives of the United Kingdom (TNA). 1967b. Minister of health, memorandum re: reintroduction of prescription charges, 18 December. T 227/2652.

The National Archives of the United Kingdom (TNA). 1967c. Treasury official letter (Rampton), 13 December. T 227/2652.

The National Archives of the United Kingdom (TNA). 1968a. Ministry of Health briefing note on prescription charges, 30 May. CAB 151/136.

The National Archives of the United Kingdom (TNA). 1968b. Treasury history of prescription charges: S.S. aspects, 24 February 1966–31 May 1967. T 227/2522.

**Published Sources**

Abelson, Julia, and Patricia A Collins. 2009. "Media Hyping and the 'Herceptin Access Story': An Analysis of Canadian and UK Newspaper Coverage." *Healthcare Policy* 4 (3). http://www.ncbi.nlm.nih.gov/pmc/articles/PMC2653700/.

Abraham, Carolyn. 2005. "Cancer Clinic Opens the Door for Private Care." *Globe and Mail*, 22 August.

Abraham, John. 2002. "The Pharmaceutical Industry as a Political Player." *Lancet* 360 (9344): 1498–502. http://dx.doi.org/10.1016/S0140-6736(02)11477-2.

Advisory Committee on Health Insurance. 1943. *Health Insurance*. Ottawa: King's Printer.

Allin, S. 2008. "Does Equity in Healthcare Use Vary across Canadian Provinces?" *Health Policy* 3 (4): 83–99.

Attlee, Clement Richard. 1937. *The Labour Party in Perspective*. London: Victor Collancz.

Australia. 2003. *Commonwealth of Australia Constitution Act*.

Bachrach, Peter, and Morton S. Baratz. 1962. "Two Faces of Power." *American Political Science Review* 56 (4): 947–52. http://dx.doi.org/10.2307/1952796.

Baumgartner, Frank R., and Bryan D. Jones. 1991. "Agenda Dynamics and Policy Subsystems." *Journal of Politics* 53 (4): 1044–74.

Bealey, Frank. 1970. *The Social and Political Thought of the British Labour Party*. London: Weidenfeld and Nicolson.

Béland, Daniel, and Robert Henry Cox, eds. 2011. *Ideas and Politics in Social Science Research*. New York: Oxford University Press.

Béland, Daniel, and A. Waddan. 2012. *The Politics of Policy Change: Welfare, Medicare, and Social Security Reform in the United States*. Washington, DC: Georgetown University Press.

Bélanger, Claude. 2001. "Canadian Federalism, the Tax Rental Agreements of the Period of 1941–1962 and Fiscal Federalism from 1962 to 1977." *Quebec History: Studies on the Canadian Constitution and Canadian Federalism*. http:// faculty.marianopolis.edu/c.belanger/quebechistory/federal/taxrent.htm.

Bell, Sonya. 2013. "Premiers to Ramp Up Bulk Purchasing of Generic and Brand-Name Drugs." *Ipolitics*. http://www.ipolitics.ca/2013/07/26/ premiers-to-ramp-up-bulk-purchasing-of-generic-and-brand-name-drugs/.

Bennett, Scott. 2003. *The Politics of Constitutional Amendment*. Ottawa: Information and Research Services, Department of the Parliamentary Library.

Berman, Sheri. 1998. *The Social Democratic Moment*. Cambridge, MA: Harvard University Press.

Berman, Sheri, Ronald Inglehart, Peter Katzenstein, David Laitin, and Kathleen McNamara. 2001. "Ideas, Norms, and Culture in Political Analysis." *Comparative Politics* 33 (2): 231–50. http://dx.doi.org/10.2307/422380.

Beveridge, Baron William Henry. 1942. *Social Insurance and Allied Services: Report of the Inter-Departmental Committee on Social Insurance and Allied Services*. London: H.M. Stationery Office.

Blyth, Mark. 1997. "'Any More Bright Ideas?' The Ideational Turn of Comparative Political Economy." *Comparative Politics* 29 (2): 229–50. http:// dx.doi.org/10.2307/422082.

Blyth, Mark. 2002. *Great Transformations: Economic Ideas and Institutional Change in the Twentieth Century*. Cambridge: Cambridge University Press. http:// dx.doi.org/10.1017/CBO9781139087230.

Blyth, Mark. 2003. "Structures Do Not Come with an Instruction Sheet: Interests, Ideas, and Progress in Political Science." *Perspectives on Politics* 1 (4) 695–706.

Booth, Alan. 1995. *British Economic Development since 1945*. Manchester: Manchester University Press.

Boychuk, Gerard W. William. 2008. *National Health Insurance in the United States and Canada*. Washington, DC: Georgetown University Press.

Bryden, P.E. 1997. *Planners and Politicians: Liberal Politics and Social Policy, 1957–1968*. Montreal and Kingston: McGill-Queen's University Press.

Bryden, P.E. 2009. "The Liberal Party and the Achievement of National Medicare." *Canadian Bulletin of Medical History* 26 (2): 315–32.

Burstein, P. 2003. "The Impact of Public Opinion on Public Policy: A Review and an Agenda." *Political Research Quarterly* 56 (1): 29–40. http://dx.doi .org/10.1177/106591290305600103.

Butler, Jim. 1991. "Health Care." In *Intergovernmental Relations and Public Policy*, ed. Brian Galligan, Owen Hughes, and Cliff Walsh, 163–87. Sydney: Allen & Unwin.

Cairns, Alan C. 1977. "The Governments and Societies of Canadian Federalism." *Canadian Journal of Political Science* 10 (4): 695–725. http:// dx.doi.org/10.1017/S0008423900050861.

Campbell, John L. 2004. *Institutional Change and Globalization*. Princeton: Princeton University Press.

Canada. 1867. Constitution Act, 1867. http://laws-lois.justice.gc.ca/eng/ const/page-1.html.

Canada. 1945. *Dominion-Provincial Conference on Reconstruction: Plenary Conference Discussions*. Ottawa: King's Printer.

Canada. 1955. "Proceedings of the Federal-Provincial Conference, October 3, 1955." Ottawa: Queen's Printer.

Canada. 1965. "Proceedings of Federal-Provincial Conference, Ottawa, July 19–22, 1965." Ottawa: Queen's Printer.

Canada. 2000. "First Ministers' Meeting Communique on Health." Ottawa: Canadian Intergovernmental Conference Secretariat.

Canada. 2001. "Health Ministers Move Forward on Improving Health Care in Canada." Ottawa: Canadian Intergovernmental Conference Secretariat.

Canada. 2003a. "Budget 2003 Supports Social and Economic Agenda While Maintaining Balanced Budgets." Ottawa: Finance Canada.

Canada. 2003b. "2003 First Ministers' Accord on Health Care Renewal." Health Canada. http://www.hc-sc.gc.ca/hcs-sss/delivery-prestation/ fptcollab/2003accord/index-eng.php#notes.

Canada. 2004. "A 10-Year Plan to Strengthen Health Care." Health Canada. Ottawa. http://www.hc-sc.gc.ca/hcs-sss/delivery-prestation/fptcollab/ 2004-fmm-rpm/index-eng.php.

Canada, Governor General. 1997. "Speech from the Throne: 36th Parliament." Ottawa: Privy Council Office, 12 July. http://www.pco-bcp.gc.ca/index. asp?lang=eng&page=information&sub=publications&doc=aarchives/sft-ddt/1997-eng.htm.

Canadian Health Coalition. 2013. "Rethinking Drug Coverage: Time for Universal Pharmacare?" *Pharmacare2013.Ca*. http://healthcoalition.ca/ main/resources/rethinking-drug-coverage-conference/?doing_wp_cron=1 412261210.6076939105987548828125.

Canadian Health Coalition. 2014. "Pharmacare: More for Less." *Pharmacarenow.
Ca.* http://pharmacarenow.ca/learn-more/the-case-for-pharmacare.

Canadian Institute for Health Information. 2011. *Drug Expenditure in Canada,
1985–2005.* Ottawa: Canadian Institute for Health Information.

Canadian Institute for Health Information. 2013. *Drug Expenditure in Canada,
1985–2012.* Ottawa: Canadian Institute for Health Information.

Canadian Pharmacists Association. 2001a. *Submission to the Romanow
Commission on the Future of Health Care in Canada.* Ottawa: Canadian
Pharmacists Association.

Canadian Pharmacists Association. 2001b. *Submission to the Standing Senate
Committee on Social Affairs, Science and Technology.* Ottawa: Canadian
Pharmacists Association.

Capoccia, Giovanni, and R. Daniel Kelemen. 2007. "The Study of Critical Junctures: Theory, Narrative, and Counterfactuals in Historical Institutionalism."
*World Politics* 59 (3): 341–69. http://dx.doi.org/10.1017/S0043887100020852.

Carpenter, Daniel P. 2010. *Reputation and Power.* Princeton: Princeton
University Press.

Castles, F.G. 1998. *Comparative Public Policy: Patterns of Post-War Transformation.*
Cheltenham: Edward Elgar Publishing.

Castles, Francis Geoffrey, and Deborah Mitchell. 1992. "Identifying Welfare
State Regimes: The Links between Politics, Instruments and Outcomes."
*Governance: An International Journal of Policy, Administration and Institutions* 5
(1): 1–26. http://dx.doi.org/10.1111/j.1468-0491.1992.tb00026.x.

Clarke, Francis Gordon. 1989. *Australia: A Concise Political and Social History.*
Oxford: Oxford University Press.

Commission on Pharmaceutical Services. 1971. *Pharmacy in a New Age.*
Toronto: Canadian Pharmaceutical Association.

Commission on the Future of Health Care in Canada. 2002. *Building on Values.*
Ottawa: Commission on the Future of Health Care in Canada.

Council of the Federation. 2013. "Pan-Canadian Purchasing Alliance."
Canada's Premiers. http://www.councilofthefederation.ca/en/initiatives/
358-pan-canadian-pricing-alliance.

Craig, Fred W.S. 1975. *British General Election Manifestos 1900–1974.* London:
Macmillan.

Craig, Fred W.S. 1982. *Conservative & Labour Party Conference Decisions,
1945–1981.* Chichester, U.K.: Parliamentary Research Service.

Crichton, Anne O.J. 1990. *Slowly Taking Control?* Sydney: Allen & Unwin.

Crossman, Richard Howard Stafford. 1975. *The Diaries of a Cabinet Minister.*
London: Hamilton and Cape.

Crowley, F.K. 1973. *Modern Australia in Documents: 1939–1970.* Vol. 2.
Melbourne: Wren.

Cutler, Fred. 2010. "The Space between Worlds: Federalism, Public Issues and Election Issues." *Regional & Federal Studies* 20 (4–5): 487–514. doi.org/ 10.1080/13597566.2010.523635.

Daw, Jamie R., and Steven G. Morgan. 2012. "Stitching the Gaps in the Canadian Public Drug Coverage Patchwork? A Review of Provincial Pharmacare Policy Changes from 2000 to 2010." *Health Policy* 104 (1): 19–26. http://dx.doi.org/10.1016/j.healthpol.2011.08.015.

Daw, Jamie R., and Steven G. Morgan. 2013. "Here Today, Gone Tomorrow: The Issue Attention Cycle and National Print Media Coverage of Prescription Drug Financing in Canada." *Health Policy* 110 (1): 67–75. http://dx.doi.org/10.1016/j.healthpol.2013.01.006.

Denzau, Arthur T., and Douglass C. North. 1994. "Shared Mental Models: Ideologies and Institutions." *Kyklos* 47 (1): 3–31. http://dx.doi.org/10.1111/ j.1467-6435.1994.tb02246.x.

Denzau, Arthur T., Douglass C. North, and Ravi K. Roy. 2007. "Shared Mental Models: A Footnote." In *Neoliberalism: National and Regional Experiments with Global Ideas*, ed. Ravi K. Roy, Thomas D. Willett, and Arthur T. Denzau, 14–25. New York: Routledge.

Department of National Health and Welfare (Research and Statistics Division). 1964. *Provision, Distribution and Cost of Drugs in Canada: Report to the Royal Commission on Health Services.* Ottawa: Queen's Printer.

Director of Investigations and Research. 1961. *Material Collected for Submission to the RTPC in the Course of an Inquiry under Section 42 of the Combines Investigation Act, Relating to the Manufacture, Distribution and Sale of Drugs ("Green Book").* Ottawa: Department of Justice, Appendix Q to Restrictive Trade Practices Commission Report.

Douglas, Kristen, and Célia Jutras. 2008. *Patent Protection for Pharmaceutical Products in Canada: Chronology of Significant Events.* Ottawa: Parliamentary Research and Information Service. http://www.parl.gc.ca/content/LOP/ ResearchPublications/prb9946-e.pdf.

Downs, Anthony. 1957. *An Economic Theory of Democracy.* New York: Harper and Row.

Duckett, S.J. 1984. "Structural Interests and Australian Health Policy." *Social Science & Medicine* 18 (11): 959–66. http://dx.doi.org/10.1016/ 0277-9536(84)90266-1.

Eastman, Harry. 1985. *Report of the Commission of Inquiry on the Pharmaceutical Industry.* Ottawa: Supply and Services Canada.

Eden, Lorraine. 1989. "Compulsory Licensing and Canadian Pharmaceutical Policy." In *International Business in Canada: Strategies for Management*, ed. Alan M. Rugman, 245–67. Scarborough, ON: Prentice Hall.

Eder, Norman R. 1982. *National Health Insurance and the Medical Profession in Britain, 1913–1939*. New York: Garland.

Editorial. 1975a. "State Must Not Miss Medibank." *Age*, 17 March.

Editorial. 1975b. "State to Blame Over Medibank." *Age*, 18 June.

Erk, J. 2006. "Does Federalism Really Matter?" *Comparative Politics* 39 (1): 103–20. http://dx.doi.org/10.2307/20434023.

Esping-Andersen, Gosta. 1990. *The Three Worlds of Welfare Capitalism*. Princeton: Princeton University Press.

Ferguson, Rob. 2013. "Dying Milton Woman Pleads for Funding of Cancer Drug." *Toronto Star*, 30 October.

Fierlbeck, Katherine. 2011. *Health Care in Canada: A Citizen's Guide to Policy and Politics*. Toronto: University of Toronto Press.

Flora, Peter, and Arnold J. Heidenheimer. 1981. *The Development of Welfare States in Europe and America*. New Brunswick: Transaction Publishers.

Forest, Pierre-Gerlier. 2004. "To Build a Wooden Horse ... Integrating Drugs into the Public Health System." *Healthcare Papers* 4 (3): 22–6. http://dx.doi.org/10.12927/hcpap..16872.

Gagnon, Marc-Andre, and Guillaume Hebert. 2010. *The Economic Case for Universal Pharmacare*. Ottawa: Canadian Centre for Policy Alternatives. https://www.policyalternatives.ca/publications/reports/economic-case-universal-pharmacare.

Galligan, Brian. 1995. *A Federal Republic: Australia's Constitutional System of Government*. Cambridge: Cambridge University Press. http://dx.doi.org/10.1017/CBO9781139084932.

George, Alexander L., and Andrew Bennett. 2005. *Case Studies and Theory Development in the Social Sciences*. Cambridge, MA: MIT Press.

Gilbert, C.D. 1980. "'There Will Be Wars and Rumours of Wars': A Comparison of the Treatment of Defence and Emergency Powers in the Federal Constitutions of Australia and Canada." *Osgoode Hall Law Journal* 18 (3): 307–35.

Gillespie, James A. 1991. *The Price of Health: Australian Governments and Medical Politics 1910–1960*. Cambridge: Cambridge University Press. http://dx.doi.org/10.1017/CBO9780511470189.

*Globe and Mail*. 1955. "CCL Asks Ottawa Check on Gouging in Drug Prices." 16 December.

*Globe and Mail*. 1960. "Price Formula Suggested: Free Lifesaving Drugs Are Urged." 6 October.

*Globe and Mail*. 1961. "Federal Body to Study Facts on Drug Prices." 4 February.

Goodin, Robert E., and John Dryzek. 1987. "Risk Sharing and Social Justice: The Motivational Foundations of the Post-War Welfare State." In *Not Only the Poor: The Middle Classes and the Welfare State*, ed. Robert E. Goodin and Julian LeGrand. London: Allen and Unwin.

Gorecki, Paul K. 1981. *Regulating the Price of Prescription Drugs in Canada.* Ottawa: Economic Council of Canada.

Gorecki, Paul K., and Ida Henderson. 1981. "Compulsory Patent Licensing of Drugs in Canada: A Comment on the Debate." *Canadian Public Policy* 7 (4): 559–68. http://dx.doi.org/10.2307/3549486.

Graham, Karen. 1998. "Conference on National Approaches to Pharmacare: Proceedings." Ottawa: Health Canada.

Gray, Gwendolyn. 1991. *Federalism and Health Policy: The Development of Health Systems in Canada and Australia.* Toronto: University of Toronto Press.

Great Britain and the Ministry of Health. 1944. *A National Health Service (White Paper).* London: Parliamentary Papers.

Grootendorst, Paul. 2002. "Beneficiary Cost Sharing under Canadian Provincial Prescription Drug Benefit Programs: History and Assessment." *Canadian Journal of Clinical Pharmacology* 9 (2): 79–99.

Grzymala-Busse, Anna. 2011. "Time Will Tell? Temporality and the Analysis of Causal Mechanisms and Processes." *Comparative Political Studies* 44 (9): 1267–97. http://dx.doi.org/10.1177/0010414010390653.

Hacker, Jacob S. 1998. "The Historical Logic of National Health Insurance: Structure and Sequence in the Development of British, Canadian, and U.S. Medical Policy." *Studies in American Political Development* 12 (1): 57–130. http://dx.doi.org/10.1017/S0898588X98001308.

Hacker, Jacob S. 2004. "Privatizing Risk without Privatizing the Welfare State: The Hidden Politics of Social Policy Retrenchment in the United States." *American Political Science Review* 98 (2): 243–60. http://dx.doi.org/10.1017/S0003055404001121.

Hall, Peter A. 1993. "Policy Paradigms, Social Learning, and the State: The Case of Economic Policymaking in Britain." *Comparative Politics* 25 (3): 275–96. http://dx.doi.org/10.2307/422246.

Hall, Peter A. 2010. "Historical Institutionalism in Rationalist and Sociological Perspective." In *Explaining Institutional Change: Ambiguity, Agency and Power*, ed. James Mahoney and Kathleen Ann Thelen, 204–23. Cambridge: Cambridge University Press.

Harris, I.C. 2005. "Disagreements between the Houses." In *House of Representatives Practice.* 5th ed. Canberra: Commonwealth of Australia. http://www.aph.gov.au/About_Parliament/House_of_Representatives/Powers_practice_and_procedure/practice.

Harrison, Kathryn. 1996. *Passing the Buck: Federalism and Canadian Environmental Policy.* Vancouver: UBC Press.

Harvey, K.J., T.A. Faunce, and B. Lokuge. 2004. "Will the Australia–United States Free Trade Agreement Undermine the Pharmaceutical Benefits Scheme?" *Medical Journal of Australia* 181 (5): 256–9.

Hay, Colin. 2011. "Ideas and the Construction of Interests." In *Ideas and Politics in Social Science Research*, ed. Daniel Béland and Robert Henry Cox, 65–82. Oxford: Oxford University Press.

Health Canada, Strategic Policy Branch. 2006. *National Pharmaceuticals Strategy: Progress Report*. Ottawa: Health Canada.

Heclo, Hugh. 1974. *Modern Social Policies in Britain and Sweden: From Relief to Income Maintenance*. New Haven, CT: Yale University Press.

Hinchliffe, Henry. 1959. *Committee on Cost of Prescribing: Final Report of the Committee*. London: H.M. Stationery Office.

Holmes, J., and C. Sharman. 1977. *The Australian Federal System*. Sydney: G. Allen & Unwin.

Hume, Mark. 2005. "B.C. Agrees to Pay for Vaunted Cancer Drug." *Globe and Mail*, 12 July.

Hunter, Thelma A. 1965. "Pharmaceutical Benefits Legislation, 1944–50." *Economic Record* 41 (95): 412–25. http://dx.doi.org/10.1111/j.1475-4932.1965.tb03059.x.

Hunter, Thelma A. 1966. "Planning National Health Policy in Australia, 1941–45." *Public Administration* 44 (3): 315–30. http://dx.doi.org/10.1111/j.1467-9299.1966.tb01589.x.

Immergut, E.M. 1992. "The Rules of the Game: The Logic of Health Policy-Making in France, Switzerland, and Sweden." In *Structuring Politics: Historical Institutionalism in Comparative Analysis*, ed. Sven Steinmo, Kathleen Ann Thelen, and Frank Longstreth, 53–89. New York: Cambridge University Press. http://dx.doi.org/10.1017/CBO9780511528125.004.

Jacobs, Alan M. 2009. "How Do Ideas Matter?: Mental Models and Attention in German Pension Politics." *Comparative Political Studies* 42 (2): 252–79. http://dx.doi.org/10.1177/0010414008325283.

Jacobs, Alan M. 2011. *Governing for the Long Term*. New York: Cambridge University Press. http://dx.doi.org/10.1017/CBO9780511921766.

Jacobs, Lawrence R. 1993. *The Health of Nations*. Ithaca, NY: Cornell University Press.

Jacobzone, S. 2000. *Pharmaceutical Policies in OECD Countries: Reconciling Social and Industrial Goals*. OECD Labour Market and Social Policy Occasional Papers, Vol. 40. Paris: OECD Publishing.

Jordan, Jason. 2009. "Federalism and Health Care Cost Containment in Comparative Perspective." *Publius* 39 (1): 164–86.

Kapur, Vishnu, and Kisalaya Basu. 2005. "Drug Coverage in Canada: Who Is at Risk?" *Health Policy* 71 (2): 181–93. http://dx.doi.org/10.1016/j.healthpol.2004.08.006.

Kewley, Thomas Henry. 1973. *Social Security in Australia, 1900–72.* Sydney: Sydney University Press.

Kingdon, John W. 2003. *Agendas, Alternatives and Public Policies.* 2nd ed. New York: Longman.

Klein, Rudolph. 2010. *The New Politics of the NHS: From Creation to Reinvention.* 6th ed. New York: Longman.

Lang, Ronald W. 1974. *The Politics of Drugs: A Comparative Pressure-Group Study of the Canadian Pharmaceutical Manufacturers Association and the Association of the British Pharmaceutical Industry, 1930–1970.* Farnborough, Hants.; Lexington, MA: Saxon House-Lexington Books.

Law, Michael R., Lucy Cheng, Irfan A. Dhalla, Deborah Heard, and Steven G. Morgan. 2012. "The Effect of Cost on Adherence to Prescription Medications in Canada." *Canadian Medical Association Journal* 184 (3): 297–302. http://dx.doi.org/10.1503/cmaj.111270.

Law, Michael, and Steven Morgan. 2011. "Purchasing Prescription Drugs in Canada: Hang Together or Hang Separately." *Healthcare Policy* 6 (4): 22–6.

Lexchin, J. 1993. "Pharmaceuticals, Patents, and Politics: Canada and Bill C-22." *International Journal of Health Services* 23 (1): 147–60.

Lexchin, J. 1997. "After Compulsory Licensing: Coming Issues in Canadian Pharmaceutical Policy and Politics." *Health Policy* 40 (1): 69–80. http://dx.doi.org/10.1016/S0168-8510(96)00886-X.

Liberal Party of Canada. 1993. *Creating Opportunity: The Liberal Plan for Canada (Red Book).* Ottawa: Liberal Party of Canada.

Liberal Party of Canada. 1997. *Securing Our Future Together: Preparing Canada for the 21st Century.* Ottawa: Liberal Party of Canada.

Lindblom, Charles E. 1982. "The Market as Prison." *Journal of Politics* 44 (2): 323–36.

Lindsey, Robin, and Douglas S. West. 1999. "National Pharmacare, Reference-Based Pricing, and Drug R&D: A Critique of the National Forum on Health's Recommendations for Pharmaceutical Policy." *Canadian Public Policy / Analyse de Politiques* 25 (1): 1–27. http://dx.doi.org/10.2307/3551399.

Livingston, W.S. 1956. *Federalism and Constitutional Change.* Oxford: The Clarendon Press.

Lofgren, Hans, and Rebecca de Boer. 2004. "Pharmaceuticals in Australia: Developments in Regulation and Governance." *Social Science & Medicine* 58 (12): 2397–407. http://dx.doi.org/10.1016/j.socscimed.2003.09.012.

Lunn, Susan. 2013. "Provinces Reach Deal to Save on 6 Generic Drugs." CBC News, 18 January. http://www.cbc.ca/news/politics/provinces-reach-deal-to-save-on-6-generic-drugs-1.1331370.

Lynch, J., and S.E. Gollust. 2010. "Playing Fair: Fairness Beliefs and Health Policy Preferences in the United States." *Journal of Health Politics, Policy and Law* 35 (6): 849–87. http://dx.doi.org/10.1215/03616878-2010-032.

Mahoney, James. 2000. "Path Dependence in Historical Sociology." *Theory and Society* 29 (4): 507–48. http://dx.doi.org/10.1023/A:1007113830879.

Mahoney, James, and Kathleen Ann Thelen. 2010. *Explaining Institutional Change*. New York: Cambridge University Press.

Maioni, Antonia. 1998. *Parting at the Crossroads*. Princeton: Princeton University Press.

Mann, John. 2004. *Life-Saving Drugs: The Elusive Magic Bullet*. Cambridge: Royal Society of Chemists.

Marsh, Leonard C. 1943. *Report on Social Security for Canada Prepared for the Advisory Committee on Reconstruction*. Ottawa: King's Printer.

Martin, Paul. 1985. *A Very Public Life*. Vol. 2. Toronto: Deneau.

Mathews, Russell L., and William Robert C. Jay. 1972. *Federal Finance: Intergovernmental Financial Relations in Australia Since Federation*. Melbourne: Thomas Nelson Publishers.

Maynard, Alan, Karen Bloor, and Nick Freemantle. 2004. "Challenges for the National Institute for Clinical Excellence." *British Medical Journal* 329:227–9.

McAllister, Ian, and Rhonda Moore. 1991. *Party Strategy and Change: Australian Electoral Speeches since 1946*. Melbourne: Longman Cheshire.

McMahon, Meghan, Steve Morgan, and Craig Mitton. 2006. "The Common Drug Review: A NICE Start for Canada?" *Health Policy* 77 (3): 339–51. http://dx.doi.org/10.1016/j.healthpol.2005.08.006.

Mehta, Jal. 2011. "The Varied Role of Ideas in Politics: From 'Whether' to 'How.'" In *Ideas and Politics in Social Science Research*, ed. Daniel Béland and Robert Henry Cox, 23–46. Oxford: Oxford University Press.

Mendelsohn, Matthew. 2002. *Canadians' Thought on Their Health Care System*. Commission on the Future of Health Care in Canada. http://www.queen-su.ca/cora/_files/MendelsohnEnglish.pdf.

Mendelson, Danuta. 1999. "Devaluation of a Constitutional Guarantee: The History of Section 51 (xxiiiA) of the Commonwealth Constitution." *Melbourne University Law Review* 14 (May): 308–39.

Menzies, R.G. 1949. "Joint Opposition Policy Speech." Canterbury, Victoria, 10 November. http://digital.slv.vic.gov.au/view/action/singleViewer.do?dvs=1412265228432~681&locale=en_US&metadata_object_ratio=

10&show_metadata=true&preferred_usage_type=VIEW_MAIN&frameId=
1&usePid1=true&usePid2=true.

Montpetit, Éric, Christine Rothmayr, and Frédéric Varone. 2005. "Institutional
Vulnerability to Social Constructions: Federalism, Target Populations, and
Policy Designs for Assisted Reproductive Technology in Six Democracies."
*Comparative Political Studies* 38 (2): 119–42. http://dx.doi.org/10.1177/
0010414004271080.

Morgan, Steve G., Jamie R. Daw, and M.R. Law. 2013. *Rethinking Pharmacare
in Canada*. C.D. Howe Institute Commentary No. 384. Toronto: C.D. Howe
Institute.

Morgan, Steve G., Meghan McMahon, and Devon Greyson. 2008. "Balancing
Health and Industrial Policy Objectives in the Pharmaceutical Sector:
Lessons from Australia." *Health Policy* 87 (2): 133–45. http://dx.doi.org/
10.1016/j.healthpol.2008.01.003.

Morgan, Steven G., and Donald J. Willison. 2004. "Post-Romanow
Pharmacare: Last-Dollar First … First-Dollar Lost?" *Healthcare Papers* 4 (3):
10–20. http://dx.doi.org/10.12927/hcpap..16871.

National Forum on Health (Canada). 1997. *Canada Health Action: The Final Report
of the National Forum on Health*. Vol. 1. Ottawa: National Forum on Health.

Naylor, Christopher David. 1986. *Private Practice, Public Payment*. Montreal
and Kingston: McGill-Queen's University Press.

Noelle-Neumann, Elisabeth. 1999. "The Effect of the Mass Media on Opinion
Formation." In *Mass Media, Social Control, and Social Change: A Macrosocial
Perspective*, ed. David Demers and K. Viswanath, 51–76. Ames: Iowa State
University Press.

Page, Earle. 1963. *Truant Surgeon*. Sydney: Angus and Robertson.

Palmer, G.R. 1979. "Health." In *From Whitlam to Fraser: Reform and Reaction
in Australian Politics*, ed. Allan Patience and Brian Head, 103–24. Oxford:
Oxford University Press.

Parsons, Craig. 2007. *How to Map Arguments in Political Science*. Oxford: Oxford
University Press.

Perry, John Harvey. 1989. *A Fiscal History of Canada*. Toronto: Canadian Tax
Foundation.

Peters, B. Guy. 2010. "Bureaucracy and Democracy." *Public Organization
Review* 10 (3): 209–22. http://dx.doi.org/10.1007/s11115-010-0133-4.

Pharmacare 2020. 2014. "Pharmacare 2020: Envisioning Canada's Future."
http://pharmacare2020.ca/.

Pierson, Paul. 1994. *Dismantling the Welfare State? Reagan, Thatcher and the
Politics of Retrenchment*. Cambridge: Cambridge University Press. http://
dx.doi.org/10.1017/CBO9780511805288.

Pierson, Paul. 1995. "Fragmented Welfare States: Federal Institutions and the Development of Social Policy." *Governance: An International Journal of Policy, Administration and Institutions* 8 (4): 449–78. http://dx.doi.org/10.1111/j.1468-0491.1995.tb00223.x.

Pierson, Paul. 2000. "Increasing Returns, Path Dependence, and the Study of Politics." *American Political Science Review* 94 (2): 251–67. http://dx.doi.org/10.2307/2586011.

Pierson, Paul. 2004. *Politics in Time: History, Institutions, and Social Analysis.* Princeton: Princeton University Press.

Pomey, Marie-Pascale, Pierre-Gerlier Forest, Howard A. Palley, and Elisabeth Martin. 2007. "Public/Private Partnerships for Prescription Drug Coverage: Policy Formulation and Outcomes in Quebec's Universal Drug Insurance Program, with Comparisons to the Medicare Prescription Drug Program in the United States." *Milbank Quarterly* 85 (3): 469–98. http://dx.doi.org/10.1111/j.1468-0009.2007.00496.x.

Pomey, Marie-Pascale, Steve Morgan, John Church, Pierre-Gerlier Forest, John N. Lavis, Tom McIntosh, Neale Smith, Jennifer Petrela, Elizabeth Martin, and Sarah Dobson. 2010. "Do Provincial Drug Benefit Initiatives Create an Effective Policy Lab? The Evidence from Canada." *Journal of Health Politics, Policy and Law* 35 (5): 705–42. http://dx.doi.org/10.1215/03616878-2010-025.

Priest, Lisa. 2011. "Breast Cancer Patient Takes Out Line of Credit to Pay for Herceptin." *Globe and Mail*, 28 August.

Public Interest Alberta. 2014. "PIA Seniors Task Force Meets with Health Minister." http://pialberta.org/content/pia-seniors-task-force-meets-health-minister.

Quirke, Vivian. 2005. "From Alkaloids to Gene Therapy: A Brief History of Drug Discovery in the 20th Century." In *Making Medicines: A Brief History of Pharmacy and Pharmaceuticals*, ed. Stuart Anderson, 177–202. London: Pharmaceutical Press.

Restrictive Trade Practices Commission. 1963. *Report Concerning the Manufacture, Distribution and Sale of Drugs.* Ottawa: Department of Justice.

Rivett, Geoffrey. 1998. *From Cradle to Grave.* London: King's Fund.

Rosenfield, D. 2011. "Zombies, Myths and Pharmacare." *Canadian Medical Association Journal* 183 (8): E465–6. http://dx.doi.org/10.1503/cmaj.109-3869.

Roskam, John. 2001. "Liberalism and Social Welfare." In *Liberalism and the Australian Federation*, ed. J.R. Nethercote, 267–86. Sydney: Federation.

Royal Commission on Health Services. 1964. *Report of the Royal Commission on Health Services*, Vol. 1. Ottawa: Queen's Printer.

Rx&D. 2010. "Where We Stand: Catastrophic Drug Coverage." Policy, Research and Analysis Department. http://www.canadapharma.org/

CMFiles/Our%20Industry/Where%20We%20Stand/WhereWeStand_
DRAFT_CatastrophicDrugCoverage2.pdf.

Ryan, Michael. 1973. "Free at Time of Use: A Study of Charges and Costs in
the National Health Service." *Social Policy and Administration* 7 (3): 219–34.
http://dx.doi.org/10.1111/j.1467-9515.1973.tb00044.x.

Sackville, Ronald. 1973. "Social Welfare in Australia: The Constitutional
Framework." *Federal Law Review* 5 (1972–3): 248–64.

Savoie, Donald J. 2003. *Breaking the Bargain*. Toronto: University of Toronto Press.

Sax, Sidney. 1984. *A Strife of Interests: Politics and Policies in Australian Health
Services*. Sydney: Allen & Unwin.

Scotton, R.B., and J.S. Deeble. 1969. "The Nimmo Report." *Economic Record* 45
(2): 258–75. http://dx.doi.org/10.1111/j.1475-4932.1969.tb00165.x.

Scotton, R.B, and Christine Rose Macdonald. 1993. *The Making of Medibank*.
Kensington, NSW: School of Health Services Management

Senate Standing Committee on Social Affairs, Science and Technology. 2002.
*The Health of Canadians: The Federal Role*. Ottawa: Parliament of Canada.

Shillington, Clarence Howard. 1972. *The Road to Medicare in Canada*. Toronto:
DEL Graphics.

Simeon, Richard, and Ian Robinson. 1990. *State, Society, and the Development of
Canadian Federalism*. Toronto: University of Toronto Press.

Skogstad, Grace. 2011a. "Conclusion." In *Policy Paradigms, Transnationalism,
and Domestic Politics*, ed. Grace Skogstad, 237–53. Toronto: University of
Toronto Press.

Skogstad, Grace. 2011b. "Constructing a Transnational Policy Paradigm in the
European Union: The Case of GMO Risk Regulation." In *Policy Paradigms,
Transnationalism, and Domestic Politics*, ed. Grace Skogstad, 3–35. Toronto:
University of Toronto Press.

Skogstad, Grace, and Vivien A. Schmidt. 2011. "Introduction: Policy
Paradigms, Transnationalism, and Domestic Politics." In *Policy Paradigms,
Transnationalism, and Domestic Politics*, ed. Grace Skogstad. Toronto:
University of Toronto Press.

Sloan, Clyde. 1995. *A History of the Pharmaceutical Benefits Scheme, 1947–1992*.
Canberra: Department of Human Services and Health (Australia).

Smiley, D.V. 1962. "The Rowell-Sirois Report, Provincial Autonomy, and
Post-War Canadian Federalism." *Canadian Journal of Economics and Political
Science* 28 (1): 54–69. http://dx.doi.org/10.2307/139263.

Snow, Dave. 2013. "The Judicialization of Assisted Reproductive Technology
Policy in Canada: Decentralization, Medicalization, and Mandatory
Regulation." *Canadian Journal of Law and Society* 27 (2): 169–88.

Special Committee of the House of Commons on Drug Costs and Prices. 1996/7. *Second (Final) Report of the Special Committee of the House of Commons on Drug Costs and Prices*. Ottawa: Queen's Printer.

Standing Committee on Industry. 1997a. *Evidence of the Committee*. Ottawa: Parliament of Canada.

Standing Committee on Industry. 1997b. *5th Report of the Standing Committee on Industry*. Ottawa: Parliament of Canada.

Statistics Canada. 2012. "Visual Census: Population and Dwelling Counts, Canada." http://www12.statcan.gc.ca/census-recensement/2011/dp-pd/vc-rv/index.cfm?Lang=ENG&VIEW=d&CFORMAT=jpg&GEOCODE=01&TOPIC_ID=1.

Streeck, Wolfgang, and Kathleen Ann Thelen. 2005. *Beyond Continuity*. New York: Oxford University Press.

Stephenson, B. 1967. *The Sugar-Coated Pill*. Toronto: Pagent Productions.

Taylor, Malcolm G. 1987. *Health Insurance and Canadian Public Policy*. Montreal and Kingston: McGill-Queen's University Press.

Taylor-Gooby, Peter. 2002. "The Silver Age of the Welfare State: Perspectives on Resilience." *Journal of Social Policy* 31 (4): 597–621. http://dx.doi.org/10.1017/S0047279402006785.

Tomes, Nancy. 2006. "The Patient as a Policy Factor: A Historical Case Study' of the Consumer/Survivor Movement in Mental Health." *Health Affairs* 25 (3): 720–9. http://dx.doi.org/10.1377/hlthaff.25.3.720.

Treff, Karin, and David B. Perry. 1997. *Finances of the Nation 1996*. Toronto: Canadian Tax Foundation.

Treff, Karin, and David B. Perry. 1998. *Finances of the Nation 1997*. Toronto: Canadian Tax Foundation.

Treff, Karin, and David B. Perry. 2002. *Finances of the Nation 2001*. Toronto: Canadian Tax Foundation.

Treff, Karin, and David B. Perry. 2003. *Finances of the Nation 2002*. Toronto: Canadian Tax Foundation.

Tsebelis, George. 1995. "Decision Making in Political Systems: Veto Players in Presidentialism, Parliamentarism, Multicameralism and Multipartyism." *British Journal of Political Science* 25 (3): 289–325. http://dx.doi.org/10.1017/S0007123400007225.

Tuohy, Carolyn Hughes. 1999. *Accidental Logics*. New York: Oxford University Press.

Tuohy, Carolyn Hughes. 2011. "American Health Reform in Comparative Perspective: Big Bang, Blueprint, or Mosaic?" *Journal of Health Politics, Policy and Law* 36 (3): 571–6. http://dx.doi.org/10.1215/03616878-1271279.

Vandergrift, Michael, and Panos Kanavos. 1997. "Health Policy versus Industrial Policy in the Pharmaceutical Sector: The Case of Canada." *Health Policy* 41 (3): 241–60. http://dx.doi.org/10.1016/S0168-8510(97)00036-5.

Weaver, R.K., and B.A. Rockman. 1993. *Do Institutions Matter?: Government Capabilities in the United States and Abroad*. Washington, DC: Brookings Institution.

Webster, C. 2002. *The National Health Service: A Political History*. Oxford: Oxford University Press.

White, Denis M. 1978. *The Philosophy of the Australian Liberal Party*. Richmond, Victoria: Hutchinson.

White, Linda A. 2011. "Institutional Stickiness and Ideational Resistance to Paradigm Change: Canada and Early Childhood Education and Care (ECEC) Policy." In *Policy Paradigms, Transnationalism, and Domestic Politics*, ed. Grace Skogstad, 202–36. Toronto: University of Toronto Press.

Whitlam, Gough. 1974. "1974 Election Policy Speech." 29 April. http://whitlamdismissal.com/1974/04/29/whitlam-1974-election-policy-speech.html.

Whitlam, Gough. 1985. *The Whitlam Government, 1972–1975*. Ringwood, Victoria: Penguin.

Wolff, Nancy. 2002. "Risk, Response, and Mental Health Policy: Learning from the Experience of the United Kingdom." *Journal of Health Politics, Policy and Law* 27 (5): 801–32. http://dx.doi.org/10.1215/03616878-27-5-801.

Wordsworth, S., Michael Ryan, and C. Donaldson. 1998. "New Labour, New Charges?" *New Economy* 5 (4): 196–201.

# Index

**Studies in Comparative Political Economy and Public Policy**